To Ed Crouch
a wonderful f̶
Janey Her

PHILIP HART

Philip A. Hart

PHILIP HART

The Conscience of the Senate

Michael O'Brien

Michigan State University Press
East Lansing

All Michigan State University Press books are produced on paper which meets
the requirements of American National Standard of Information Sciences—
Permanence of paper for printed materials ANSI Z39.48-1984

Michigan State University Press
East Lansing, Michigan 48823-5202

03 02 01 00 99 98 97 96 95 1 2 3 4 5 6 7 8 9

Library of Congress Cataloging-in-Publication Data

O'Brien, Michael. 1943-
    Philip Hart : the conscience of the Senate / Michael O'Brien.
       p.   cm.
    Includes bibliographical references and index.
    ISBN 0-87013-407-8 (alk. paper)
    1. Hart, Philip A. (Philip Aloysius). 1912-   . 2. Legislators—United
States—Biography. 3. United States. Congress. Senate—Biography. I. Title.
E840.8.H287037   1995
328.73'092—dc20
[B]   95-33291
                                                               CIP

All photographs courtesy of Janey Hart and her children, Ann, Clyde, and
James.

For my children

Tim
Sean
Jeremy
Carey

Contents

Acknowledgments   ix

Introduction   1

Chapter 1: Early Life, 1912-1941   5

Chapter 2: World War II and Aftermath, 1941-1946   27

Chapter 3: Road to the Senate, 1947-1958   55

Chapter 4: Gaining Respect, 1959-1970   79

Chapter 5: Profile: Personality, Character, Family   131

Chapter 6: Conscience of the Senate   167

Epilogue   219

Sources   221

Index   227

Acknowledgments

Once again, I have incurred many debts in preparing a book and am delighted to express my deep gratitude. I owe a primary debt for the valuable assistance of librarians and archivists, including Nancy Bartlett at the Bentley Historical Library at the University of Michigan and Nancy Fallgren at the Georgetown University Library.

Several persons graciously gave me (or loaned me) valuable papers at their disposal. Among them were James Hart, Bill Herd, Wallace Long, and Burton Wides. For their kindness and assistance special thanks to Basil Briggs, Clyde Hart, Werner Kleeman, and Ann Bronfman.

This is not an authorized study. I did not ask permission of the Philip Hart family to write my book, preferring instead to write independently. Nonetheless, I appreciate the consideration and hospitality of Janey Hart for permitting me to inspect extremely important family papers in her possession and helping to secure valuable educational and military records of her husband.

Several people criticized manuscript versions of the book, catching errors, helping me overcome problems of writing and interpretation, and offering their encouragement. For their efforts I deeply appreciate Lewis Fiset, Saul Friedman, Janey Hart, Jerry Kabel, Sally O'Brien, and Sidney Woolner.

As in my previous books, I have placed a heavy burden on the staff at the University of Wisconsin Center—Fox Valley who have, nonetheless, responded with good humor and patience. For the second time Kathy Hosmer typed many drafts of the book and Patricia Warmbrunn efficiently processed hundreds of interlibrary loan requests. Former Dean Robert Young kindly supported my project from the start and offered his advice and assistance.

In the early stages of my study I received important and timely grants from the University of Wisconsin Center Fox Valley and the University of Wisconsin—Fox Cities Foundation, Inc. In addition, the University of Wisconsin awarded me a sabbatical during the critical, last stage of my writing.

My voluntary research assistants, Connie Gamsky and Marguerite Hagen, located and photographed many important articles and newspaper clippings. I have been very fortunate to have a special voluntary typist, Reighe Nagel, who for over two years expertly and quickly typed many drafts of the manuscript.

My wife, Sally, was a valuable critic and graciously endured her husband's third book with patience, encouragement, and love. Also thanks to Tim, Sean, Jeremy, and Carcy for all the love and enjoyment they bring me.

Introduction

"The most important left/liberal in Congress for the last 18 years is someone you never heard of," wrote Joe Klein in the December 1976 issue of *Rolling Stone*. Klein was referring to Democratic senator Philip A. Hart of Michigan. First elected to the Senate in 1958, and reelected two more times, Phil announced in June 1975 that he would retire at the end of his third term. Tragically, six weeks after his announcement he learned he had cancer; and by the fall of 1976, as he was about to leave the Senate, he was terminally ill.[1]

Phil Hart was easily overlooked. Because he was thin and his right arm had been damaged in World War II, some thought he looked weak. He did not have a forceful personality, did not bombard newsrooms with press releases to gain political advantage, and did not hold a Senate leadership position. His exceptional modesty partially explained why few people knew about him outside Michigan and Washington, D.C. "He lived by the Golden Rule of Washington," said Senator Edward Kennedy (D-Mass.), "that there is no limit to what you can accomplish in this city, if you are willing to give someone else the credit."[2]

Although not widely known by the public, Hart was well known by his Senate colleagues and close observers of Washington politics. In their tributes to him in the fall of 1976, fellow senators pointed out that he had supported or authored many bills, particularly in the areas of civil rights, antitrust enforcement, and consumer and environmental protection. (Hart took special pride in leading the Senate fight for the Voting Rights Act of 1965, a law, he said, "which has really made a difference.")

1

Although impressive, Hart's legislative record was not the feature that made him extraordinary. Rather, the fulsome praise of colleagues focused primarily on the manner and quality of the man himself. He became known as the "Conscience of the Senate." He was what a senator was *supposed* to be, and colleagues knew it and were influenced by it. "His mere presence on the floor could sway votes," said one senator. "There is something about Phil Hart that has an element of intellectual purity that is hard to find in most individuals," said Senator John Pastore (D-R.I.).[3]

On 27 August 1976, Senator Kennedy suggested to Senator Mike Mansfield (D-Mon.) that the new Senate office building be named after Hart. (The building under construction was an annex to—but twice as large as—the Everett M. Dirksen Senate Office Building.) Three days later, on 30 August, the bill sponsored by eighty-five senators passed the Senate, and the new building became the Philip A. Hart Senate Office Building. The honor was unusual for two reasons. All the other congressional buildings bore the names of Senate and House leaders, but in his eighteen years in the Senate, Hart had risen no higher than chair of a subcommittee and never even sought a leadership post. Also, he was one of only a few after whom a building or a monument in Washington was named while he was still alive.

Hart's friends in the Senate rushed around getting signatures from ninety-nine senators on the architect's watercolor rendering of the building. Senator Edmund Muskie (D-Maine) quietly passed the word to a small number of senators that Hart would come for a reception and photographs. But word of the reception spread and so many senators showed up that the reception had to be moved to a larger room, which also quickly filled. (Some senators sat on the floor.) Phil was surprised with the watercolor, which lacked one signature. "I told him to sign it," recalled Muskie. Seated there, Hart did, and as he did, he obviously bloomed. "Phil was so weak by then he could barely thank us," Senator Jacob Javits (R-N.Y.) later said, "but we could read his feeling and appreciation in his eyes as we shook hands with him and said what we all knew would be our final farewells." Naming the building for Phil was a nice gesture, wrote columnist Mary McGrory, "and if they could build his qualities . . . into the walls, we would have a Senate that would astound the world with its civility and enlightenment."[4]

Senator Mansfield was also retiring, and at the end of September his colleagues threw a farewell reception for the much-loved majority leader. When Hart arrived, the party had already begun. His eyes met Mansfield's and the two embraced. "For several seconds," observed reporter David Rosenbaum in the *New York Times*, "these two men who have been close friends for years stood there speechless, hugging, with tears in their eyes, and when they broke apart, several other Senators were also fighting back tears."

On his last day in the Senate, a reporter asked Senator Mansfield who was the most outstanding senator he had met during his long career. Without a pause, Mansfield replied: "Phil Hart. He is a man of great courage, great compassion, great determination. Don't be fooled by the exterior. He is a man of steel."[5]

NOTES

1. Joe Klein, "The Saint in the Senate," *Rolling Stone*, 30 December 1976, 35.
2. *Congressional Record*, 100th Cong., 2d sess., 1988, vol. 134, pt. 21:5; *Washington Post*, 29 December 1976; Richard Ryan, telephone interview, 19 May 1988.
3. *Memorial Addresses and Other Tributes in the Congress of the United States on the Life and Contributions of Philip A. Hart*, 95th Cong., 1st sess., 1977, S. Doc. 95, 37; *The Ann Arbor News*, 27 December 1976; *New York Times*, 27 December 1976; Klein, "Saint," 35.
4. Clipping, unprocessed Janey Hart Papers, Washington, D.C.; *The Ann Arbor News*, 27 December 1976; *New York Times*, 1 September 1976, 3 October 1976, 27 December 1976; Senator Jacob K. Javits, *Javits: The Autobiography of a Public Man* (Boston: Houghton Mifflin Company, 1981), 262; Janey Hart, interview, Washington, D.C., 1 and 2 April 1989; Edmund Muskie, telephone interview, 13 July 1988.
5. *New York Times*, 3 October 1976, 27 December 1976.

Early Life, 1912-1941

Accounts of Phil Hart's ancestors and the early life of his parents are sketchy. His paternal grandfather, a Catholic from County Dublin, fought with the British Army during the Crimean War (1854-1855). Shortly after the war he and his wife, Bridget, moved to the United States where he eventually settled in Bryn Mawr, Pennsylvania, and worked as a landscape gardener and manager of a private estate. Their son Philip A. Hart, Sr. was born in 1872. After attending the Lower Merion public schools, Philip studied at Pierce Business College in Philadelphia and then in 1889 accepted a position as a clerk at the newly formed Bryn Mawr Trust Company.

In 1910 Philip Hart, thirty-eight, married Anna Clyde, thirty-four. Anna's parents, the Samuel Clydes, were Scotch Presbyterians who arrived in the United States in the late 1850s and settled near Philadelphia. Anna graduated from high school, an academic accomplishment for a woman in her day, and possessed a keen mind. A notable feature of her personality was her tolerance, a virtue that may have derived partially from the religious friction with her family when she announced her conversion to Catholicism shortly after her marriage. The wedding may have been delayed several years because of her family's strong objection to her marrying a Catholic.[1]

The Harts had two children, Philip, born on 10 December 1912, and Clyde, who arrived five years later to the day. The family settled in Bryn Mawr at 1009 Old Lancaster Road in a three-story, five-bedroom home. Bryn Mawr was an attractive suburban community located in

Lower Merion township in Montgomery County, nine miles west of Philadelphia. Since colonial times the area had been a prime location for estates, and when the Pennsylvania Railroad's main line was constructed, wealthy residents, some of them railroad officials, built more large estates.[2]

Philip Hart worked diligently at the Bryn Mawr Trust Co. and moved up the ranks until he was appointed president in 1921. The 1920s ushered in a new era of prosperity. With rapid expansion of industry and an increase in construction activity and real estate values, the Bryn Mawr Trust Co. flourished, broadening its services to meet a wide range of banking, trust, title insurance, and real estate needs. In 1927 deposits exceeded $4 million.

Although not wealthy, the Harts were comfortable financially. Besides their large home, they owned a cottage, golfed at a private country club, and sent their children to expensive private schools. Philip's principal indulgence was his automobile—a beautiful Pierce Arrow. "Phil was a little embarrassed because his father did indulge himself in [the luxurious] car," recalled Hart's friend and neighbor, Russell MacMullan. Despite their material advantages, the Harts usually lived a simple, modest life.

As a youth Hart had two serious illnesses—a bout with scarlet fever at age eight and another with pneumonia at age nine. (One illness forced him to miss over a month of grade school.) For the most part, Phil had warm memories of his childhood. He had plenty of friends, enjoyed delightful summers, attended excellent schools, and loved and respected his parents. "I knew a childhood," he later said, "which no amount of revision or reliving could make one minute happier."[3]

Together, the Hart family attended the theater, football and baseball games, and the country club. "It seemed there was just a natural family togetherness in our growing up," said Clyde, adding, "The most meaningful values came from mom and dad." Anna was a Norman Rockwell mother—an outstanding housewife, mother, housekeeper, and cook. Philip was a quiet, gentle, thoughtful man. Conscientious at work and at home, tactful and diplomatic, he was well liked in the community and active in civic affairs. "His gracious manner, his friendly consideration, his keen insight into human nature and his sound business judgment made him highly esteemed and respected by all with whom he came in contact," the local Bryn Mawr newspaper later said. At work he could say 'no' to a client and that person would leave and not feel resentful or angry. Eleanor MacMullan, Russ's sister, liked both of Phil's parents: "They were easy to talk to. They did not frighten me as a child as some mothers and fathers . . . used to." Both parents abstained from alcohol and did not serve alcohol to guests. They counseled their children against lying and hypocrisy. "If you say something, mean what you say," was a quietly imparted admonition. Both were also fair-minded and charitable. In 1930, 4.4 percent of the township was made up of blacks who had settled where they could find work in the wealthy homes in the area. Like many of their Bryn Mawr neighbors, the Harts had a series of black maids, but Philip and Anna were not bigoted, believing everyone should be accorded dignity. They also assisted the poor in the community, most of whom were servants of the wealthy. Both Phil and Russ MacMullan delivered baskets of food to the poor.[4]

As a child Phil read, arranged his stamp collection, played baseball near the Catholic Church on Old Lancaster Road, and golfed with his father. The Harts usually spent their summer at Longport, New Jersey, a picturesque resort community on the Atlantic Ocean. At first the family rented an old hotel but later purchased a large, simple cottage on the beach. Anna stayed with the children and Philip joined the family on weekends. Phil swam and played tennis and golf. When he was in high school, his family purchased a motorboat they christened *Phi-Cly* (after the first letters of the children's names). Phil and Clyde competed in boat races. "We both enjoyed it for many summers," said Clyde. An avid and expert body surfer, Phil would catch a wave and let it carry him to the beach. Friends from Bryn Mawr, including Eleanor and Russ MacMullan, were occasional guests. "We had an awful lot of fun," said Eleanor. Summers at Longport were idyllic times for Hart and he fondly recalled them many years later. The beauty of Longport inspired a deep concern for preserving the natural environment, particularly pristine beaches.[5]

On 9 September 1918, Phil entered grade school in Merion, about four and a half miles from his home. The Sisters of Mercy had founded a school in Merion in 1885, and after improving the facilities and expanding the program, they opened a new school in 1923, the Waldron Academy for Boys (named after Mother Patricia Waldron, who had founded the Sisters of Mercy order in Philadelphia). A horse-drawn bus occasionally drove Hart to Waldron but usually his father took him by car.

Waldron was an exclusive, expensive, Catholic school attended mostly by sons of the wealthy. There were only seven students in Hart's graduating class of 1926. Waldron's most unique feature was its heavy emphasis on languages—Latin, German, Greek, and French. The nuns prided themselves on challenging students to measure up to their capabilities, urging them to develop spiritually, academically, socially, and physically as outstanding Christians. The official history of the school contends that "the spirit of self-sacrifice was so prevalent in the sisters that it penetrated the heart and the character of the pupils."[6]

On 7 September 1926, Hart entered West Philadelphia Catholic High School for Boys, a parochial school with 1,700 students, run by the Christian Brothers. Renowned for their dedication to teaching, the Christian Brothers educated their students so they would be able to enter excellent colleges and placed a premium on teaching a solid course in moral ethics. "You were taught right from wrong," said Paul Slattery, a fellow student. "It seemed to permeate all your education."

Hart's interests ranged widely. He served as an officer in the literary club and in student government, starred in the class play, wrote for the school newspaper and the yearbook, helped organize the prom, and managed athletic teams. He was a quiet force in all his activities. "He was always the leader," said Russ MacMullan. "Whatever he was in, he was in a sense directing it without your recognizing he was directing it. He had that rare ability to get things done without any screaming, yelling, pushing, shoving, demanding."

The Kilmer club, the elite literary association for excellent students, improved his writing abilities and provided valuable experience in public speaking. Every other Thursday, members took turns reading poems or delivering talks. A new feature instituted in Hart's senior year called for members to deliver speeches in front of floodlights in the auditorium in order to "cast aside a conquered fear."

Hart modestly understated his own accomplishments. He had a major role in the senior class play *The Triumph*, and a reviewer specifically singled out his performance, praising him for having "carried his part perfectly." Later, however, when Phil described the drama club's activities for the yearbook, he praised the director and the hard-working cast, but did not mention his own role. Of the nine principal actors in the play, he listed himself last.[7]

In some respects Hart differed from his classmates. "He . . . had an air of aristocracy about him," said a fellow student. He dressed better than other boys, the sons of mostly working-class parents. His manner and bearing were also conspicuous. "He had culture," recalled

William Cotterall, another classmate. "He had good breeding and training."

Nonetheless, Phil was popular and respected. "He was a gentleman," said Cotterall, "Everybody liked him. There was nothing snobbish about him." Phil had a "marvelous personality," said Eleanor MacMullan, and was "fun to be with." The editors of the senior yearbook described Hart as "A real man among men. Always willing, always doing. His character true as a fine steel rapier, undaunted, successful, admired."[8]

In his junior year Hart began driving a car and on Friday and Saturday nights he and his friends attended dances, played bridge, or went to a movie or the ice cream parlor. He startled his friends by his attitude toward unattractive girls. At the dances some of the girls were wallflowers. Overweight, ungainly, none of the boys would dance with them. Except Phil. He asked them to dance, brightening their evening. Some of the other boys never understood Hart's motive. "It was typical of him," said Russ MacMullan, who did understand. "To be kind. To give them some fun."

Hart earned a B+ average in his college preparation courses, which included four years of Latin and three of German. Both Phil and Russ MacMullan were near the top of their class. "I do not think he was a genius," reflected MacMullan, whose grades were higher than Phil's. Yet MacMullan conceded Hart had an advantage in another quality. "I was very highly intelligent," MacMullan said, "but [I] did not have the street smarts that he had."

Hart's verbose but sincere editorial in his senior yearbook thanked the Christian Brothers for instilling "high and elevating ideals" and for having "carried us along in our troubles, stepped aside in our glories and given us every opportunity for recognition."[9]

As Phil grew up he identified primarily with his Irish-Catholic background, and his heritage stimulated his distaste for discrimination and his love of politics. In northeastern states before the Civil War, the Know-Nothing movement organized political assaults on the citizenship and equal status of Irish-Catholics, and after the war the Irish remained objects of contempt and discrimination. As unskilled newcomers to older established communities, the Irish found themselves on the lowest rung of the economic ladder. By 1880 half the Irish population of Philadelphia was still engaged in unskilled jobs. Consequently, "the Irish consistently suffered the disdain that society reserves for its poor and marginal members." Hostility to the Irish was more extreme, however, partly because of the violent resistance of the Irish to denigration and their pugnacious and successful efforts to achieve influence. In the late nineteenth century, higher-toned newspapers and periodicals and reformed-minded journalists perpetuated the stereotype of the "corrupt, drunken, ignorant, and priest-ridden Irishman." Thomas Nast savagely caricatured the Irish in his cartoons, portraying them as subhuman species, more apes than men. "There is no doubt that my Irish background has helped shape my attitudes on . . . civil rights," Phil Hart later said. Stories heard at home made him "keenly aware of the kind of discrimination my grandparents faced when they arrived in this country."[10]

As large numbers of Irish Americans became U.S. citizens and familiar with the nation, they became increasingly active in politics. With its egalitarian outlook and strength among the lower classes, the Democratic party attracted the Irish, and the Irish politicians came to dominate politics in New York and Boston. Although often corrupt, Irish politicians capitalized on ethnic identity and served constituents by facilitating naturalization, finding employment, offering relief services, and acting as the intermediary with higher authorities.[11]

Phil's father intensely enjoyed politics—"as all Irish are supposed to," Phil later observed. Bryn Mawr was overwhelmingly Republican. In 1920 Montgomery County gave Republican presidential candidate Warren Harding an almost three-to-one margin, but Philip, Sr. was a Democrat, partly because his own father had probably been a Democrat. "He was pretty definite about his politics," observed Russ MacMullan, whom Mr. Hart often teased. "I was welcome in his home," said MacMullan, "despite the fact that I came from a very Republican family."

For awhile Phil Hart, Sr. was chairman of the Lower Merion Township Democratic Committee, and his counsel was sought by county and state Democrats. Animated, stimulating, uncontrived political conversation dominated the dinner table at the Hart home. Never vehement or dogmatic, Philip discussed political issues intelligently and tolerated other opinions. He believed in tolerance and justice to such a degree that he bought Phil an unusual gift on his seventeenth birthday: a membership in the National Association for the Advancement of Colored People (NAACP).

Young Phil grew up steeped in the lore of Woodrow Wilson, who in the mid-1880s briefly taught history at nearby Bryn Mawr College before going into politics and the presidency. At school Hart's friends teased him about his political interests. "Phil," said one, "you are going to be a senator someday."[12]

When Phil was eleven, his father took him to Madison Square Garden for the 1924 Democratic Convention, one of the most exciting and bitter conventions in United States history. It was a "knockdown, dragout fight" illustrating many of the social conflicts of the 1920s. Democrats were showing signs of falling under the sway of "racists, bigots and xenophobes" in their southern and western wings. The powerful Ku Klux Klan angered eastern Democrats, many of whom were Catholic and from immigrant backgrounds. Many delegates from the South and West were Klansmen or worried about the Klan's influence in their state. When the convention's platform committee refused to condemn the Klan by name, eastern delegates wrote a minority report, singling out the Klan for strong criticism. The convention bitterly fought over the minority report and barely defeated it, preventing the party from going on record against the Klan.

The convention's presidential nomination pitted Alfred E. Smith against William G. McAdoo. Phil and his father supported Smith, the governor of New York, a Catholic and the darling of eastern city masses. Popular and talented, Smith had earned a reputation for honesty and sincere interest in alleviating the problems of the poor and the working class of the great metropolitan areas. McAdoo, a Protestant from Tennessee, evoked the enthusiastic support of the South and West. Eastern delegates wanted Smith and would not compromise; southern and western delegates insisted on McAdoo and would not budge. Noisy Smith partisans in the galleries hooted at speakers who opposed their hero. Fist fights broke out. After several days, on the 103rd ballot the weary delegates turned to a compromise candidate, John W. Davis, an archconservative Wall Street lawyer, who ended up losing to incumbent President Calvin Coolidge. The exciting convention left a lasting impression on the young Phil Hart. Reflecting on the convention thirty years later, he observed that "The most thrilling spectacle is not a World Series or an Army-Navy football game—it's a national convention of one of our major political parties." In 1932 Phil attended the Democratic Convention in Chicago during which Franklin D. Roosevelt was nominated to run against President Herbert Hoover. Hart predicted Roosevelt would be a weak candidate. "We live and learn," he later confessed.[13]

In the fall of 1930, Phil entered Jesuit-run Georgetown University. Founded in 1789, the university was located on seventy-eight acres in

Georgetown Heights, a twenty-minute ride from the White House, with a noble view overlooking Washington, D.C. and the Potomac river. Tuition, room, and board, cost $1,250 in Phil's senior year, making Georgetown the most expensive Catholic college in the country. The school highlighted the advantages of its location in the nation's capital: access to major libraries and scientific collections, plus "the presence of the National Government" which "in itself [is] a most powerful agent of education."[14]

The Jesuit system of education was thorough, organized, efficient, and exacting. Jesuits have the reputation for turning out persons of strong will power and long vision. At Georgetown philosophy and religion courses were compulsory. Scholastic philosophy permeated the academic atmosphere, and its principles molded Hart's moral and intellectual development. "Philosophy was the compulsory major," said Herman Heide, one of Phil's classmates; "we got a very good course in scholasticism." Scholasticism was the method of learning in the medieval cathedral schools. St. Thomas Aquinas, its principal formulator, brought together into a formidable synthesis the insights of classical philosophy (mainly Aristotle's) and Christian theology. The system's method relied on strict logical deduction taking the form of an intricate system; one established premises that led inexorably to a conclusion. Religious instruction was the "first importance," said the Georgetown catalogue. In the Scholastic system, philosophy was directly and immediately subordinate to Catholic theology. Riches, pleasure, power, and knowledge were all good and legitimate objects of the appetites, but perfect happiness was found not in created things but in God, the supreme good.

The Jesuits regulated student life and the classroom to establish the conditions for rigorous work. Hours were fixed for students to rise, take their meals, and attend chapel and Mass. On some days during the week mass was required, and a student who missed was denied weekend privileges. Any student possessing liquor or "immoral books," warned the college catalogue, would be liable to expulsion, "as will any grave offense against morals or discipline." If a student missed more than fifteen percent of his classes, he failed the course. Through such rules, Georgetown's Jesuits hoped to produce dedicated, self-sacrificing students.[15]

With Hart they succeeded. Quiet, serious, and rule-abiding, he worried about every exam he took, but he did not need to worry. In class he was always prepared, answered questions and engaged in class discussions. "He was an excellent student," recalled Father Vincent Hart (no relation), Dean of the College of Arts and Sciences during most of Phil's college years. Of twenty-three courses Phil took, he received only one grade below B+ (a C+ in German) and earned a four-year average of A-.[16]

For over three years Hart roomed with Walter O. "Spike" Briggs, Jr., the son of a wealthy industrialist from Detroit. A cheerful, amiable, and popular student, Briggs became Hart's closest friend. But Spike was not earnest in his academic work; he liked to drink and to sneak off the campus. Spike's father thought his son would have never graduated had Phil not "chained him in" occasionally and made him pay attention to his studies.

Extracurricular activities occupied much of Hart's time. His interests ranged from student government to debate, from religion to managing athletic teams. At meetings of the Current Events Club he listened to lectures on major national and international issues. As a sophomore he served as vice president of his class and president of the Gaston Debating Society; as a junior he was class president and assistant manager of the football team.

He went to Mass almost every day and for four years he belonged to the Sodality of the Blessed Virgin, whose members were usually the most devout Catholics. The Sodality encouraged piety and honored the Mother of God with special devotions and activities. Because the Jesuits were intensely interested in social reform, they encouraged students to work with the poor. "Their preferential option is for the poor," said Father Hart of the Jesuit's philosophy. Hart focused his efforts on working with the Catholic charities in Washington, D.C. that were trying to help poor, wayward boys—both black and white. John Murray, a leader in Sodality and the student coordinator of its work with the Catholic charities, described Phil as "extremely busy" but "always available whenever there was something to be done."[17]

Hart's primary interest was debate, and at Georgetown debate was a major activity. The college had three debating societies, plus an intercollegiate debating team, and reports on debates filled the student newspaper. The debate program was designed to develop the student's skills in applied logic and argumentation. After thoroughly studying an issue, the debater took the affirmative or negative position and rebutted the arguments of debaters on the other side of the issue. Judges determined the winner.

Father John Toohey, the genius behind Georgetown's successful debate program, was the master of logic, who taught philosophy and religion and became Hart's primary mentor. In his highly respected logic course, Toohey taught students about apprehension, judgment, inference, the syllogism, truth, skepticism, and theories of knowledge. Exceptionally organized and methodical, for over two decades he had been the academic advisor to the Philodemic Society, the most prestigious debating club at Georgetown.

Hart debated the pros and cons of inflating the United States money supply, canceling the war debts from World War I, intervening militarily in Latin America, and nationalizing coal mines. "He was a public speaker of great merit," said Father Hart. Indeed, Hart became an exceptionally persuasive debater. He took both sides of the same question on the same evening and won both debates. A debating colleague knew Phil was an outstanding debater simply because "he was on the winning team so often." In his sophomore year he and three other students debated in Latin, and a priest observer remarked that Hart's delivery was so outstanding it made him think that he had been listening to a "modern-day Cicero."[18]

Hart won major debating contests in both his sophomore and junior years. As a junior, in competition with seven other debaters, he earned the Garvan Oratorical Medal for his eight-minute, original speech on cancellation of war debts. The school newspaper described it as "exceptionally well composed" and presented with "force and eloquence as stirring as it was impressive. Very rhetorical in nature, it perfectly suited Mr. Hart's manner of speaking."

In Hart's junior year he was asked to join the Philodemic Society. Over a century old, rich in tradition, the Philodemic Society arranged contests among Georgetown's members and debated major eastern universities including Harvard and Columbia. It had not lost an intercollegiate debate since 1921.[19]

"What a versatile fellow [Phil] was," said Wilmer Bradley, a classmate. Bradley's assessment particularly applied to Hart's final year and a half at Georgetown, during which his combined efforts in courses and in extracurricular activities rank among the most remarkable in the history of the university. Although one incident blemished his record, Hart was president of the Yard, president of the Student Council, president of the Philodemic Society, president of the Athletic Association, the school's most illustrious orator, an award-winning senior officer in the Reserve

Officers' Training Corps (ROTC), an editor of the yearbook, associate editor of the school newspaper, and the principal speaker at the senior class day exercise. To top it off, he earned a straight A average in all his senior courses.[20]

For four years Hart took courses and trained in ROTC, and earned a reserve commission. In his final year he was a top officer in Georgetown's unit. Not all his efforts succeeded. While commanding a unit marching in a parade, he directed his men down a narrow dead-end street and had difficulty getting them back into the parade.

But another ROTC experience was a major accomplishment. In the summer of 1933, before his senior year, Phil attended two weeks of training at Fort George G. Meade near Laurel, Maryland. Rising early in the morning, he endured a rigorous series of drills and exercises and learned about the 30-caliber rifle, the rifle range, and tactics. "We were soldiers for those two weeks," recalled Wilmer Bradley, a fellow trainee.

Near the end of Hart's training an important exercise put into practice the theories he had learned. Given command of a battalion, he was to engage in a surprise attack on an "enemy" unit. The observers—all regular army men—sat Hart down and handed him the problem on paper, told him to study it and execute a plan, and rated him on his performance.

Hart performed brilliantly. "He did such an excellent job," recalled Bradley, "that the top brass on the scene were forced to admit that it was just about 'tops' in anything like it they had ever seen." He was awarded a special medal, but, Bradley said, "to him it was not all that great—that was typically Hart."[21]

In May 1933, at the end of Hart's junior year, Georgetown's students selected three members of the junior class as their "Yard Officers." After a week-long campaign conducted with the assistance of friends, Hart won the election as president of the Yard, the highest student position at Georgetown, making him the "official spokesman" for the students during his senior year. (The position also placed him in charge of the Student Council.)

In the eyes of the faculty and the administration, by being elected president of the Yard Hart had shown his leadership qualities and was entitled to special privileges. He could leave campus at any time. (On about ten occasions in his senior year the administration asked him to meet visiting dignitaries at the train depot.) No student petition could be presented to the faculty or the administration without his approval.

He could enter the dean's office or the president's office at his pleasure. "He was never rejected whenever he wanted to see the president," observed Father Hart.[22]

As president of the Yard, Hart was supposed to provide guidance for new students. In a windy statement published in *The Hoya* in the fall of Phil's senior year, he urged the new freshmen class "to aspire to emulate the example of their upper class brothers." There were "traditions and rules the observance of which is expected and conformity with which will assure immediate and unreserved acceptance of that class by others." If the freshmen cooperated, Hart predicted, their support would be all that was needed "to assure a year unrivalled in achievement and glory." He also tried to inspire students to support the football team. At a pep rally attended by 500 students in the fall of 1933, he spoke of the "famed Georgetown spirit" and pleaded with the students to "get entirely behind the team and to cheer as they have never cheered before."

Hart won praises for his year-long work as president of the Yard. "He was an excellent president," said Father Hart. "His judgment was excellent." The yearbook's editor agreed, commending his methods and success: "With always a kind word and a gracious appearance, with at times a gentle but firm and just criticism, he was able to inspire alike, the trust and confidence of the faculty and the students."[23]

Hart's articles in the student newspaper dealt mainly with the football team. One well-written piece (co-authored by the chief editor) effectively smoothed ruffled feathers of another college. Stories in Washington, D.C. newspapers quoted the coach of Carnegie reacting bitterly to alleged unsportsmanlike behavior by Georgetown's fans at a recent football game. Georgetown's cheerleaders, the coach charged, had purposely and rudely drummed up noise to drown out the signals of Carnegie's quarterback and a major "melee" had resulted in the "disappearance" of Carnegie's football. Hart's article diplomatically contended that the Georgetown fans had cheered in response to their own team's outstanding defensive play and that the cheerleaders had stopped the cheering as soon as possible. Moreover, after the game Georgetown's coach had entered Carnegie's locker room to apologize for the fighting and to present the Carnegie coach with a new football. Concluding gracefully, the article called Carnegie a "friend to be most highly regarded" and offered "sincere" apology for the misunderstandings.[24]

In December 1933, the Philodemic Society sponsored the most prestigious oratorical competition of the year, the annual Merrick

Debate. Hart and his partner debated two fellow students on the question: "That the present system of tax exemption for federal, state, and municipal securities should be abolished." Phil took the affirmative and, said *The Hoya*, his speech was delivered "in the heat of outrage" against the unfair practice that resulted from the tax exemption. He primarily argued that the exemption allowed the government securities to compete unfairly with the securities of businesses and corporations. The system had a depressing effect upon businesses, burdening them with high carrying charges. Moreover, the exemption enabled the wealthy to dodge their tax obligations, allowing the burden to fall on the already overburdened middle-class taxpayer. Hart concluded with a quote from a financial periodical, stating that "an awakened public opinion should demand the taxation of those securities now exempt . . . both as a source of new revenue and as a means of limiting excessive fortunes in a land where multitudes are in dire stress."

Later in the debate Hart impressively rebutted the negative position. "He clearly and concisely gave competent and stirring answers to practically every argument advanced by the negative," reported *The Hoya*. Judges awarded the victory to the negative position, but the "Merrick Medal" for the single outstanding debater went to Phil. He won, said *The Hoya*, because he combined a "complete mastery of the facts . . . with an ability to present well-developed and pertinent arguments with force, conviction, and fluency."[25]

Most persons who knew Phil at Georgetown described him as warm, kind, friendly, and always interested and concerned for the welfare of others. "Phil was much loved," said Father Hart. John Murray lived across the hall from Hart, and when Murray's father died in 1932, Phil wrote Murray a note of condolence. "He was definitely a man of outstanding character and ability," Murray recalled. Robert Hall, another classmate and friend, judged Phil as "a man of unwavering integrity and impeccable character." Modesty was one of his virtues, added Hall: "I . . . never heard him brag about his accomplishments, though myriad." While Phil was running for president of the Yard, in most classes he sat next to Hall. Yet Phil never personally asked for Hall's vote. After the election, when Hall told Hart he had voted for him, Phil expressed appreciation and added that he had not said anything earlier because he wanted Hall "to vote his conscience." Concluded Hall: "This was an example of his consideration for others."[26]

Not everyone liked Hart. A few classmates thought he used transparent friendliness to ingratiate himself with everyone at Georgetown in order to advance his standing as the leading campus politician. "Phil Hart was a consummate politician from the first day of school," contended E. Kirby Hayes. "He was liked by his classmates because he was always pleasant, did not take opposite stands from the students and joined every organization on the campus." Herman Heide, another classmate, agreed: "He was basically, in the proper sense of the word, a politician from the start."27

One embarrassing public incident seemed to confirm the view of Hart's critics. In early February 1934, the Philodemic Society held its election meeting. Phil chaired the meeting and sought election as president. Assuming he deserved the office, he expected no challenge. But Spike Briggs and Herman Heide had secretly organized to oppose him. Apparently they perceived an irritating smugness in Phil's demeanor and were going to teach him a lesson. The pair arranged for Briggs to run against Hart for president. Heide recalled that they wanted to put a "little scare" into him. Hart was more than scared; he was enraged. How could Briggs, his roommate and closest friend, have the gall to challenge him? Unfortunately, a reporter for the school newspaper covered the election and recorded Hart's arrogant response to the challenge. "Forewarned by his astute political nose," reported *The Hoya* of the chaotic election, "Hart descended from the rostrum to deliver a particularly bitter invective against those he termed his 'political enemies.'" Phil ridiculed the oratorical ability of Briggs and reminded everyone that he "was eminently qualified for the job since he had been president of the Gaston [Debating] Society, winner of many debating and oratorical awards, and was in general very much the superior of Mr. Briggs."

Hart won the election—by only one vote. The temporary chair, who had been appointed by Hart, cast the deciding vote in his favor. Heide, whom Hart had charged with being one of his enemies, was nonetheless elected vice president. (Phil "blasted me from here to kingdom come," Heide recalled many years after the incident.) What had caused Phil's uncharacteristic angry outburst? Heide speculated that Hart desperately wanted to win the election because normally the president of the Philodemic Society was chosen by the administration to deliver the Conhonguroton Address, the prestigious student oration delivered during the week of June graduation exercises. "Of course," said Heide, "he wanted to give that [oration]." Arrogance was a feature of Hart's personality, Heide thought. Normally Phil was modest and pleasant, Heide added, "except when his dander [was] up." The election squabble left no lasting scars. Hart subsequently resumed amiable relations with both Briggs and Heide. And despite being attacked by Phil, Heide thought the motives for his political activities on campus were good— that he wanted to serve the needs of students and the university.[28]

The administration did select Hart to deliver the Conhonguroton Address, named after a famous Indian chief of the Potomac. On 9 June 1934, wearing Indian regalia, Hart delivered the oration from the balcony over the esplanade of the White-Gravenor Building. Two days later he received his Bachelor of Arts, cum laude, at Georgetown's 135th commencement ceremony.[29]

Thirty years after graduation Hart reflected on the values taught him at Georgetown. He praised his alma mater for teaching intellectual honesty and for encouraging independent thought. After many years it was difficult for him to separate the influences Georgetown had on his life, even though he knew they were considerable. Whatever lessons he learned at Georgetown "in humanity, justice, fellowship, and love of God become so woven into your natural being that their origins can no longer be accurately catalogued." Hart concluded: "And is not that what truly good teaching is all about?"[30]

While Hart established a sparkling record at Georgetown, a melancholy development cast a pall over his college years. In October 1929, stock prices collapsed, and when the nation plummeted into severe depression, thousands of banks closed their doors, including thirteen in Montgomery County, Pennsylvania. Would his father's institution survive? Phil wondered with deepening concern. "He was very concerned about the banks," said a friend. By March 1933, deposits at the Bryn Mawr Trust Co. had dipped to a little more than two million dollars. The company remained solvent but with a heavily depressed real estate market, the recovery was slow and painful. The burden of guiding the company through the depression weighed heavily on Philip Hart, Sr. Worried, working feverishly so none of his depositors would lose any money, he felt intense pressure that may have contributed to his fatal heart attack at age sixty-two in November 1934. A memorial service in Bryn Mawr eulogized him for his "sterling qualities, splendid character, [and] unfailing honesty." Although deeply saddened, young Phil was proud of his father's five-year struggle to save his company and his sensitivity to his customers. Six years later his mother died of colon cancer.[31]

On 24 September 1934, Hart entered law school at the University of Michigan in Ann Arbor. Under the brilliant guidance of its president, Alexander Ruthven, the University of Michigan had become an outstanding center of scholarship and its law school was one of the most eminent in the nation. At the University of Michigan Hart not only received an excellent education in law, but further cultivated his interest in liberal Democratic politics during the height of Democrat Franklin Roosevelt's New Deal.

During his three years at law school Hart studied diligently, but because he grasped assignments quicker than most of his classmates, he did not have to exhaust himself. He earned a B+ average in his freshman year; slumped to a C+ his second; and rebounded his senior year, earning an A-. He could have done better had he not enjoyed reading and discussion with friends more than he enjoyed just studying. "It is far from the easiest thing conceivable," he wrote a priest friend at Georgetown in December 1935. "Thanks to Georgetown's foundation and my Irish luck, I have been very successful so far, and was one of the twenty to be invited from the second-year class to 'go on' the *Law Review*."

The faculty invited the brightest students to become editorial assistants on the *Michigan Law Review*. It was an honor and an advantage in securing an excellent job after graduation. For two years Phil worked on the *Law Review*, writing esoteric articles on the legal status of airplane flight, trademarks, the capacity of an unincorporated association to act as a trustee of a charitable trust, and the rules of evidence when a wife testified against her husband.[32]

Because of the rigorous course work, students had little time for social life, and Hart socialized even less than most. He maintained his friendship with Spike Briggs, who had returned to Detroit to work in his father's business. On weekends students congregated at the Pretzel Bell, a large beer hall and restaurant in Ann Arbor, but Hart seldom drank and did not enjoy the raucous atmosphere. Instead, he played rummy or went to a movie with friends. He seemed shy around women and dated infrequently. For awhile he dated Betty Firestone, wealthy heir to the founder of the Firestone Tire Co., but their relationship never developed into a serious one. "I never saw him in the presence of a woman," said Charles Moon, a fellow student, adding, "I would have thought sometimes that his life on campus might have been a little lonely."[33]

Most of Hart's social life centered around his fraternity. In his first year he lived in a dormitory with other law students; the following year he joined Phi Delta Phi and lived at the fraternity house. (Tragedy struck the second year. He woke up one morning to find his roommate had died of a heart attack.) Phi Delta Phi was a prestigious legal fraternity pledging mostly excellent legal scholars. "It was a very fine group of men," said one of Phil's classmates. In his senior year Hart became president of the fraternity, an honor but not a burdensome task since the fraternity had a manager who handled day-to-day operations. One unpleasant burden, though, did fall to Phil: the responsibility of controlling heavy drinking at parties by a few fraternity brothers. "I think he had a little trouble understanding . . . some of the members of the fraternity," said Moon. When parties became wild, Hart would "endeavor to lecture some of the members about their behavior," but his efforts proved unavailing.

Hart's classmates enjoyed and respected him. A "wonderful guy that everyone loved," said one; a "delightful personality, [with] highest character and exceptional intelligence," said another. George Balter recalled Hart as "slender, almost frail looking, quiet, laid-back, refined, a great listener, very, very bright, and completely candid."[34]

One student Hart associated with in classes, *Law Review*, and the fraternity was Gerhard Mennen Williams, and the pair became kindred spirits in Democratic politics. A native of Detroit and a year ahead of Hart in law school, Williams was an heir to the Mennen soap fortune, hence his nickname "Soapy," which he had since boyhood. Big, charismatic, outspoken, and brilliant, Williams attended an exclusive prep school, then Princeton University, where he graduated with high honors and was recommended for a Rhodes Scholarship. At law school he would also graduate with honors.

Although his family were staunch Republicans, by the time Williams entered law school he had become a liberal Democrat. "It was sort of a paradox," said a law school classmate, "because everybody knew Soapy came from a wealthy family." Williams later claimed that his study of the misery brought on by English serfdom and the growth of a grinding and heartless factory system in England helped to convert him into a determined champion of the underdog. Infected with liberal idealism, Williams made vociferous speeches on campus supporting the New Deal of Franklin Roosevelt.[35]

Hart, like Williams, was caught up in the turmoil of theories, ideas, debate, and controversy. "There were a lot of new ideas kicking around," Phil recalled thirty years after law school. "Radical ones. Social security. Medicare. Minimum wage. Ideas such as those, all of them troublesome." But Hart vigorously supported all of them and was usually in the minority. "Phil Hart and Soapy Williams were part of a very small group of 'liberals' in an overwhelmingly conservative student body of Republicans," said Balter, a fellow democrat. The faculty was mostly conservative Republican as well. But Hart and Williams gravitated toward other liberal Democrats, such as Prof. John P. Dawson, one of the few Democrats on the faculty. "At that time," recalled Dawson of the political controversy on campus, "there was a series of great events; the London Economic Conference, the Agricultural Adjustment Administration, NRA, the Wagner Labor Relations Act, the beginnings of the Reciprocal Trade Program, passage of Social Security. New concepts were arrived at every day, and put into national legislation or international commitments."

Hart and Williams helped organize the Lawyers' Liberal Club, which met regularly to hear highly controversial talks by such prominent figures as Socialist leader Norman Thomas, to discuss military and international affairs, and to analyze the reform programs of the New Deal. An avid reader of newspapers and magazines, Hart kept himself fully informed on current events. "I marched in the '30s in campus protests," Phil said many years later. He may have protested occasionally but his primary passion was discussing and arguing with friends. "I certainly remember many, many discussions with him . . . in which he was a very strong supporter of FDR and of his policies and programs," said Moon. He had "empathy for the underdog," said Milton Howard, a liberal Democrat. Arguments with classmates occasionally became heated, especially during the 1936 election campaign between FDR and Alf Landon. "Our group wore our FDR buttons with pride," said Balter.[36]

On 19 June 1937, Hart graduated with his Juris Doctor, an honors degree, having ranked in the top twenty-five percent of his class. After graduation, he accepted an offer to join the blue-chip law firm Beaumont, Smith, and Harris, located in downtown Detroit. Busy at work, he did not bother to study for his Michigan Bar exam and paid the price for his overconfidence: he flunked one section. "He did not study, did not take it seriously," said a former classmate. "It was a surprise to all of us"—and an embarrassment to Hart. Six months later he retook the entire exam and passed.[37]

NOTES

1. *Dublin* [Ireland] *Sunday Independent*, 24 July 1966; Nena Vreeland, *Philip A. Hart,* Ralph Nader Congress Project: Citizens Look at Congress (Grossman Publishers, 1972), 2; Ann Anderson, interview, Washington, D.C., 26 March 1988; Clyde Hart, telephone interview, 8 August 1988; Janey Hart, interview, Washington, D.C., 1 and 2 April 1989.

2. Jean Barth Toll and Michael J. Schwager, eds., *Montgomery County: The Second Hundred Years* (Montgomery: Montgomery County Federation of Historical Societies, 1983), 1:308; Clyde Hart, telephone interview, 8 August 1988; Russell MacMullan, telephone interview, 5 July 1988.

3. Philip Hart to Janey Hart, 16 April 1944, unprocessed Janey Hart Papers, Washington, D.C.; "Report of Physical Examination," 27 June 1941, Philip Hart File, Veterans' Administration Papers, Milwaukee, Wisconsin; "Academic Records of Philip A. Hart," unprocessed Waldron Academy Papers, Merion, Pennsylvania; *Blue and White 1929* [Yearbook, West Philadelphia Catholic High School for Boys]; *Bryn Mawr Bank Corporation: 1988 Annual Report*, 5-8; Ann Anderson, interview, Washington, D.C., 26 March 1988; Clyde Hart, telephone interview, 8 August 1988; Janey Hart, interview, Washington, D.C., 1 and 2 April 1989; Russell MacMullan, telephone interview, 5 July 1988.

4. Clyde Hart to author, 9 April 1988; clipping, Janey Hart Papers; Toll and Schwager, *Montgomery County*, 1:309; Clyde Hart, telephone interview, 8 August 1988; Russell MacMullan, telephone interview, 5 July 1988, Eleanor Richards, telephone interview, 20 March 1989.

5. Clyde Hart to author, 1 June 1989; Ann Anderson, interview, Washington, D.C., 26 March 1988; Clyde Hart, telephone interview, 8 August 1988; Russell MacMullan, telephone interview, 5 July 1988; Eleanor Richards, telephone interview, 20 March 1989; Paul Slattery, telephone interview, 16 May 1988.

6. "Academic Records of Hart"; "A History of Waldron Academy," unpublished article, Waldron Academy Papers; Russell MacMullan, telephone interview, 5 July 1988.

7. "Transcript of Phil Hart's Grades," unprocessed West Philadelphia Catholic School for Boys Papers, Philadelphia, Pennsylvania; *Blue and White, 1928*; *Blue and White, 1930*; William Cotterall, telephone interview, 5 July 1988; Albert Keefe, telephone interview, 17 May 1988; Russell MacMullan, telephone interview, 5 July 1988; Paul Slattery, telephone interview, 16 May 1988.

8. Thomas Hannigan to author, 25 June 1988; *Blue and White, 1930*; William Cotterall, telephone interview, 5 July 1988; Eleanor Richards, telephone interview, 20 March 1989.

9. "Hart's Grades"; *Blue and White, 1930*; William McGarvey, telephone interview, 7 May 1988; Russell MacMullan, telephone interview, 5 July 1988; Paul Slattery, telephone interview, 16 May 1988.

10. *Dublin* [Ireland] *Sunday Independent*, 24 July 1966; Thomas Archdeacon, *Becoming American: An Ethnic History* (New York: The Free Press, 1983), 97, 98, 101; Jean Barth Toll and Michael J. Schwager, eds., *Montgomery County: The Second Hundred Years* (Montgomery: Montgomery County Federation of Historical Societies, 1983), 2:975.

11. Archdeacon, *Becoming American*, 99-101.

12. Clyde Hart to author, 9 April 1988; clipping, Hart Scrapbooks, Philip A. Hart Papers, Bentley Historical Library, Ann Arbor, Michigan; *Chicago Tribune*, 29 September 1968; Toll and Schwager, *Montgomery County*, 2:975; Vreeland, *Philip A. Hart*, 2; Clyde Hart, telephone interview, 8 August 1988; Janey Hart, interview, Washington, D.C., 1 and 2 April 1989; Jerry Kabel, telephone interview, 24 February 1988; Russell MacMullan, telephone interview, 5 July 1988; Paul Slattery, telephone interview, 16 May 1988.

13. Clipping, Hart Scrapbooks, Hart Papers, Bentley Library; *Labor*, 25 October 1958; Archdeacon, *Becoming American*, 191; George Mowry, *The Urban Nation: 1920-1960* (New York: Hill and Wang, 1965), 52-54; David Shannon, *Between the Wars: America, 1919-1941* (Boston: Houghton Mifflin Company, 1965), 60-61.

14. *Georgetown University Catalogue, 1933-1934.*

15. Ibid.; Michael O'Brien, *Vince: A Personal Biography of Vince Lombardi* (New York: William Morrow and Company, Inc., 1987), 37-39; Herman Heide, telephone interview, 29 April 1988.

16. Unpublished letter enclosed in Walter Doherty to author, 8 July 1988; "Academic Records of Philip Aloysius Hart, Jr.," 1934-1937, University of Michigan Law School Papers, Ann Arbor, Michigan; Janey Hart, interview, Washington, D.C., 1 and 2 April 1989; Vincent Hart, telephone interview, 16 May 1989.

17. John Murray to author, 12 July 1988; *Ye Domesday Booke, 1934* [yearbook, Georgetown University]; Janey Hart, interview, Washington, D.C., 1 and 2 April 1989; Vincent Hart, telephone interview, 16 May 1989.

18. Robert Hall to author, 18 July 1988; *The Hoya*, 5 April 1933, 17 May 1933, 18 October 1933, 31 January 1934; *Georgetown University Catalogue, 1933-1934*; Vincent Hart, telephone interview, 16 May 1989; Herman Heide, telephone interview, 29 April 1988; Thomas Williams, interview, Washington, D.C., 28 March 1988.

19. *The Hoya*, 5 April 1933, 31 January 1934; *Georgetown University Catalogue, 1933-1934.*

20. Wilmer Bradley to author, 17 June 1988.

21. Ibid.; Janey Hart, interview, Washington, D.C., 1 and 2 April 1989.

22. *Ye Domesday Booke, 1934;* Vincent Hart, telephone interview, 16 May 1989.

23. Ibid.; *The Hoya*, 27 September 1933, 18 October 1933.

24. *The Hoya*, 22 November 1933.

25. Ibid., 13 December 1933.

26. Robert Hall to author, 18 July 1988; John Murray to author, 12 July 1988; Vincent Hart, telephone interview, 16 May 1989; Herman Heide, telephone interview, 29 April 1988.

27. E. Kirby Hayes to author, 6 June 1988; Herman Heide, telephone interview, 29 April 1988.

28. *The Hoya*, 14 February 1934; Herman Heide, telephone interview, 29 April 1988.

29. Clipping, Philip A. Hart File, Georgetown University Papers, Georgetown University Library, Washington, D.C.; *The Hoya*, 10 May 1934.

30. Philip Hart to Edward Bunn, 2 June 1965, Hart File, Georgetown University Papers.

31. Clipping, Janey Hart Papers; *Bryn Mawr Bank Corporation: 1988 Annual Report*, 6; Janey Hart, interview, Washington, D.C., 1 and 2 April 1989; Paul Slattery, telephone interview, 16 May 1988.

32. Stanley Smoyer to author, 7 February 1989; Phil Hart to (?), 1 December 1935, Hart File, Georgetown University Papers; "Academic Records of Philip Hart," 1934-1937, University of Michigan Law School Papers; *Michigan Law Review* 35 (1936): 329-33; *Michigan Law Review* 35 (1937): 656-59, 1403-6, 1123-30; Frank McNaughton, *Mennen Williams of Michigan: Fighter for Progress* (New York: Oceana Publications, Inc., 1960), 58; Richard Barrett, telephone interview, 25 January 1989; Milton Howard, telephone interview, 15 February 1989; Charles Moon, telephone interview, 23 February 1989.

33. Richard Barrett to author, 14 January 1989; Richard Barrett, telephone interview, 25 January 1989; Janey Hart, interview, Washington, D.C., 1 and 2 April 1989; Milton Howard, telephone interview, 15 February 1989; Charles Moon, telephone interview, 23 February 1989.

34. George Balter to author, 4 February 1989; Stanley Smoyer to author, 7 February 1989; Richard Barrett, telephone interview, 25 January 1989; Janey Hart, interview, Washington, D.C., 1 and 2 April 1989; Milton Howard, telephone interview, 15 February 1989; Charles Moon, telephone interview, 23 February 1989.

35. George Balter to author, 4 February 1989; McNaughton, *Mennen Williams*, 55, 58; Charles Moritz, ed., "G. Mennen Williams," *Current Biography Yearbook 1963* (New York: The H.W. Wilson Company, 1963), 466-67; Richard Barrett, telephone interview, 25 January 1989; Milton Howard, telephone interview, 15 February 1989.

36. George Balter to author, 4 February 1989; *New York Times*, 23 February 1969; *Washington Post*, 3 May 1970; McNaughton, *Mennen Williams*, 59-60; Milton Howard, telephone interview, 15 February 1989; Richard Barrett, telephone interview, 25 January 1989.

37. Janey Hart, interview, Washington, D.C., 1 and 2 April 1989; Milton Howard, telephone interview, 15 February 1989; Charles Moon, telephone interview, 23 February 1989.

World War II and Aftermath, 1941-1946

Philip Hart had not been a lawyer for long when World War II interrupted his career for five years. During the war he was not a glamorous hero—in combat he never fired his pistol and seldom used his rifle. Yet in some ways he did act heroically. In any case, he was a dedicated infantry officer who diligently performed his tasks and was a sensitive, keen observer of the war and the soldiers who fought it. There were tragic moments as well—a serious injury and his heartbreaking, depressing return home after the war.

World War II had broken out on 1 September 1939 when Nazi Germany invaded Poland. A storm of fire and steel battered the Poles throughout the month as the powerful Germans completed an easy victory. On 10 May 1940, Hitler's forces broke through defenses in the West, forcing France to capitulate six weeks later and leaving Great Britain isolated. After the fall of France, Great Britain fought alone against the Nazi onslaught until Germany invaded Russia in June 1941, after which the Russians and the British became allies.

Meanwhile, the United States was gradually awakening from its isolationist slumber. With the British near financial bankruptcy, President Roosevelt inaugurated Lend-Lease, which became law in March 1941, enabling the United States to funnel supplies to the British. Japan's attack on Pearl Harbor on 7 December 1941 unified Americans and precipitated U.S. entry in the war against Japan, Germany and Italy.

Hart had been unenthusiastic about U.S. intervention, later observing "I was a whole lot less aggressive (and certain)" than others. After his

ROTC experience at Georgetown, he had no further contact with the military until 1 July 1941, when the Army, short of trained officers, called him to active duty. He was sent to Fort Sheridan, Chicago, as a supply and evacuation staff officer, helping to process new draftees. (He shepherded the inductees by train from their physical exam to basic training.)[1]

It was dull duty and surprisingly hazardous. Given a shot for yellow fever, he suffered a severe reaction and landed in the hospital for eleven days. "A man of superior type and character," the officer at Fort Sheridan wrote on Hart's efficiency report in March 1942. Phil was adaptable, versatile, and modest, reported the officer, but "a little doubtful of his own ability."

Ready for more exciting work, in June 1942, while reading *Stars and Stripes*, Hart noted that General Raymond O. Barton had been given command of the 4th Infantry Division at Camp Gordon near Augusta, Georgia. Hart knew Barton because nine years earlier, as he entered his senior year at Georgetown, Barton had joined the faculty as Professor of Military Science and Tactics. Hart wrote Barton, reminding him that the general had told the Georgetown ROTC graduates that if there were ever a war, he wanted them as officers in his command. He requested reassignment to the 4th Division. Barton responded quickly, arranged for Phil's transfer, and Hart joined Barton at Camp Gordon on about 11 August 1942.

At that time Hart was a first lieutenant and Barton's senior aide; the junior aide was First Lieutenant Lew Fiset, who became Phil's closest friend in the war. Fiset, a Chicago native, had attended Northwestern University and Officer Candidate School. Both of them developed a deep respect and affection for General Barton. Raised in Oklahoma, a graduate of West Point in 1912, Barton was a thickset, strong man with a military mustache and a severe ulcer. He was considerate, fine social company, and an astute, hard-driving commander. "He treated us more like sons," said Fiset of Barton's fatherly manner.[2]

The 4th Infantry Division had a glorious history, but soldiers in the division worried they would sit out World War II at garrisons in the States. The division's three infantry regiments had been fighting for generations. The 12th regiment fought in the War of 1812, with General Winfield Scott in Mexico, in the Civil War, Indian campaigns, the war with Spain, the Philippine Insurrection, and World War I.

In June 1940, a new 4th Division was activated. Organized and trained at Fort Benning, Georgia, it initially served as a guinea pig in experiments with motorized infantry divisions. The 4th moved to Camp Gordon early in 1942 when that infantry training center opened. In the fall of 1942, the division packed up for the invasion of North Africa but was squeezed out by a shipping shortage. For the next six months, the 4th was one of the most frequently alerted units in the army. But while fighting raged in Africa, Sicily, and Italy, the division resumed training at Camp Gordon. In the spring of 1943, the experiment as a motorized division scuttled, the 4th moved north to Fort Dix, New Jersey, to retrain as a conventional infantry division. Rumors circulated of impending overseas duty, but instead the men of the 4th spent much of their time raking lawns and painting garbage cans. Then came amphibious training at Camp Gordon Johnston in Florida and a brief stretch at Fort Jackson, South Carolina. Every time the division moved it seemed to get no nearer to the war. "We're over-trained!" the men complained. "What're we waiting for?" Meanwhile, during 1942-1943, Hart was preoccupied with something far more personal than the 4th Division and World War II—his courtship with Jane (Janey) Briggs.[3]

Janey Briggs, nine years younger than Phil, was the sister of Hart's Georgetown roommate, Walter O. "Spike" Briggs. Born on 20 October 1921, she was the fifth child of the multimillionaire industrialist, Walter O. Briggs, Sr. Her father had quit school at fourteen to work, drifted into the automobile business, and in 1909 founded the Briggs Manufacturing Co. of Detroit, which became the largest independent auto-body manufacturer in the world. Her father also owned the Detroit Tigers baseball team and Briggs Stadium in Detroit.

Born into a world of French governesses and jaunts to Europe, Janey rode horses, show-jumped, sailed, and earned a pilot's license. From age ten to seventeen, her parents sent her to Eden Hall, an exclusive private school in Torresdale, Pennsylvania. After graduating in 1939, she attended Manhattanville, an exclusive Catholic women's college in New York.

They first met about 1930 when Spike Briggs invited Hart to join the Briggs family at its vacation retreat in Miami Beach. Phil was eighteen and a freshman in college; Janey was nine. Eight years later, while Phil was practicing law in Detroit, Spike and his wife hosted dinner parties, and Phil and Janey, now a debutante, were among the guests. "I think [Spike] was hoping something would happen," Janey recalled. From 1938-1941, they occasionally dated.

In the fall of 1942, Janey was working for the Red Cross in Detroit, having dropped out of college after her freshman year. She had not heard from Phil in almost a year, but he had been thinking deeply about her and analyzing their relationship. "I had thrashed around," he later told her, "with so many questions and complications, some of which I knew never could be adjusted, hence had to be decided as not essential before I felt free to say just how I did feel." Finally he decided to propose marriage ("promising myself never later to question that decision"). While visiting Detroit, Hart phoned her, arranged for dinner, and three days later he asked to marry her. "What a joke!" recalled Janey, laughing at the suddenness of his proposal. "It shows you what war will do to somebody!"

Janey worried that she did not know Phil well enough. Now she took stock of him. She knew he was intelligent, kind, funny, and "that I was very comfortable with him." Her mother worried that Hart was too serious-minded. But her brother Spike had always admired him. Janey's father did too. Indebted to Hart for helping his son through Georgetown, Walter Briggs, Sr. "thought it was the smartest thing I could do in my whole life," said Janey. Having thought it over, she wrote Phil a letter and said yes. Hart was delighted, observing later "how wonderful it was and how about the only disappointment was the clearer understanding of how much I had missed in so long delaying." On 19 June 1943, a sweltering day, they were married at Blessed Sacrament Cathedral in Detroit.

In some ways they were oddly matched. Her high spirits and outspokenness contrasted sharply with Hart's reserve and judiciousness. Phil was a liberal Democrat; Janey's family were conservative-Republican, anti-union, haters of "that man" Franklin Roosevelt and his New Deal. Yet in their over thirty-three years of marriage they would develop common interests, value each other's companionship, and care deeply for each other.[4]

Janey joined Phil during the last portion of his training. After their wedding, the Harts lived in a second-floor, walk-up apartment in an old house in Moorestown, New Jersey, and Phil commuted to Fort Dix. While at Camp Gordon Johnston, they rented a room in a fishing lodge shared by married military. In Florida, General Barton invited Janey to dine at the General's mess, allowing her to become acquainted with Phil's fellow officers. Janey also briefly joined Phil in South Carolina, but then, suddenly, he was gone. "One day he didn't come home,"

Janey later said. "He couldn't [write]. Nobody could tell anything." Finally, on 18 January 1944, after two years of restless waiting, the 4th Infantry Division embarked for England, assigned a major role in the invasion of Europe.[5]

After leaving for Europe, Phil wrote hundreds of letters to Janey. Because of strict censorship guidelines not to reveal sensitive information, Hart had to be circumspect about his military observations. Nonetheless, his letters were exceptionally sensitive, literate, and astute, revealing his unassuming dedication, cooperative spirit, courage, fear, and especially his intense longing for home, Janey, and the new baby.

Soon after he arrived in England, Hart ceased being General Barton's aide and became the assistant to Colonel D. W. Stone, the 4th Division's Commander of G-5, Civil Affairs. The Civil Affairs Section (later changed to the Military Government Section after the 4th Division entered Germany) was activated in England on 20 February 1944. (Lew Fiset was also transferred to G-5.) In early March, Hart and Colonel Stone began six weeks of study at the British Civil Affairs College in Wimbelton. Colonel Stone, one of the oldest officers in the 4th Division, was a lawyer in a large New York law firm. Arrogant and overbearing, few people liked him. Hart was among the minority who tolerated Stone and got along with him. "Phil got along with everybody," said Fiset.[6]

Hart was pleased when his work was recognized but never boasted or dwelled on his promotions. He started service as a Second Lieutenant and ended as a lieutenant colonel. After being promoted from Captain to Major in the winter of 1944, he told Janey, "I honestly never gave it a thought. (No, I'm *not* lazy or unambitious—just keenly conscious that a lot of infantrymen would be made even more unattractive insurance risks if I moved any further.)"

He tolerated the foibles of his comrades and seldom criticized anyone. But he did have one pet peeve: the man of fighting age who thought he was winning the war in his downtown office in Detroit, and the young man in the States, "draped in a uniform," who dictated "weighty studies on assorted items which a guy 50 could do about as competently." If an acquaintance in Michigan ever made it to Europe, Hart said, "by all that's holy I will expose him to an infantryman's life and let him go back an honest soldier."[7]

He instructed Janey in the historic value of the infantry soldier, partly to communicate more effectively with her, and partly "to speak for the sometimes mute boy down in the rifle company." He did not want to denigrate the contributions of other soldiers—the air fighter, tank gunner, medical, signal, or engineer soldier or any other soldier. But the infantryman habitually had the crucial assignment of closing with the enemy in a way no other soldier can. He carried the battle to the enemy and drove him from places machines of war could not reach. "The infantryman . . . feels that no other soldiers have the tough, demanding battle assignments which are his every hour he fights. In nearly every battle, his is the longest and most continuous fight of all."

As a "kid-glove infantryman," Hart said, "I can't be charged with self-seeking," but he grew angry at the frequent failure to recognize the primary worth of the infantry soldier. "In all those fancy newspaper maps of The Campaign, The Situation, or `We thrust deep into the Hun,' . . . that wavering, irregular line on the map is, really, just a bunch of doughboys. And the public ought to realize it." To complete his lesson, he sent along a poem he picked up during training:

> To finish the job that the rest begin,
> The foot divisions come sloggin' in.
> So it was, and is, and ever will be,
> That the basic rhythm of victory
> is the beat of the feet of the Infantry.[8]

Life as a soldier in England was difficult, but he tried to joke about its worst aspects. He was served powdered eggs every morning for three weeks. He stopped eating them because after six weeks they began to represent "Hitler in Person." Eating a powdered egg was like eating ground glass, only worse because "it takes longer to act." He issued explicit legal instructions to Janey: "Mrs. P.A. Hart, her agents, assignees, representatives and/or persons under her direction or control, will not deal in, possess, handle, control, or in any manner or fashion traffic with powered eggs."[9]

Along with the impending invasion of Europe and his responsibilities in England, Hart's thoughts were on home. "Phil [expressed] a great desire to be home," observed Fiset. Indeed, more than anything else, he thought of Janey and awaited anxiously the birth of their first child due in the spring of 1944.

"Just how much do you weigh—honest?" Phil asked Janey on 4 March 1944. "And how about a profile of yourself, if I promise promptly to keep it locked?" Two months later the photo arrived with Janey in profile, eight months pregnant. "Pure horror," Hart responded. "I told [General Barton] you sent me the picture (*told* him, didn't show him). He claims that proves you a good sport. The more I look at this picture the more I believe he is right. My imagination simply wasn't equal to the job."

He sought to visualize the details of Janey's life in their new home. "*Please* tell me when you are set, how things look—down to little details: where you like to sit, how the sun comes in, is there a radio, are there pictures, *everything*." As he climbed into bed he expected to dream of her. "Will I see you? And will you be smiling? And will you be naturally slender, or with child obviously, or a mother? And will I dream a boy—or a girl? So long as it's of you, it will be fine." Sometimes he felt her physical presence. "I can see you so very clearly—and not in profile either—that to stop writing seems just like turning my back on you and leaving the room. . . . You seem so close that it's silly to write that I love you because I'm sure you can hear me say it."[10]

When Janey expressed her pride in Phil, he thanked her but did not feel he deserved it. "As for being proud of me," he wrote, "I love you so completely that I want you to believe all impossible things of me. It crowds my conscience to realize that you deserve just that sort of husband and to know full well I don't fill the customary definitions." He worried that he was expressing himself inadequately, that while his letters were designed to break the monotony of Janey's life, they were, instead, the "very sort which create monotony." "For the thousandth time," he wrote on another occasion, "with complete lack of originality—I miss you dreadfully, Janey."

"You probably can't imagine," he wrote two months before Janey delivered their baby, "but merely talking about that child and that event throws me into a pleasant daze." As Janey's due-date approached, Phil was hopeful: "I just feel that any minute a cable is bound to arrive," he wrote on 3 May 1944. "And I'm absolutely convinced you are in [the hospital] this minute—you are fine and so is the baby." Hart had been correct. On 1 May 1944, Janey delivered a baby boy, Philip, Jr. ("Flip"), and the new father learned the news via cable five days later. A glow of happiness surrounded him as friends in the division sent him flowers, General Barton raised a toast at dinner, and Catholic Chaplain Cajetan Sullivan said a Mass for the boy. It was unusual "to thank your wife for becoming a mother," Hart said, "but I want to anyway."

Military restrictions prohibited him from sending Janey an arrangement of flowers, so he did the next best thing, closing a letter, "Simulate some . . . flowers, please."[11]

Hart's letters were often clever and funny. "The time sequence is bad," he told Janey in May 1944, "so you will have to keep your letters filled with answers to the questions you must imagine I am asking. Otherwise, in your August letters you will be answering the questions in my letters written in June and received in July, but concerning events of May. Or, should I start that sentence over again?"

When Janey informed Phil that the new baby had his ears—which were large—he replied with mock indignation. "Lay off that ear story. . . . a full two sentences on his ears (both sentences were slanderous too.)" A few days later, after Janey again mentioned the boy's ears, Hart responded: "And more comment on *his (my) ears*, but still nothing on the color of his eyes or the unmistakable brilliance of his mind!"[12]

The birth of Flip had been wonderful, but there was still a major distraction. "All that remains," wrote Hart sardonically after the birth, "Is the matter of a war."

The planned Allied invasion of Europe appeared to be an exceptionally hazardous venture. "The Allied troops had to disembark on a coast that the enemy had occupied during four years, with ample time to fortify it, cover it with obstacles and sow it with mines," observed military historian B. H. Liddell Hart. "For the defense, the Germans had fifty-eight divisions in the West, and ten of these were panzer divisions that might swiftly deliver an armored counterstroke." That the attack on Hitler's Atlantic Wall might be thrown back in the sea seemed like a real danger.

Ways had to be devised to conceal the concentration of troops and landing craft in England; weather conditions over the English Channel had to be calculated carefully because an untimely storm could ruin the entire operation. Two hundred thousand allied troops and all their vehicles and equipment had to be successfully landed within forty-eight hours. A narrow margin separated success from failure.

As a civil affairs officer, Hart was expected to land on the Normandy beach on the first day of the invasion of Europe to shepherd civilians safely into a small sector away from the fighting. His job was dangerous, and he knew he might be killed. Thinking about the invasion frayed his nerves. He never expressed irritation with Janey except before the invasion. After she requested advice about a problem with their home, Phil replied testily, "I'd like to ask you again, please, not to bother me on these minor details." At other times he tried to remain lighthearted. "I did do some firing this morning, and feel perfectly satisfied I can do business with any average Kraut we meet. I plan on avoiding any who are above average." He reported the existence of a new disease among the troops: "Invasion Plague or Channelitis." Symptoms included feelings of love for England, hunger for dirt underfoot, involuntary urination, castanet teeth, and love of the prone. Church attendance was increasing among the troops. "Religion is getting a mighty big play these days," he said. His favorite prayer was to the Blessed Mother. "If you really work for Her," Phil told Janey, "She will see that what is best, now and always, will be."

On 25 May 1944, Hart thanked Janey for her recent expression of love. "Over here right now," he added, "our emotions are very close to the surface. That doesn't mean we fail to understand things, or falsely picture things. But it does mean that we don't manufacture distractions or pretend indifference to strong personal feelings. Really it gives you a more accurate sense of *values*. The most wonderful thing life can hold is strong belief, deep love. I can't understand why we sometimes hesitate to acknowledge it." As the troops awaited the invasion, there was nothing to do except think. "I try to specialize on you and the boy," Hart wrote; "on the happy past and things to do when we begin again."

On 1 June, five days before D-Day, Phil's thoughts were on Janey, Flip, God, and his own possible death. "If the baby prospers, and it should happen that *I'm not there*, please tell him how very much I wanted to have a son. Tell him, too, that there are only a few times in life when a man has the chance to get a proper perspective on *values*. Right now, for me, is one of those times and he can accept it as absolutely certain that the only piece of advice I would have you give him is true and correct: make sure that you and your *God* are old friends. . . . I love you, Janey, and shall always. You are going to be very close these next few days and you will help me."[13]

On 2 June 1944, Hart boarded the USS *Bayfield*, along with General Barton, Colonel Stone, and the staff. The following day they lifted anchor and headed for France. Foul weather and choppy seas delayed the invasion. But at 0630 on 6 June, assault waves of the 4th Infantry hit Utah Beach. About six hours later Hart also landed and began crossing the beach. However, he never fired a shot or started his assignment. As he crossed the beach, a German artillery shell exploded near him, and a piece of shrapnel smashed into the inside of his right arm, above the elbow. The shrapnel missed his bone but severed the main artery in the arm, and blood spouted out. Fortunately, Hart remained conscious (or he might have bled to death). He managed to drag the bag off his back, rummaged through it for something to block off the blood, found a pair of socks, wadded them under his arm and pushed. The procedure slowed the flow of blood. "It worked rather well," he later said. A medic arrived, put a tourniquet around the injured arm, and gave him a shot of morphine.[14]

Near Hart lay a more seriously injured soldier. As medics were about to lift his stretcher and carry him away, Phil motioned toward his injured comrade and told the medic, "Take him instead." Then he rolled off the stretcher, allowing the other soldier to be carried away first. Later, as Hart was being hoisted aboard a ship for the return trip to England, a spectacular air and artillery battle exploded shells all around him. He subsequently laughed as he described the scene and his thoughts. "Floating" on morphine, sitting in his hoist in midair with deadly fireworks exploding, he thought to himself: "Well, isn't that nice!" He ate small cans of cold oatmeal as the evacuation ship took four days to cross the channel back to England. Summarizing his experience on D-Day, Hart told Janey: "I was just one of many who landed early and didn't stay long."

On 10 June 1944, Hart was admitted to the 18th General Hospital in Plymouth, England, and shortly after was transferred to the 203rd Hospital in Oxford. The primary damage had been to the ulnar nerve that controlled the use of his fourth and little fingers. Neither hospital had a nerve specialist capable of working on his injury, and he received no therapy. He lay in bed with his arm strapped to his side, taking painful penicillin shots every four hours. On 22 June, sixteen days after his injury, he sat up in a chair for five minutes.[15]

Meanwhile, Janey received a War Department telegram, indicating that Phil had been "seriously" wounded, but no other information. Not knowing the nature of his wound, his overall condition, or even where he was hospitalized, she frantically mobilized family resources to find answers. Her father badgered the War Department for information. A family friend, James M. Cox, provided invaluable assistance. Cox, the former governor of Ohio and Democratic candidate for president in 1920, owned a chain of newspapers and recruited an Associated Press correspondent in England to search for Hart in hospitals. The correspondent found him and reported the nature of his injury and his stable condition to Janey, relieving some of her anxiety. The pressure from Janey's father on the War Department succeeded in getting Hart transferred on 3 July to a better hospital, the 160th near Cheltenham, which had a nerve specialist. (All the family's maneuvering to get Hart to a better hospital was without his knowledge.) Almost immediately doctors performed an operation, taking skin from his stomach and grafting it onto his arm. "Result," reported Hart, "tender stomach and sore arm." The graft succeeded, but on 3 August surgeons performed a three-hour exploratory operation. The surgeon found the nerve firmly bound down in scar tissue but finally freed it. The nerve was partially severed and densely scarred and showed only slight response to stimulation. The surgeon repaired the damage the best he could. After two bouts with infections, doctors finally took Hart off the penicillin in September 1944.[16]

The first letters home from the hospital Hart scratched awkwardly with his left hand. "A few days ago I ducked too late," he wrote on 16 June 1944, "which deprived Ike of one infantryman. The net result on the course of the war won't be affected." He told her that he still had his arms and legs. As for his ears, no, the Germans "did *not* use them as artillery registration points."

Two months after the injury his arm hurt like a toothache, more so in cold weather. ("In another few weeks I should be able to predict the weather at a 48-hour distance.") The doctors told him the arm should be adequate for normal life but not for shot putting or mule skinning. "It is a case where it doesn't make any difference if the customer is satisfied or not, as he might just as well take it in stride."

He tried to maintain perspective on his injury and not slip into self-pity. "The person doesn't live who could feel too sorry for himself so long as he is as complete as I am when he is in a nerve center hospital filled with battle casualties. Head and spine injuries make stray arm nerve cases look like a slight headache or an ingrown hair."[17]

After he made the casualty list in a Philadelphia newspaper, he received thirty-four letters from long-forgotten acquaintances. "It makes for a pleasant sensation," he said. Friends in Michigan thought Phil was a hero, Janey wrote. "On the hero side," Hart responded, "I have to confess taking dishonest pleasure from that. . . . But there's nothing heroic in failing to guess where the next burst is going to fall. If I could get home in time for the [Democratic National] Convention I'd be willing to masquerade the hero if it would get me the V.P. nomination instead of [Henry] Wallace."

From his hospital bed Hart followed the progress of the men of the 4th Infantry Division and was proud of their valor and success. After D-Day the 4th battled through France, during one period fighting twenty three days without rest. "Today we saw who were the first U.S. troops in Paris," Phil informed Janey in August 1944. "It was the Fourth, of course!" He pumped newly arrived patients for information about the war. When a veteran of the 4th Division entered the hospital in October 1944, Hart gathered news about friends and was shocked with the reports. "The men who are no longer with [the 4th Division] absolutely curls your hair."[18]

Life in the hospital was often boring and sometimes depressing. Powdered eggs were the usual diet at breakfast, and all the jokes had been repeated at least once. "Thirty-four-odd men in the ward and nothing to do but growl," Hart said. New casualities arrived daily, some of them badly "chewed up." Phil could predict their nightmares. One soldier howled for his jeep driver, another fought the same machine gun every night. "Two of them fought their last fight all over again during the night," Phil told Janey. "I would be on the verge of diving out of bed as one of them would yell something about tanks along the ridge line, or 'Sure you're scared but so are they'; then a fierce 'Let's go!'" Hart added: "You would be struck at the frequency of reference by these fellows to fear."

He had plenty of time to observe and reflect. "The guy who doesn't think a battlefield causes changes in people . . . should wander through one of these hospitals—or a battle. The revision of values is the biggest change, and if that change is as lasting as the physical scars there will be a whole lot less selfishness loose."[19]

Some of his observations and reflections modified his stereotyped bias against Jews. Somewhere Hart had acquired a distaste for Jews. He had grown up in the exclusive WASP community of Bryn Mawr and had probably been exposed to anti-Semitism in Catholic schools. He had also observed Jewish lawyers and businessmen in Detroit and at the horse-racing track in Chicago and disliked them. "He grew up fully brain-washed, stereotyping all Jews," recalled Janey Hart, adding, "I, too, grew up burdened with the same problem." In one letter, Phil referred to Jews as "purple suit, cigar-smoking, wise-money boys of you-know-what clan." In another, he made an ambiguous reference to being a "Jew partner," meaning someone who hands out "mean treatment." Lew Fiset, who was a Catholic but had Jewish friends, noticed Hart's anti-Semitism. "I was quite surprised," said Fiset. "Phil had an odd attitude [about Jews]," one shared by "many of the higher-ranking officers." Since blatant anti-Semitism was undiplomatic, Hart and others occasionally disguised their references to Jews by referring to them as "Arabs." Pfc. Werner Kleeman, who was Jewish and had been assigned to G-5 because he spoke German, never considered Hart anti-Semitic; yet he did observe anti-Jewish sentiment among other officers in the division. "Us Jewish boys, we would never get an award," said Kleeman.

One encounter with a Jewish soldier profoundly affected Hart, causing him to reassess his prejudice. Shortly after the birth of Flip, the baby needed serious surgery. After he recovered, Janey wrote Phil that she was so grateful she had resolved to pray to the Blessed Mother and to stop "Jew-baiting." On 2 September 1944, Hart referred to her resolution concerning Jews. "I've had a fine lesson in the bed next to me here," he said. The man had arrived at the hospital six weeks earlier seriously wounded. "That man has been suffering *greatly*, every day and every night, since he got here. There is drainage from eye, arm, leg, ears. Yet there isn't a more courageous man in the ward and he never utters a word of complaint, never asks for a thing. And he is 100% Jew." The man was a lawyer and could have finessed a safe administrative position during the war. "Not him," Hart said; "he was an infantryman, went to Inf. OCS, and had *a company when hit*. His sort make up for some of the green-suited, smart-money boys at the race track, and I've promised myself to remember him whenever I run into the other type."[20]

Hart had infrequent contact with black soldiers. Those he did observe he usually referred to as "colored" or "chocolate." A group of black soldiers' brutality he witnessed at the end of the war disturbed him. "Some of our colored soldiers run the [Russians] a close . . . race when it comes to objectionable strong-arm dealings with anyone who looks *either* cross-eyed and objectionable or blue-eyed and attractive." The few blacks he saw in the hospital he partially viewed in stereotype. One had a "typical negro sense of humor" and two others he expected to come "out of the fog with rare remarks. If so, censor permitting, I'll send them along." Yet, like that of Jews, the dedication and suffering of black soldiers caused him to modify his views. After describing a wounded black man in the hospital, Hart concluded, "These, and dozens more, are the lessons which are apt to make me intolerant of self-designated 'superior' people."[21]

Kind and helpful, Hart often visited with badly injured patients. He arranged baseball and volleyball games, though the endeavor stimulated some dark humor. "I had to do some figuring," he wrote. "For example, if you have 19 men with amputated left arms, and 7 with a leg gone, how many men do you have for a volleyball game?"

The 160th Hospital had a fine library and Hart spent much of his time reading books and periodicals. He devoured *The New Yorker*, the stories of humorist Robert Benchley, and biographies of Napoleon and St. Frances of Assisi. From a battered copy of the *Ladies Home Journal* he quoted for Janey an article on "The Rights of Infants," which argued that a baby's deepest psychological need was a mother's caressing love.[22]

His primary interest was reading and rereading Janey's many letters. "Pleasant isn't the word for it—it's wonderful and the best medicine in the world." He worried about her and the baby and was sorry she had to worry about him. He thanked her for the "understanding way you look at this business of participating in a war. If doing what you would like to do was the only consideration in life, then I wouldn't be dynamited from home."

In all the letters during his recuperation Phil again poured out his love for Janey and his longing for home. "I love you, Janey—and it seems more than ever I want to be with you, and the baby. Do file an extra prayer this thing settles soon, and they return war back to the historians." He concluded one letter: "Janey, I want to get home. That puts it short and sweet."[23]

As the 1944 presidential election approached between Democrat Franklin D. Roosevelt and Republican Thomas Dewey, Phil conducted a long-distance debate with Janey on U.S. politics. He teased her about her recent "Political Bulletin" in which she endorsed Dewey and bitterly attacked FDR, warning of the danger in store for America if FDR won a fourth term. "Before the day was over," Hart joked, "they had me back on penicillin—literally. *Maybe* it would have happened anyway. But, again, maybe it was the horror picture you gave me."

Janey argued that the New Deal had been too radical and poorly administered. Phil pointed out that critics at the beginning of the twentieth century judged as radical or socialist anyone who suggested some limit be fixed by law on hours of employment; conditions under which children could work; old-age pensions; unemployment insurance; and equalization of price fluctuations in agriculture. Yet Dewey's speeches during the 1944 campaign indicated acceptance in principle of all of those measures. In essence, Dewey had accepted the New Deal and only proposed to administer it more effectively. "That it has been *badly* administered I have no doubt," Hart added. "I believe equally that it is right in principle. *If* a majority reject the Republican's invitation to introduce proper administration, it may be that the controlling emotion behind the rejection is an unwillingness to believe that the party which for so long rejected the principle now honestly has been converted."

Not only had Dewey and the Republicans accepted the New Deal, Dewey even proposed to extend old-age pensions and survivors insurance to 20,000,000 farmers, domestic workers, government employees, and others not covered by the Social Security Act. That being the influence of FDR's New Deal, Phil warned Janey, "don't be too disheartened if a majority of Americans have not yet . . . become willing to turn it over to the party which opposed the inception."

"Remember," Phil wrote a few days before the 1944 election, "when the perfect democracy dawns, we will be able to distinguish the faulty from the sound. Pressure groups and time-serving politicians will then be out of business. Actually we are in the earliest stages of attainment of a perfect democracy. Our way of attaining it, the so-called American way, by which people get excited over issues, make mistakes, sometimes are persuaded by false arguments, and sometimes fail to understand the right ones, doesn't guarantee that the voters will graduate in democracy on some fixed future date. But it does promise that learning as they go along, they will make continuous progress towards graduation."

Despite his disagreement with Janey, he applauded her concern. "Thank heaven," he told her, "you are damn serious about the impact of the election on life ahead." After the reelection of FDR, however, Hart could not resist chiding her for her failure to comment. "Why didn't you mail the post-election letter? I'd have enjoyed it; probably agreed with much, if not all of it."[24]

Phil often prayed for a full recovery and asked for Janey's prayerful assistance: "I used up most of my credit with heaven trying to get off the beach and in keeping the arm. So any spare prayers you can promote for full return of the hand will not be wasted." By 11 September 1944, Hart was fully mobile and attended Mass at a chapel hut three hundred yards down the road from the hospital. He received communion—"My campaign to rebuild some heavenly credit is in full swing."[25]

Unquestionably, the highlight of his convalescence occurred in late September 1944, when he received a pass to attend a ceremony in Tiverton. For five months before D-Day, the 4th Infantry Division had been stationed near Tiverton, and General Barton wanted to present a plaque to the town residents in appreciation for their warm hospitality. Barton selected Hart to make the presentation ("One more thoughtful gesture" by the General, said Phil). Aldermen, councilors, and the public watched the thirty-minute ceremony at the Tiverton Town Hall. John Lewis, the town's mayor, who bore striking resemblance to Winston Churchill, introduced Hart as "one of the heroes who fought for his country, with marks of the fighting on him."

Hart's speech recalled the official welcome at the town hall upon the division's arrival and General Barton's request for patience from town residents as the soldiers adjusted. "I know now that our adjustment was not completely successful, and I realize why. One cannot be taught the fury which is war until one has seen it, and I ask you to realize that and use it as a filter when you think of us and our days with you. If you do us that courtesy, we will remember the days on which the 'sun' shone." Security prevented the soldiers from saying farewell as the division slipped out of Tiverton on a gray morning in May 1944, "when we left you to begin that for which we had come." After describing the successful battles fought by the division since it landed at Normandy, Hart concluded that he hoped the plaque "will remind all of us that we must continue together with the same intense energy and tolerant understanding to maintain the peace which, together, we seem about to win." Then he presented the plaque to the mayor amid applause.

After he returned to the hospital, Phil explained to Janey his reaction to the five-day outing. "If you can imagine three and a half months in a series of army hospitals; then a sudden cross-country trip with nothing to do but admire green hills and [breathe fresh] air, you can understand my reaction to the trip. It was wonderful."[26]

As his wound slowly healed, Hart pondered his future. Would he stay in Europe or be sent home? Much depended on the degree of healing. If he needed further surgery to repair nerve damage to the arm, then he was likely to be sent home—"be promoted to civilian, with emphasis on husband and father." The uncertainty was not enjoyable. "I am holding my breath until they tell me I'm headed home," he wrote on 18 July 1944.

Finally, on 1 September 1944, Phil admitted to Janey that he had requested return to the division. Of course, he would prefer to be home and at work. "But war happens to be one of the few times you shouldn't . . . take the road self-interest dictates. . . . I know how many thousands of men are here and in the same fix, and worse. If we all announced that, since our personal comfort in the future demanded we get home and to work, we were taking a powder, this war wouldn't look so rosy." Still, the prospect of returning to the war "has all the charm of a dentist appointment."[27]

General Barton accepted him back on "limited assignment," meaning he would not be fit enough for combat, but could perform other assignments. "Normally, a man like that would have been sent home" observed Kleeman. "But he pulled strings with [General Barton]." On 2 November 1944, Hart left the hospital to return to his division. "Feel fit and ready," he told Janey the following day. But it was to be a far more confusing and exhausting trip than he anticipated. After shipping out from Southhampton, England, he disembarked at Le Havre, journeyed south of Paris, then to Liege and Verviers Belgium, and finally to the city of Luxembourg where the 4th Division was stationed. He found transportation only when the army was not shipping tanks, ammunition, men, and rations. The transportation he did find—in a box car for four days— was horrible: "roof leaking, cold and no straw on the floor; filthy; K rations and no way to heat water; legs and arms entangled with assorted portions of the body of the man alongside and across from you."

"I'm still stalled," Hart wrote on 1 December 1944, almost a month after he left the hospital. "Somewhere in France." His attempt to rejoin the division had become snarled in red tape. Barton's letter requesting his return had been lost, and instead he found himself reassigned to a safe job at a "super-plush blouse and pants" spot. It was the sort of responsibility Hart could have easily performed. "But the temptation wasn't as great as you might think," he wrote, because the "*real* need" was near the front line. "Once in a desk-type job you figure a dozen reasons why you're more valuable than on the line. Usually, it's all eyewash. Some older man could do at least almost as well—and he couldn't do that in the line. . . . I should give it a try." A few days later he found a "big shot" to change his orders from the plush position to the 4th division.

"Finally—*rejoined*!" Hart wrote on 13 December 1944, more than five weeks after he had left the hospital. He was delighted to see old friends and equally delighted, they were happy to see him. "If one is allowed to boast to his wife, I want to report sincere pleasure shown by everyone around here. And calls have even come in from the line."[28]

The seriousness of his arm injury, plus the exhausting five-week trip, left him looking haggard. His "arm was practically [useless]," said Kleeman. "He couldn't lift anything or carry anything." Fiset thought Hart should never have returned to the division: "He should have gone back to the States. Phil was going around just on guts . . . [and] was still a weak person when he rejoined us. He just didn't want to be known as some rich man getting out of hazardous duty."[29]

After a bloody, exhausting battle with the Germans in the Hurtgen Forest in November, on 4 December 1944, the 4th Division had been pulled out of the line and rested at a billet near the city of Luxembourg. It was there Hart rejoined his comrades. Almost everyone—from General Omar Bradley, General Dwight Eisenhower, and British Field Marshal Bernard Montgomery to Major Philip A. Hart—thought the Germans were permanently on the defensive and incapable of launching a major offensive. "Couldn't have rejoined at an *easier time*," Phil reassured Janey on 14 December 1944. "Life is comfortable and safer than crossing Woodward with the green light. For me they can spend the rest of the war doing this." Hart's easy time lasted less than two days.

On the morning of 16 December 1944, the German High Command launched a surprise, powerful mechanized drive against the U.S. First Army in the Ardennes, where the slender defense line had been thinned out in order to amass the maximum force against Germany in other sectors. The Germans hoped to split the Allied forces and drive through to Antwerp. The 4th Division, widely dispersed along a thirty-five-mile front in Luxembourg, took the first impact on the southern front. During the Battle of the Bulge, German forces swarmed around small units of the 4th, often outnumbering them five to one. Some platoons were overwhelmed. General Barton immediately issued an order: "There will be no retrograde movement in this sector." With no reserves to call upon, soon cooks, quartermasters, MPs, and possibly Phil Hart, were in the line. The 4th fought brilliantly, helping to thwart the southern wing of the thrust, checking the attack after it had gone only three or four miles. "Very busy," Hart wrote on 21 December; he promised to write more when "things are a little quieter." It took ten days to check the German advance. After the attack was blunted and the Allies resumed the offensive, Hart reflected on the chaos that prevented any Christmas shopping: "Whenever someone mentions 'an exciting

Holiday season' you'll undoubtedly notice a momentary vague look in my eye."[30]

The famous novelist Ernest Hemingway traveled extensively with the 4th Division and Hart met him shortly after the Battle of the Bulge. An accredited correspondent, Hemingway had attached himself to the division after the breakthrough in Normandy and saw considerable action. On 24 December 1944, Hemingway, Hart and other officers dined at General Barton's mess, a schoolhouse in Luxembourg. The Christmas turkey, with mashed potatoes and cranberry sauce, must have made the atmosphere seem almost like home. Over drinks the group spun stories and Hart later judged the novelist as having "real courage" under fire and as "remarkable . . . because he is so quiet, pleasant and indifferent to favorable notices which he must have been conscious of for years."[31]

Hart gave General Barton much of the credit for the 4th Division's success and judged him the most able division commander in Europe. Hart had a "very, very private and good relationship with the General," observed Kleeman. "He went to [Barton's] trailer every night to discuss things with him." Barton respected Hart's "brain and directive genius," and cherished his personal advice. "I want you with me," Barton wrote while Hart was recuperating in the hospital, "not only because I need you officially but little though you may have realized it, I need you near me personally." "No combat record exceeds his own," Hart said of Barton. "His exactness, seeming unreasonableness at times, and driving demands, proved invaluable. The stand before Luxembourg City was *his*. . . . His determination to stay put, come hell or Germans, was contagious." Because of his troublesome ulcer, however, after the Battle of the Bulge, General Barton was reassigned to the United States and was succeeded by General Harold W. Blakeley.[32]

Reports by Hart's commanding officers consistently highlighted his character, intelligence, and attention to duty. "This officer is exceptionally intelligent and personable," Colonel Stone wrote in Hart's report. Kleeman remembers Hart as "very human and very kind . . . [and] very, very humble." He "never let anything go to his head." When Lew Fiset "broke" a sergeant to private for missing an assignment, Hart successfully urged Fiset to give the young man another chance. "He convinced me," Fiset recalled. "Phil was being kind to the boy." It amazed Fiset that Hart, having "been raised the way he was, with everything he ever needed," was nonetheless a "very kind, and a very understanding, and a very pleasant person."[33]

When Hart returned to the Division he was still in G-5. As Allied forces captured territory in Germany, new government and social services had to be created out of the chaos. Hart's job was to establish order and provide services in the newly captured towns. Often he went from cellar to cellar looking for the mayor or someone who was not a Nazi to assume the role of controlling civilians. He appointed judges, collected weapons, assisted refugees, provided food, enforced rationing, and established hospital services, police forces, and schools. He even helped Chaplain Sullivan arrange Masses in German Catholic churches. Fiset, who had the same assignment as Hart, observed: "I became the law." Hart nonchalantly referred to other soldiers in the 4th Division as the "real fighters," yet found his responsibility a "fine, interesting job." On 10 April 1945, Colonel Stone was reassigned and Hart replaced him as the Chief Military Government Officer of the division. Shortly after, Phil learned of his promotion to lieutenant colonel. "I hope it gives you a pleasant feeling," he told Janey; "it surely did me."[34]

He hoped his faith would protect him from injury during his second tour of duty in the war. At church he "bombarded Heaven" for an early victory. While visiting a Catholic church in Belgium and praying at the altar rail, an old man knelt next to him and gave him a Sacred Heart medal. Hart added it to other personal and religious items in his crowded breast pocket. "Soon that pocket will bulge enough to turn back direct, high velocity artillery."

Hart was shocked by the devastation caused to Germany and predicted massive postwar problems. "Germany will be without leadership; its resources will be at rock bottom; it will have a lost generation: armless, legless, sightless, plus dead and [shortages of] food, soap, items of hygiene, houses—this place is junk and so are the humans." The postwar problem was not only Germany's or Europe's—"it's everyone's." And before people started discussing settlements and rehabilitation, "they should see, actually see and understand, the enormity of the problem."

The deluge of civilian problems disturbed Hart. He saw babies born in rocky caves sheltered from artillery; infants die in barns crowded with other infants; sick women and feeble-minded old men; children orphaned by one shell; home, cattle, and all possessions destroyed in one fight. "I wish I was a German linguist, surgeon, midwife, undertaker, building carpenter and food producer all in one," Hart said wearily on 7 March 1945. "Plus a man of even temper and disposition, who didn't need more than a few hours' sleep a week."[35]

On 28 April 1945, Hart helped to liberate Jews in a German concentration camp and, again, the experience was eye-opening. He explained that "For years I read of concentration camp atrocities; of planned elimination of Jews; of brutality and inhuman conduct. Always I felt it was propaganda." He had been "very wrong," he said. He took photographs of the camp so "I can see what my eyes for the past week have tried to tell me. This incident was no 'plant'—I was very nearly the first there. Since then I have had to [deal] with thousands . . . of humans who have been made permanent *wrecks*. It's something which has to be seen if it is to be believed in full. I never dreamed a human could so revile another human." The horrible sight, the enormity of the wrongs done to millions of people, taught him a lesson: "Once in a war, better not [lose] it." On Flip's first birthday, Phil offered two hopeful bits of wisdom: "Pray he won't see a repetition of this. Pray just as hard that he won't blind himself in order not to see it, if it should again occur."[36]

"You don't need to worry about me falling in love with Russia or Russians," Hart wrote in May 1945, in what was probably the most bigoted statement ever made by this normally understanding and tolerant man. "Try handling a gang variously estimated between 17,500 and 40,000 rampaging around—animals, almost all of them. . . . I regard them as a race apart. The women are the nearest thing to cows this side of the barnyard. Germans are terrified of 'em—and I'd love to have them agin us in a war."[37]

After rejoining the division, Hart tried to maintain a cheerful attitude. "Around here the guy who doesn't have a good disposition serves only to make it a little more unpleasant for everyone else without accomplishing anything for himself." But the war was taking its toll on him physically and psychologically. Like other soldiers, he suffered the war's discomfort and discouragement. For most of February 1945, he was laid up with severe dysentery. During his illness he seemed depressed: "War is [as] destructive of gray matter as it is of life and limb. My memory has gone from unsatisfactory to intolerable. Maybe daylight will help, plus one more day of convalescence."

He worried that he was forgetting the law. But mostly, as the war ground on, his letters to Janey reflected his deep frustration and unhappiness with his separation from her and from home. "News has gotten through which makes me fear my attempt to get a Christmas present to you probably failed," he wrote Janey on Christmas Day 1944. "That's a small incident in this thing called history, yet it shows clearly how harsh and unreasoning are the consequences of a war." A week later he said: "No husband at Christmas, no flowers on time, no this, no that. Only colorless letters from miles away. That raises hell with my digestion."

After Janey related that heavy rain had caused leaks in their home, Phil replied: "I wish I could make it better, Janey. I know that doesn't stop a single leak and I feel uncomfortable that all I do is tell you I wish it was nicer. Worse yet, there is much that I must do once this present job has been finished before I can make it better. It adds up to an unhappy prospect."

He began referring to himself as the "war-weary stranger who claims to be your husband." Occasionally he seemed desperate: "I want to see you, to be with you. I miss you. I want to see the boy. I'm a sissy—I want to come home!"[38]

Germany officially surrendered on 8 May 1945, and on their second wedding anniversary (19 June 1945), Phil thought he was almost home, complete with two arms. "I'll never be able to express the long ing for you which, month by month, has accumulated. Because of a lifetime of things which went on during this past year, I know how very much I shall need you *always*." But a few days later he learned his status was still in limbo, and that he might not be home indefinitely. If he returned to the United States with the 4th Division and the 4th was reassigned to the Pacific theater, he was sure his damaged arm would get him a discharge. He was depressed, though, at the conventional wisdom that if the 4th returned to the United States, his Military Government Section would *remain* in Europe. "Not cheerful [news]," Hart wrote, giving him a "low feeling."

Finally, in July 1945, Hart was reassigned to the States. His efforts in World War II earned him the Purple Heart, Bronze Star with Clusters, the Invasion Arrowhead, four campaign stars, and the French Croix de Guerre. On leave from the Army, he returned home to Detroit. But the long-awaited, joyous reunion with his family quickly turned to ashes.[39]

"We had to get to know each other all over again," said Janey. "We were both scared to death." While in Detroit Hart suffered such severe pain in his injured arm that he could not sleep at night. "He would get up [from bed] and run around the room," said Janey. These nerve spasms continued for several more years. After the victory over Japan, Hart still had one more assignment from the army—to help compile a history of the 4th Infantry Division in the war. He rejoined the division at Camp Butner, North Carolina, but instead of working on his assignment, in

early September 1945, he entered the hospital complaining of two problems. Hart told the doctors that beginning in January 1944, about the
time he arrived in Europe, he had developed a strong urge to urinate
often. At its worst, he urinated twenty times a day and occasionally at
night. Doctors referred to his problem as "marked urgency [and] frequency." Hart also complained of general malaise and a worn-down feeling; sometimes he described feelings of fogginess and loss of energy. The
malaise and other symptoms intermittently declined and reappeared but
became particularly intense in June 1945. Jane definitely noticed he had
slipped into depression. "The depression got him to the point where he
was imagining all kinds of things wrong with him," she said, "none of
which was true."[40]

After a week in the hospital, with no particular treatment, Hart was
released but returned again in mid-November complaining of the same
two problems. To relieve his urgency and frequency, on 10 December
1945, doctors removed a small section of his prostate. Following his
recuperation from the surgery, though, a medical officer reported
"there did not seem to be any improvement in the condition, and he
was told that there was nothing more that could be done." After a
twenty-day leave, he returned to the hospital on 11 January 1946 for
more tests. Still, doctors could find nothing seriously wrong. "Medical
workups reveal nothing but the nerve injury [to the arm]," said a medical report on 29 January. Because Hart kept complaining of illness, Dr.
Maskin, the psychiatrist attached to the 4th Infantry at Camp Butner,
recommended he undergo further observation and tests. He was sent to
the Percy Jones General Hospital in Battle Creek, Michigan, and arrived
there on 15 February 1946.

At Percy Jones doctors reinspected his damaged arm and found
marked atrophy in his right hand. There was little prospect of improving the situation, and Hart rejected further surgery. Doctors also performed a battery of tests on his prostate but found "no evidence of any
urinary pathology." He remained at Percy Jones for over three months.
In sum, Hart spent seven-and-a-half months in two different hospitals
and the medical staffs found nothing significantly wrong with him
except the obvious damage to his arm.[41]

So what was wrong with him? A combination of genetic and environmental factors undoubtedly explained his depression. Witnessing the
horrible conditions of Jewish prisoners in the concentration camps
apparently left an indelible impression on him. "That depressed him for

a long time," recalled Janey. "The vision of those camps." He told Janey that he felt he had been contaminated in some way by being at the camps. Lew Fiset, Werner Kleeman, and Chaplain Cajetan Sullivan had not noticed that Hart suffered any depression in Europe. He may have been depressed but showed no outward symptoms. "None whatsoever," said Fiset. Yet his letters to Janey at the end of the war expressed increasing frustration and unhappiness.[42]

Hart's medical records, however, reveal the most likely scenario that triggered both his depression and his insistence on tests of his prostate. In June 1945, while Phil was in Germany, he complained to a medical officer about his urinary problems. The officer shocked Hart by suggesting his illness might be venereal disease. The officer told him he would require special tests—including urine and blood tests—after he returned to the States. "[At] this time," a doctor later wrote in Hart's medical record, "he began to feel his first general symptoms [of malaise] which consisted . . . of fogginess, and lassitude."

In fact, Hart had good reason to fear that he may have picked up venereal disease. In November 1944, while he was laboriously trying to rejoin the 4th Division, some of the men he was traveling with put together a party that included drinking and prostitutes. After World War II, Phil told Janey that he did have sexual relations with a prostitute at the party and that it was a "horrible" experience. He never mentioned, though, his extraordinary fear of having contracted venereal disease from the prostitute.

In Hart's case his fogginess and lassitude were euphemisms for the deep depression he felt after contemplating the doctor's shocking diagnosis. Most likely fear of having contracted venereal disease explained his postwar problems. Ashamed and guilty, he refused to tell anyone, including Janey, of his worst fear—with one exception. In early September 1946, under questioning by a medical officer at Camp Butner, he admitted being worried about having the disease. "Further questioning," said the perceptive doctor's report, "brings out the point that this officer, having been told his condition might be venereal, has developed a very anxious attitude toward this, and this seems to be quite a bit at the root of his trouble at the present time."

Indeed, fear of having venereal disease may explain why he felt contaminated, why he insisted on the battery of medical tests and why he could not share his secret with anyone. One doctor may have speculated correctly when he reported that Hart suffered "chronic anxiety with psychosomatic localization [in his urinary tract].” There was never any proof that Phil ever had venereal disease. At both Camp Butner and Percy Jones, he was routinely checked for the disease and all the tests were negative. There never was any medical proof and his worst fear undoubtedly was baseless.[43]

Apparently, few patients at Percy Jones knew that Hart suffered from depression. He acted as the handyman around the ward for patients who were immobile. He ran errands and bought cigarettes at the PX. He took patients who were ambulatory to Detroit Tigers baseball games. Two seriously injured patients at Percy Jones later became U.S. Senators—Daniel K. Inouye (D.-Hawaii), and Robert Dole (R.-Kans.). Dole recalled Hart as exceptionally kind. He “did a lot of things for a lot of us when we couldn’t do for ourselves,” said Dole. “He did everything he could, notwithstanding his own injuries, to make us feel comfortable,” and therefore “endeared himself to every man in that ward.” Inouye was most impressed with Hart’s modesty: “Phil was a simple, unassuming veteran in the hospital, not a flashy one like the rest of us who wore our ribbons and flaunted our patriotism.”[44]

Because doctors found nothing physically wrong with Hart, except for his right arm, the army wanted to discharge him. But he refused to sign his discharge papers, fearing his signature would relieve the army of responsibility for treating his illness. He refused to sign, said Janey, because “he was so sure that there was something wrong with him [and] that he was going to become disabled and become a burden to me.” Bewildered and frustrated, Janey consulted Dr. Maskin, the psychiatrist at Camp Butner, who happened to be visiting Detroit, and the doctor went to Percy Jones to talk with Hart. He later phoned Janey and strongly urged her to get Phil out of the hospital. Otherwise, said Dr. Maskin, “He is going to become so locked into being a professional invalid that you’re never going to get him out.” Taking the psychiatrist’s advice, Janey angrily confronted Phil and insisted he sign his discharge papers. He agreed, left the hospital in late May 1946, and returned home to Bloomfield Hills.[45]

Ahead in the next thirty years would be more tragedy for Phil—the death of Flip at age three and another, more severe, bout with depression. But there would also be eight more children and an extraordinarily distinguished career in the U.S. Senate.

NOTES

1. Philip Hart to Janey Hart, 3 February 1945, 29 May 1945, unprocessed Janey Hart Papers; B. H. Liddell Hart, *History of the Second World War* (New York: G. P. Putnam's Sons, 1971), 65; Gordon Wright, *The Ordeal of Total War: 1939-1945* (New York: Harper Torchbooks, 1968), 17, 26, 28, 167-68; Janey Hart, interview, Washington, D.C., 1 and 2 April 1989.

2. "Efficiency Report," 15 March 1942, Philip A. Hart File, Department of the Army Papers, St. Louis, Missouri; Lew Fiset, telephone interview, 11 May 1989; Janey Hart, interview, Washington, D.C., 1 and 2 April 1989.

3. Clipping contained in Philip Hart to Janey Hart, 12 July 1944, Janey Hart Papers; *Famous Fourth: The Story of the 4th Infantry Division* (n.p., n.d.), 3-5, 22; Lew Fiset, telephone interview, 11 May 1989; Janey Hart, interview, Washington, D.C., 1 and 2 April 1989.

4. Philip Hart to Janey Hart, 7 May 1944, Janey Hart Papers; *Detroit News*, 6 November 1958; *Lansing State Journal*, 16 January 1955; *Washington Star*, 5 December 1976; Janey Hart, interview, Washington, D.C., 1 and 2 April 1989.

5. Philip Hart to Janey Hart, 18 January 1944, Janey Hart Papers; *Lansing State Journal*, 16 January 1955; *Famous Fourth*, 22; Janey Hart, interview, Washington, D.C., 1 and 2 April 1989.

6. "G-5 Diary, Headquarters 4th Infantry Division," 1, unpublished diary of J. K. Owen, unprocessed Werner Kleeman Papers, Flushing, New York; Lew Fiset, telephone interview, 11 May 1989; Werner Kleeman, telephone interview, 23 May 1989.

7. Philip Hart to Janey Hart, 16 March 1944, 3 May 1944, Janey Hart Papers; Janey Hart, interview, Washington, D.C., 1 and 2 April 1989.

8. Philip Hart to Janey Hart, 22 March 1944, Janey Hart Papers.

9. Philip Hart to Janey Hart, 10 May 1944, Janey Hart Papers.

10. Philip Hart to Janey Hart, 4 March 1944, 3 May 1944, Janey Hart Papers; Lew Fiset, telephone interview, 11 May 1989.

11. Philip Hart to Janey Hart, 16 March 1944, 3 May 1944, 4 May 1944, 10 May 1944, Janey Hart Papers.

12. Philip Hart to Janey Hart, 11 May 1944, 14 May 1944, Janey Hart Papers.

13. Philip Hart to Janey Hart, 14 April 1944, 7 May 1944, 14 May 1944, 21 May 1944, 25 May 1944, 1 June 1944, Janey Hart Papers; Hart, *History of the Second World War*, 543; Wright, *Ordeal of Total War*, 197-98.

14. Philip Hart to Janey Hart, 17 October 1944; "G-5 Diary," 4, Kleeman Papers; Lew Fiset, telephone interview, 11 May 1989; Janey Hart, interview, Washington, D.C., 1 and 2 April 1989; Werner Kleeman, telephone interview, 23 May 1989.

15. Philip Hart to Janey Hart, 22 June 1944, 10 July 1944, Janey Hart Papers; Lew Fiset, telephone interview, 11 May 1989; Janey Hart, interview, Washington, D.C., 1 and 2 April 1989.

16. "Casualty Message Telegram," 18 June 1944, Hart File, Department of the Army Papers; Philip Hart to Janey Hart, 7 July 1944, 10 July 1944, 4 August 1944, 28 August 1944, 11 September 1944, 28 May 1945, Janey Hart Papers; "Operations," August 1944, Philip Hart File, Veterans' Administration Papers; Janey Hart, interview, Washington, D C , 1 and 2 April 1989.

17. Philip Hart to Janey Hart, 16 June 1944, 19 June 1944, 23 July 1944, 11 September 1944, 15 September 1944, 4 October 1944, Janey Hart Papers.

18. Philip Hart to Janey Hart, 18 July 1944, 26 July 1944, 28 August 1944, 29 October 1944, Janey Hart Papers; *Famous Fourth*, 3, 17.

19. Philip Hart to Janey Hart, 10 July 1944, 30 August 1944, 11 September 1944, 15 September 1944, Janey Hart Papers.

20. Philip Hart to Janey Hart, 2 August 1944, 2 September 1944, 1 December 1944, 28 June 1945, Janey Hart Papers; Lew Fiset, telephone interview, 11 May 1989; Janey Hart, interview, Washington, D.C., 1 and 2 April 1989; Werner Kleeman, telephone interview, 23 May 1989.

21. Philip Hart to Janey Hart, 2 September 1944, 2 October 1944, Janey Hart Papers.

22. Philip Hart to Janey Hart, 28 August 1944, 24 September 1944, 4 October 1944, 17 October 1944, Janey Hart Papers.

23. Philip Hart to Janey Hart, 9 July 1944, 15 July 1944, 18 July 1944, 30 August 1944, 29 October 1944, Janey Hart Papers.

24. Philip Hart to Janey Hart, 6 September 1944, 28 October 1944, 3 February 1945, Janey Hart Papers.

25. Philip Hart to Janey Hart, 23 July 1944, 11 September 1944, Janey Hart Papers.

26. Philip Hart to Janey Hart, 15 September 1944, 24 September 1944, clipping inside 27 January 1945, Janey Hart Papers.

27. Philip Hart to Janey Hart, 15 July 1944, 18 July 1944, 1 September 1944, 11 September 1944, Janey Hart Papers.

28. Philip Hart to Janey Hart, 4 November 1944, 23 November 1944, 3 December 1944, 11 December 1944, 14 December 1944, Janey Hart Papers; Janey Hart, interview, Washington, D.C., 1 and 2 April 1989; Werner Kleeman, telephone interview, 23 May 1989.

29. Lew Fiset, telephone interview, 11 May 1989; Werner Kleeman, telephone interview, 23 May 1989.

30. Philip Hart to Janey Hart, 14 December 1944, 21 December 1944, 1 January 1945, Janey Hart Papers; *Famous Fourth*, 1, 2, 26-29; Hart, *History of the Second World War*, 653-54.

31. Philip Hart to Janey Hart, 20 February 1945, Janey Hart Papers; Carlos Baker, *Ernest Hemingway: A Life Story* (New York: Charles Scribner's Sons, 1969), 440; Philip Young, *Ernest Hemingway* (Minneapolis: University of Minnesota Press, 1959), 24.

32. Philip Hart to Janey Hart, 20 February 1945, 28 February 1945, Janey Hart Papers; Raymond Barton to Philip Hart, 13 August 1944, Janey Hart Papers; *Famous Fourth*, 29; Werner Kleeman, telephone interview, 23 May 1989.

33. "Efficiency Report," July 1945, Hart File, Department of the Army Papers; Lew Fiset, telephone interview, 11 May 1989; Werner Kleeman, telephone interview, 23 May 1989.

34. Philip Hart to Janey Hart, 22 January 1945, 18 March 1945, 22 March 1945, 19 June 1945, Janey Hart Papers; "G-5 Diary," 38-45, Kleeman Papers; Lew Fiset, telephone interview, 11 May 1989; Janey Hart, interview, Washington, D.C., 1 and 2 April 1989; Cajetan Sullivan, telephone interview, 15 June 1989.

35. Philip Hart to Janey Hart, 11 December 1944, 1 January 1945, 3 February 1945, 23 February 1945, 7 March 1945, Janey Hart Papers.

36. Philip Hart to Janey Hart, 1 May 1945, 3 May 1945, Janey Hart Papers.

37. Philip Hart to Janey Hart, 29 May 1945, Janey Hart Papers.

38. Philip Hart to Janey Hart, 9 December 1944, 2 January 1945, 3 February 1945, 8 February 1945, 20 February 1945, 28 February 1945, 2 March 1945, Janey Hart Papers.

39. Philip Hart to Janey Hart, 28 May 1945, 19 June 1945, Janey Hart Papers; clipping, Box 551, Hart Papers, Bentley Library.

40. R. E. Schwab to Sidney Adler, 17 October 1947, Philip Hart File, Veterans' Administration Papers; "Chief Complaint . . . Previous Personal History," Philip Hart File, Veterans' Administration Papers; "Progress Notes" [November 1945], Philip Hart File, Veterans' Administration Papers; Janey Hart, interview, Washington, D.C., 1 and 2 April 1989.

41. Schwab to Adler, 17 October 1947, Philip Hart File, Veterans' Administration Papers, "Progress Notes" [1945-1946], Philip Hart File, Veterans' Administration Papers.

42. Lew Fiset, telephone interview, 11 May 1989; Janey Hart, interview, Washington, D.C., 1 and 2 April 1989; Werner Kleeman, telephone interview, 23 May 1989; Cajetan Sullivan, telephone interview, 15 June 1989.

43. Janey Hart to author, 1 July 1991; "Chief Complaint," Philip Hart File, Veterans' Administration Papers; "Progress Notes," Philip Hart File, Veterans' Administration Papers; Janey Hart, interview, Washington, D.C., 1 and 2 April 1989.

44. *Congressional Record*, 100th Cong., 2d sess., 1988, vol. 134, pt. 21:5-6.

45. Janey Hart, interview, Washington, D.C., 1 and 2 April 1989.

Road to the Senate, 1947-1958

On 30 August 1947, Labor Day weekend, Janey and her relatives were at the Briggs summer cottage on Bois Blanc Island, near Mackinac Island. Philip Hart was in Detroit and about to drive north to join them. Janey briefly left, thinking her relatives or a nursemaid were watching Flip, but the three-year-old wandered out on the dock unnoticed, fell into the water, and drowned. Both Phil and Janey were devastated. Phil helped Janey recover from her grief. "He was strong and supportive," she recalled.

After Flip's death, the Hart family grew rapidly. Ann was born on 9 July 1947, two months before Flip's death, and in the next decade seven more healthy children followed: Cammie (1948), Walter (1950), James (1951), Michael (1952), Clyde (1954), Mary (1956), and Laura (1957).[1]

Meanwhile, after leaving Percy Jones General Hospital, Hart resumed his law career, joining with prewar friends to form the Detroit law firm of Monaghan, Clark, Crawmer, and Hart. There were seven lawyers in the firm, including two Monaghans—Peter, Jr. and Joseph. Hart shared much in common with the Monaghans who were Catholic and friends of the Briggs family. (Joseph Monaghan graduated from the University of Michigan Law School one year ahead of him.) Hart worked long hours at the firm, but to his surprise he soon became bored with law practice. "He wasn't . . . happy practicing law at all as he had been before the war," recalled Janey. "His enthusiasm for law practice was down to zilch." He needed a new direction for his career.[2]

On the morning of the 1948 fall primary election in Michigan, Hart voted at an old firehouse near his home in Bloomfield Hills. When he noticed no one listed on the ballot for Democratic precinct delegate, he wrote in his own name. After arriving at his law office, he phoned Janey and told her to do the same and to round up a few other votes from friends. Janey called scores of friends. Even so, he was surprised to discover that thirty-two persons of both parties had written in his name. With this auspicious victory, Hart inaugurated his career in Michigan politics.

Phil and Janey had recently discussed his passion for public service, but he had two serious reservations about entering politics. How would he support his growing family if he gave up his lucrative law practice to enter the low-paying field of politics? Janey advised him not to worry about financial matters; she had plenty of money to support the family. Hart mulled over the problem for several years, not fully convinced that such a breadwinning arrangement was proper for him. He also worried that his involvement with the Democrats would embarrass Janey and her Republican relatives. Again Janey downplayed the problem. Her own loyalty to the Republicans had been tenuous anyway; she was ready to convert to the Democrats. Moreover, the prospect of working in politics fascinated her. "I think *I* would enjoy it," she told him. She kept nudging him into politics. With his law career unfulfilling, he needed something else. "I always knew he wanted to be in politics," she said. "Janey . . . pushed him into politics as kind of therapy," recalled a Michigan Democratic leader. "It seemed to have worked."[3]

Fortunate timing and circumstances smoothed Hart's rise in Michigan politics, but he had the talent and the personality to capitalize on his opportunities. After World War II, Michigan Democrats swept into power through a combination of strong labor and minority support, brilliant party organization, and the charisma of Hart's law school friend, G. Mennen Williams. By the late 1940s the industrial and political power of Detroit and the United Auto Workers had matured. Over its violent and formative phase and having joined in the war effort, the UAW had become more respectable. Walter Reuther had consolidated his control of the UAW and used the power of the union to help turn Michigan's Democratic party into supporting the liberal programs of Franklin Roosevelt's New Deal and Harry Truman's Fair Deal. August Scholle, the powerful director of the Michigan CIO, openly abandoned nonpartisanship and threw his support behind the Democrats in

Michigan. Scholle and his fellow labor leaders raised money and recruited votes for Democratic candidates.

Brilliant party organization led by Neil Staebler of Ann Arbor, who chaired the Democratic State Central Committee, and the support of Michigan's black voters also spurred the party's resurgence. Before the 1930s, blacks allied with the Republicans, the party of Lincoln, but FDR and his New Deal converted them to Democrats. After World War II, blacks perceived the Democrats in the North as far more zealous than Republicans in support of civil rights. Michigan's liberal-labor coalition was in the forefront nationally in fighting to keep the Democrats strongly committed to civil rights.[4]

On 21 November 1947, two young Detroit attorneys, Hicks Griffiths and G. Mennen Williams, together with Neil Staebler and several others, met at Griffiths' home to lay plans for a coalition of liberal intellectuals and labor leaders to take advantage of the votes of the union members that Scholle and Reuther represented. Williams, 36, was on the verge of becoming a political phenomenon.

After graduating from law school, Williams assumed various state and federal positions before entering the Navy in World War II. Discharged with the rank of lieutenant commander in February 1946, he returned to Detroit and became law partners with Hicks and Martha Griffiths. Ironically, Republican governor Kim Sigler, a future gubernatorial opponent, boosted his political career by appointing him as a Democratic member of the bipartisan Liquor Control Commission. Normally an insignificant position, Williams used it to advance himself in Michigan politics.

In the spring of 1948, the newly organized group of liberals formed the Michigan Democratic Club, and Williams announced his candidacy for governor. Although not given much of a chance for victory, his campaign was bolstered by the support of the AFL and the CIO who were seeking a candidate independent of James R. Hoffa, who had thrown the support of the International Teamsters Union behind his own candidate. With labor's backing, Williams won the Democratic nomination by only 8,000 votes. In the general election in November, Williams faced Governor Sigler, and although Republicans carried Michigan for presidential candidate Thomas Dewey and captured the legislature, Williams won the election by 163,000 votes. In 1950, Williams defeated former Governor Harry F. Kelly by 1,154 votes after a recount, and two years later he again narrowly won after a recount.[5]

Hart started to be active politically during Williams' meteoric rise. He contributed $500 to Williams' 1948 campaign, but did not beat the bushes for him and was surprised that he won. During the 1948 election campaign, Hart attended a meeting of the Oakland County Democrats and volunteered his services. He volunteered Janey's as well. In mid-September, while she was in the hospital to give birth to Cammie, Phil visited her and announced, "You've been elected Vice Chairman of the Democratic County Committee!" Initially shocked, Janey nonetheless accepted. "I found [after] I started that I just loved it," said Janey. "We then became 'the team.'"[6]

Meanwhile, Hart was becoming active in the community. Because his law firm had represented the Detroit Lions football team, he was named to the board of directors. Because of his connection with the Briggs family, he was named a director of the Detroit Baseball Company, which owned the Detroit Tigers. Walter O. Briggs, Sr. detested blacks and refused to allow them on his Tigers' team, but after he died in 1952, Hart worked vigorously to change the team's philosophy, emphasizing the importance of developing black players through Detroit's minor league farm system. He also supported civic organizations, particularly those assisting the disadvantaged. In 1949, he and Janey joined the newly formed Pontiac Urban League in which he served on the governing board, and she worked for the women's auxiliary. The organization focused on securing housing for blacks and employment at traditionally all-white stores. Hart personally negotiated with a Pontiac hospital that had few black employees and admitted few black patients. "He leaned on them and their conscience and had some minor success in opening the hospital for [blacks]," Janey recalled. He also helped establish Bosco House, a recreational center for black and white ghetto children near downtown Detroit. He attended its meetings and social events and enthusiastically supported its interracial goals.[7]

After the 1948 election, Williams needed new, talented Democrats to fill many vacancies in his administration. At first he asked Hart to become Michigan's boxing commissioner, but Phil was unenthusiastic. Then Williams offered him the position as corporation and securities commissioner, and Hart accepted. Never again did he engage in the private practice of law, but in his new position from 1949-1950 he dealt mostly with legal issues that ranged from registering securities to licensing real estate dealers and beauty parlors. "He enjoyed it a lot," Janey observed.

In 1950, Michigan Democrats recruited Hart to run for secretary of state against Fred Alger, an entrenched Republican incumbent. Hart was trounced by 195,000 votes. Losing was not unexpected, but some wondered if Hart would ever overcome the serious limitations he displayed as a candidate. Initially, leading Michigan Democrats suspected Hart because of his marriage into the Briggs family. "It took me a long time to be sure of Phil," said Adelaide Hart, a state Democratic leader. "He was married to Janey Briggs. . . . I was a little nervous about that." "He was married to the employer," a labor official said bluntly.[8]

Hart seemed to lack the aptitude for politics, particularly the ability to adopt the methods a politician normally uses to get elected. Because it was common knowledge that Janey was extremely wealthy, Phil could not bring himself to ask for campaign funds. Even more disturbing was his extreme diffidence and modesty. Unlike most politicians, who were delighted to be front and center at meetings, when Hart arrived at a forum, he refused to call attention to himself. Instead he hung out in the back of the room until his campaign assistants took him by the arm and marched him to the front. "Phil preferred hiding someplace," said Carolyn Burns, a Democratic leader.

The dynamic, extroverted Williams found it difficult to understand Hart's reticence. "Phil did not like the whole campaign scene," observed Nancy Williams, Soapy's wife. "He found it very difficult to talk to people he didn't know and [to] meet perfect strangers. He would go into a room and sit in the back and be very quiet, and my husband was always having to get him to stand up and say, 'My name is Phil Hart, and I'm running for office.'"

Hart was even reluctant to ask people to vote for him and apologized for running for office. Helen Berthelot, a labor official and campaign manager for Governor Williams in the 1950s, angrily grabbed Phil by the shoulders and shook him. "You've got to stop that!" she shouted. "Don't apologize for running for office!" Another disturbing trait was his apparent indecisiveness. "You asked for his opinion, and he had to think about it awhile," said Berthelot. "It was irritating to a lot of people. He would not give you answers. . . . He saw both sides of everything."[9]

Even Janey agreed that Phil had serious limitations as a campaigner in 1950. "He didn't have the style," she thought. "He didn't know how to campaign. . . . He was too reticent [and] didn't [know] how to work a crowd." Others judged Hart's style more sympathetically. "I read it as a consideration of others and a distaste of pushing himself," observed Sidney Woolner, campaign director for Michigan's Democratic party in the 1950s.

In his first campaign Hart could not effectively use his primary attributes—his ability to discuss and debate issues. He had no political record to defend, and running for secretary of state afforded few scintillating issues to discuss. "It is one thing to debate a question, and it's something else to try and sell everybody [on] how wonderful you are," Janey observed. Hart loved to debate issues but was too modest to sell himself. "What am I going to tell these people," he seemed to be thinking, "that makes them think I'm good enough to ask them to vote for me?" Despite his defeat in 1950, Hart learned about politics and enjoyed the campaign. So did Janey, who drove him to meetings and helped organize Democrats in Oakland County. "It was fun," she said.[10]

After the 1950 election, Williams secured Hart a federal position as director of Michigan's Office of Price Stabilization. Traveling extensively throughout Michigan, he diligently explained federal price guidelines to a myriad of businesses. "He learned a whole lot about meat," said Janey of Phil's attempt to explain the rules to butchers. But because the rules were complicated, the bureaucracy stifling, and the travel exhausting, Hart was unhappy. "It was a painful time," Janey recalled.

In 1951, Hart received a better federal position as U.S. attorney for eastern Michigan and won praise for his efficiency and judgment. He enjoyed the job except for one controversial assignment. Part of his duties included prosecuting six Michigan communists under the Smith Act, the controversial law of 1940 making it a crime to advocate or teach the overthrow of government in the United States by force or violence. Although critics charged that the Smith Act violated the First Amendment right of free speech, members of the American Communist party were convicted under the law. Hart was also troubled, but like many other liberals, he succumbed to the anticommunist hysteria. During the McCarthy era, the liberals in Michigan and elsewhere engaged in their own anticommunist hunt in the labor movement and other organizations, unwittingly feeding the fires of the "McCarthyist Monster" they had come to detest. Hart fed the fires and successfully prosecuted the communists. Later he regretted his role.[11]

After Eisenhower's inauguration Hart resigned his post, allowing the new Republican administration to fill the position. In 1953 Williams appointed him as the governor's legal advisor. The Hart family moved to Lansing, and Phil advised the governor on a variety of state legal issues. Early the following year, Hart began eyeing the race for lieutenant governor. He had become reconciled to the financial limitations of elective office. As Williams' legal advisor he earned $12,000; if he were elected lieutenant governor his salary would drop to only $6,400 (plus another $9,000 from his investments and 60 percent military disability pay). Janey's wealth would have to cover much of the family's expenses if he were elected to office. "He didn't have to be making money," Janey recalled of their understanding. In the late 1930s, Walter Briggs, Sr. established trust funds for each of his five children. Each received interest from the trust; the corpus of the funds would go to the grandchildren upon the death of the children. In the mid-1950s, after the death of both of her parents, Janey received a twenty per cent share of the Briggs' $20,000,000 estate (after taxes) which was placed in another trust fund. Estimates of Janey's total wealth varied widely; nonetheless, she was at least a multimillionaire. But she did not have access to the principal of her trust funds. She later estimated that her cash flow was $4,000 per month after World War II. Hart used his income to take care of some of the family's daily living and household expenses. Janey's income also helped pay for the family's expenses; otherwise, she spent her money as she pleased, such as on her used airplane and occasional trips to Europe. "I couldn't justify being in politics at my salary except for the provisions made for my children," Phil said candidly when reporters questioned him about the Briggs fortune.[12]

In April 1954, Hart resigned as legal advisor to Williams and announced his candidacy for lieutenant governor. His opponent in the Democratic primary, George B. Fitzgerald, the attorney for the Teamsters Union and former Democratic National Committeeman, was a seasoned candidate of the old-line Michigan Democrats. "It was a vicious campaign," said a reporter; "the Teamsters on occasion tried the use of a little muscle against Hart's supporters." Governor Williams helped Hart by breaking precedent and endorsing him in the primary.

When Hart's campaign was desperately short of money, preventing his aides from buying much-needed promotional ads, Janey secretly contributed $50,000 to his campaign. Busy touring the state, he never noticed—"I never told him," said Janey. The aides used the money to purchase the ads. Hart won the nomination easily by a three-to-one margin. The result "surprised everybody," said the *Detroit News.* "It surprised me, too," said Hart.

On the second night after the primary, as Hart dined at a Detroit restaurant with Alfred Fitt, a campaign supporter, he was called to the phone and informed that his daughter Ann, seven, had fallen victim to the raging polio epidemic. She had been on Mackinac Island, and Janey took her to a nearby hospital. Hart was deeply troubled and immediately left the restaurant to go to the hospital. "We had been having such a good time," recalled Fitt. "It was really heartrending." (Ann would spend almost a year in two hospitals and suffered severe paralysis to her gluteus media and the calf muscles of her legs.)[13]

Hart's opponent in the general election was Republican incumbent Clarence A. Reid, a former state senator and a veteran campaigner who had been elected lieutenant governor in 1952. Campaigning on four major themes, Hart pledged to be an active, full-time lieutenant governor, defended the record of Governor Williams, argued the virtues of the Democrats' domestic policy, and presented a civic lesson on politics. He promised to spend full time at what had been traditionally a part time job. To a Democratic lieutenant governor, he argued, would fall many of the governmental chores that heretofore Williams could not entrust to anyone.

Hart defended Williams from his critics, particularly from the GOP charge that Michigan needed a Republican governor to cooperate with the Republican legislature. Williams had not cooperated with the Republican legislature, Hart said, only when he thought his opposition was necessary to block bills that throttled progress. "In 1947 a Republican governor and legislature abolished the Mackinac Bridge Authority," Hart argued, but because of Williams' persistence the bridge was under construction. "This is the kind of program Michigan wants."[14]

In mid-October 1954, at the Pontiac Rotary Club, Hart credited the New Deal reforms with preserving the American competitive system and praised politics as an honorable profession. "I believe in the New Deal," he said; yet "I'm as conservative a man as any in the building today." He had faith in the free enterprise system and credited the New Deal for ironing out "excesses" and "abuses," thereby sustaining the competitive business structure. Time would demonstrate that the "hideous predictions for America expressed by Republican leaders in the thirties have proved very false." He cited social security as an example of a New Deal program that made sense, although it was termed socialistic by its opponents in the thirties. Condemning the current plague of McCarthyism, he urged an end to misleading slogans that appealed to prejudice and prevented intelligent examination of issues. "There's danger in having such slogans as 'it smacks of Communism' broadcast whenever someone comes up with a new approach."[15]

Hart often spoke of the place held by politics in the minds of citizens. "I like politics and I am not ashamed to be in politics. I have no use for people who think they are above politics and then complain about the way the country is run." Hart told the Rotarians that parents should not give their children the impression that government service was too dirty to consider as a career. "Politics make a community vibrant and vital. It's not a dirty word, but the day-to-day housekeeping job of a democracy." He criticized two types of persons found in both political parties. One thought that questions were too complex and the machine too big to take a stand; the other thought he was the person who already had all the answers and simply slapped a label on every issue. He denounced the cries of "socialism" from the Republican right aimed at the Democrats and shouts of "fascism" from the Democratic left directed at the Republicans. "Generally the answer lies right down the middle of the road," he said.

To some Hart still seemed ill-fitted for politics. "Hart has none of the aplomb of a Harry Truman, the authority of a Dwight D. Eisenhower or the glad-handedness of a 'Soapy' Williams," observed a reporter for the *Detroit Free Press*. Despite his limitations, by 1954, Michigan Democrats were beginning to appreciate his attributes. They found him refreshingly articulate and knowledgeable and liked his personality and kindness. "He was wonderful company," said Mildred Jeffrey, a labor leader and member of the Democratic National Committee with whom Hart teased and joked; "There was not a malicious bone in his body." Phil's honesty and simplicity were also attractive. "He didn't need any window dressing," said Carolyn Burns. "He didn't need any salesmanship."[16]

Because he was so dedicated to a career in public life, Hart knew he had to interact with people and project himself more effectively. By the end of the 1954 campaign he had improved as a campaigner and impressed political observers with his disarming style and grace. "Typical of Hart's modesty," said the *Detroit News*, "is his World War II record. Only a handful know he was wounded as an infantryman at Normandy and was decorated for bravery by France, Belgium and the U.S." He seemed to disdain one of the most attractive features of public life. "He is completely unimpressed about seeing his name or picture in the paper," observed *The Detroit Times*.

Because he was a more willing handshaker, voters usually accepted his handshake and little card. But whenever a person refused to accept a card, Hart countered with a subtle argument. "Well, why don't you take a card so you can find out about the guy you're going to vote against?" The voter usually relented. "Everybody who met him liked him and had the feeling he liked them in return," said Al Fitt.

Instead of a rabble-rousing speech, voters found themselves hearing an earnest, slender man in light, horn-rimmed glasses say, "No party has a monopoly on wisdom, integrity and sincerity. But in the long run, I think we Democrats better serve the people because our target is the welfare of everybody." Then he would step down, shake hands, flash his smile and depart, leaving, said the *Detroit News*, "the men thoughtful and the women sighing."[17]

Voters favored all Democratic state officers in the 1954 election, and Hart defeated Reid by 184,000 votes, polling a state-ticket majority second only to Williams himself. Suddenly pundits were proclaiming Hart the second most powerful Democrat in Michigan. "One of the brightest stars in the Democratic sky," "the key figure in state government for the next two years," and Williams' "hand-picked successor" were typical post-election comments. When reporters told him that Democratic strategists referred to him as Williams' heir apparent, Hart blushed and grinned with boyish embarrassment.[18]

For six years Hart's career had been bolstered by Governor Williams, and starting in 1955, the two top government officials in Michigan worked closely together for four more years. Considering his family and educational background, Williams had amazing ability to establish rapport with the ordinary working man and minority groups. During his first campaign, Williams picked up his political trademarks—a green and white polka dot bow tie and a talent for calling square dances. Effervescent, boyishly friendly, he seemed willing to shake every hand in Michigan.

In some ways Hart and Williams differed markedly. Abrasively partisan, Williams gave passionate, rousing, slogan-filled speeches; Hart shared none of those traits. Dressing conservatively, Hart affected none of the trademarks like the bow tie worn by Williams. Despite their different styles, the pair shared much in common and became friends and confidants. Both were sincere, dedicated, liberal Democrats. Hart admired Williams' intelligence, kindness, integrity, and ideals, and Williams appreciated the same qualities in Phil. Williams welcomed dissent from his advisors and Hart argued with him, but when Williams decided on a course of action, Hart loyally supported him, winning the governor's gratitude. Occasionally, Hart and Williams spent time together at their vacation retreats on Mackinac Island, and the informal contact cemented their close relationship.

As governor, Williams promoted a strong program of civil rights, leading the state to enact fair employment practices and prohibit discrimination in the buying and selling of real estate. He also appointed blacks to his cabinet and judgeships. He made effective use of study commissions. Consisting of prominent persons of both parties, his commissions planned the Mackinac Bridge project, recommended aid to the physically handicapped, proposed election reforms, and improved the youth correction system. "He championed the cause of the little people, advocated more support for education, and in general was sensitive to human needs," said historians Willis Dunbar and George May. "His appointments were excellent; there was hardly a breath of scandal during his dozen years as governor."[19]

Because the term for state offices was only two years, Williams and Hart constantly campaigned. Although he remained in the shadow of the governor, in his quiet way Hart built alliances with Democrats, blacks, and labor. "He had a lot of bridges," said Jerald terHorst, political reporter for the *Detroit News*. "He was always cooperative with us," Adelaide Hart observed of Phil's assistance to Michigan Democrats. Phil spoke to many groups about race relations. He focused on conservative groups that ordinarily did not support racial integration. At the 50th anniversary meeting of a real estate board, he boldly told the starchy gathering that an auspicious start for the next fifty years would be to open all housing to purchase by people of all races and creeds. "Phil was one of the few who would go out and talk with the conservative side," said John Feild, director of Michigan's Civil Rights Commission.[20]

Hart enjoyed speaking to groups of youths, trying to spark their interest in political affairs. "You may have good ideas," he told 180 leaders in Kalamazoo, "fine instincts, good will, and an understanding of brotherhood, but all of these will not be exploited unless you determine that you will actively participate in public business." He was ahead of his time on some issues. In 1957, before the Peace Corps or VISTA, he urged the state's Young Democrats to find solutions to "poverty in Asia and Africa and prejudice in America." In 1958, six years before creation of the Equal Employment Opportunity Commission, he wrote

Vice President Richard Nixon, requesting that more facts be made available on the success or failure of eliminating discrimination in government contracts.[21]

Hart's duties as lieutenant governor included presiding over the state senate, serving as acting governor when Williams was out of the state, and sitting as a member of the State Administrative Board. The lieutenant governor's position had the potential, however, for being a dead end in politics. Despite being competent and popular, Hart's predecessor had been unable to glamorize the job. Except as a standby for the governor, the position did not even rate with the state senators or the representatives. At least they voted and passed laws. The lieutenant governor had no vote and could not even vote to break a tie as could the vice president of the United States or the lieutenant governors in some states. Republicans still controlled the legislature after the 1954 election and would run the show. Although some potent politicians had held the lieutenant governor's post, none had ever been elected governor in Michigan. Phil had pledged during the campaign that he would work full time, but some were skeptical. "The office gets about one stray visitor a month as par for the course," said a reporter for the *Detroit Free Press*, "and he is usually lost and looking for another place to light."[22]

But Hart did work full time. People seeking advice on state affairs stopped at his cramped office behind the Senate chamber, a cubbyhole so small he had to tape record his weekly radio broadcast while perched on a sink in his washroom. Janey contributed money to a fund that allowed Phil to hire a secretary and a researcher. He used the extra assistance to prepare legislation on labor, highways, and other important issues. "This office had been sort of a fifth wheel before," he observed of his attempt to improve its influence and effectiveness.

When Williams took a two-week tour of the Near East and Hart served as the acting governor, Williams' personal publicity machine busily rolled out statements that "Lt. Gov. Hart says this. . . . " and "Lt. Gov. Hart does that. . . . " Through it all, Phil grinned as if to say, "Shucks, fellows, this is all kinda embarrassing to me."

Hart's first proposal as acting governor was masterful. He called in the media and suggested that the legislature provide a million dollars to give free polio vaccine to all Michigan children, regardless of their financial status. Making it clear he did not consider his proposal a partisan suggestion, he had earlier invited Republican leaders into his office to see if they would accept authorship of his plan. All he wanted to do was help the children. Republicans were perplexed. "Accustomed to being kicked in the shins and socked behind the ear as they walk past the governor's office," observed a reporter, Republicans "were sort of left gasping by this approach." A tight fisted, veteran, Republican state senator found himself on the senate floor relaying to the members what he and Hart thought ought to be done. Concluded the reporter of Hart's approach, "It's kind of hard to get mad at a guy who just stands there and grins at you in a friendly way or who has a twinkle in his eye as he slips a knife under your ribs so very gently you think he is tickling you." Capitol observers were interested in seeing how the Republicans would handle "this Tom Sawyer in a button-down collar."[23]

Hart's dedication, intelligence, and demeanor earned the respect of his peers. "Hart is well-regarded by Senate members," reported the *Detroit Free Press*, "although he wields a gavel over a Republican majority. He presides with quiet decorum and close attention to correct form, occasionally easing tensions with a flash of nimble wit." Political reporters also respected him. Some politicians in Lansing sought to sway the press by doing favors. If a newspaper was pushing a pet project, a legislator would offer to introduce a bill advancing it. In return, of course, the legislator expected favorable publicity in the newspaper. "[That] was fairly common," said terHorst. "Except Phil Hart never did it." Reporters had to seek out Hart. "He was not a person who sought headlines, unlike many other political figures in Lansing," terHorst observed. When Hart gave a speech or granted an interview, he did not use clichés or slogans. "When he had something to say, it was usually quite thoughtful," said terHorst. "He was so genuine."[24]

Hart and Williams both won reelection in 1956. During the campaign Hart sharply criticized Williams' Republican opponent, Detroit Mayor Albert E. Cobo, spurring the charge that Hart had executed a "verbal hatchet job." The charge was exaggerated but newspapers resurrected the accusation for almost two years. Hart criticized what he said was the Cobo Myth, declaring the mayor a manufactured statesman who had burdened Detroit with heavy debts and was financed by big business and sold by professional hucksters. (Williams' staff apparently prepared the attack, and Hart delivered it.)[25]

As the 1958 election approached, Williams faced a crucial decision: should he run for governor or for U.S. senator? The Democrats had captured one Michigan Senate seat in 1954 when Detroit labor official Patrick McNamara defeated incumbent Republican Homer Ferguson.

The other seat was held by Republican Charles Potter, who was first elected in 1952. Since Potter had a nondescript Senate career, his seat seemed vulnerable in 1958 to any Democrat with stature.

Williams and his advisors wanted to position him to run for president in 1960. The dilemma was this: as the springboard to the presidential nomination, was it preferable to run for an unprecedented sixth term as governor, or challenge the U.S. Senate seat held by Potter? The decision was crucial for Hart as well, since whichever position Williams did not select, he could attempt to obtain. Williams' advisors were sharply divided on the best course of action. Some urged him to run for governor. "I tried to get him to run for senator," said Neil Staebler.[26]

Meanwhile, Michigan's Democratic leaders were confident that Hart's talents were best-suited for the Senate. "We thought Phil would be an infinitely better U.S. senator than he would be an executive," said Mildred Jeffrey. "Phil Hart walked around every issue . . . was infinitely fair, infinitely judicious and those qualities are better suited to be a legislator than an executive." Privately, Phil and Janey also preferred the senatorial position. In any case, Hart's goals did not matter. He could not say anything publicly about his own wishes or intentions until Williams made up his mind. It seemed like an eternity as Williams contemplated. Janey hated the period of indecision, but Phil waited patiently, saying only of Williams, "He and he alone set me on the road. He built the party. I'll wait."

In a burst of frankness, Williams told a reporter he had not yet made up his mind to run again for governor or for the U.S. Senate, adding that Hart would "fill in" whichever job he did not want. The embarrassing comment made Hart vulnerable to the charge that he was merely Williams' "handmaiden." A Republican leader chided Hart as "always a bridesmaid, never a bride." Phil countered stoutly, "I've enjoyed being a bridesmaid," adding a bit wistfully, "I also understand it's pleasant to be a bride."[27]

Finally, in February 1958, Williams announced he would run again for governor. He apparently thought his reputation and programs were at stake and that his career would be damaged if he stepped down from the governor's position. Conventional wisdom held that as a springboard to a presidential nomination, a governorship, especially a sixth-term governorship, was vastly preferable to a freshman senatorship. Williams was probably thinking of the Democratic governors in the 1950s who were powerful and prominent in the party, like Governor

Adlai Stevenson of Illinois. In any case, the way was now clear for Hart to run for the Senate, and in mid-February 1958, he summoned newsmen to his Lansing office and announced his senatorial bid.[28]

The 1958 election looked promising for Democrats because the Eisenhower administration was reeling from a series of setbacks. When industrial production dropped and unemployment increased in 1957, Democrats blamed the Republican administration for the recession. Growing tension over civil rights also damaged the president. In 1957, he dispatched paratroopers and National Guardsmen to Central High School in Little Rock, Arkansas, to escort black students and protect them from violence. Eisenhower's confrontation with segregationist Governor Orval Faubus of Arkansas damaged Ike's image as a symbol of national unity and common purpose. Following the Little Rock crisis, Eisenhower backed away from the civil rights struggle in the South, refusing public comment on the problem, which spurred liberal Democrats to attack his weak leadership.

On the heels of Little Rock came the electrifying news on 4 October 1957 that the Russians had launched Sputnik, the first space satellite. Shocked and apprehensive, politicians and the public questioned our scientific superiority and the adequacy of federal aid to education. Scandal added to the headaches of the Eisenhower administration. Sherman Adams, Ike's close friend and chief of staff, was forced to resign in September 1958 after being accused of influence-peddling on behalf of a sleazy millionaire friend, Bernard Goldfine.[29]

Hart's opponent, Charles Potter, forty-two, had lost both legs in 1945 when he stepped on a land mine while leading an attack on a German position. After World War II, he was a vocational rehabilitation advisor until he was elected a U.S. congressman in 1947. Potter moved about on artificial legs with the help of canes. He greeted Hart's candidacy with the charge that Phil was a "stooge" of Governor Williams, who was a "puppet" of the UAW's Walter Reuther. Hart declined to reply to the charge and indicated he might never reply.

On 10 March 1958, Hart was in Washington soliciting support among Senate and House Democrats. When he met with reporters, they assumed he would attack Potter. Instead Hart praised him. "First of all," he told the reporters, "I want to make it clear that I think Charles Potter has done a fine job. He is an honest conservative, and I think he has represented his philosophy well in Washington." He did not intend to engage in a personal campaign against Potter. "It is not in my personal makeup to conduct a bitter campaign," he said. Nor would he seek out evidence of Republican corruption to spice up his campaign. Then he went on to explain why he thought his liberal Democratic philosophy would better serve the needs of Michigan than Potter's conservative views. The Republicans "lack imagination and do not move swiftly enough to meet the challenges of the changing times," Hart said.

Hart had practical reasons as well for not shooting major fireworks at Potter. "Who knows Charlie Potter?" he told a reporter, jabbing at Potter's obscure record. "Sure, I'll take an occasional verbal poke at Potter," he said, "but the basic issue is that he has done nothing as a senator in Washington to suggest imagination and leadership. So why publicize him now?" Unlike Potter's, Hart's war injury was not apparent to voters. "If I attack him bitterly," he said candidly during the campaign, "it might generate sympathy, as an underdog, for a disabled war veteran. It might help him more than hurt him."[30]

Hart still refused to capitalize on his own World War II record. When he attended a campaign dinner in which the sponsors had printed a program dramatizing his war record, he was embarrassed and upset. "I want it clearly understood that I just happened to be there on D-Day," he told the gathering. "What happened to me happened to other people. I want no false note developed in relation to that." Never again did Hart discuss his war record on the campaign trail, and his advisors and supporters never again sought to glamorize it.[31]

Janey left their eight young children in the care of a housekeeper in order to devote more time to assisting Phil. Looking for a way to boost the campaign, she learned to pilot a rented helicopter and flew Hart to some engagements. The tactic drew extensive publicity for the campaign, especially from smaller newspapers. "I never believed he'd win," Janey recalled. "It was a great uphill fight."[32]

From June to November, Hart campaigned almost every day, matching Williams' stamina. He talked, smiled, and shook hands at endless rounds of banquets, shopping centers, coffees, and rallies. "Politics is one of the most important fields a man can enter," Hart often said during the campaign, "and I like excitement. I contemplate being in politics as long as the people want me. I want to make every minute count and leave a record that is worthwhile." Making campaign promises was usually not his style. He criticized the "Republican" recession, favored federal aid to education, federal help for depressed areas, expansion of social security to provide hospitalization, medical aid, and more effective assistance for the elderly, the blind, the disabled, and dependent children.

In late October, to a Lansing television audience, Hart referred to Potter's slogan "Keep your voice in Washington." Hart questioned if Michigan could afford a voice that voted against income tax cuts for low-income families and against money for hospitals and medical research. "I fear the voice my Republican opponent is talking about is the voice of big business bosses," he said. "My opponent says he is the best friend labor ever had. He can't sell that to Michigan's 450,000 unemployed, the hard-pressed merchant, the housewife whose grocery bill is skyrocketing, or the farmer caught in the price squeeze."

Nationally, many Democratic candidates seized upon the Soviet Union's sputnik to spread the alarm about a missile gap. But Hart approached the issue from a different angle. "Catching up in the missile race is child's play compared with bringing our values up to standard," he said, developing a major theme of his campaign. "In the U.S. the material is too often prized over success in research, youth over wisdom, athletic prowess over knowledge." Ideas that advanced the individual were just as essential as rockets. "The individual may join in the fight for freedom in other areas than fighting a Soviet tank in Budapest," he said. "We reject guilt by association. It's the individual who's good or bad, not religions, classes or races. But until we can stand up and plead not guilty to racial bitterness and prejudice—to the betrayal of freedom and justice which they breed—the individual's job is far from complete."[33]

Hart also focused on Eisenhower's tepid approach to civil rights. Four years after the Supreme Court's *Brown* case, southern schools were still segregated. Most black citizens still were not allowed to register to vote, and segregated buses, restaurants, hotels, theaters, and even drinking fountains remained the order of the day in the South. Hart argued that the Eisenhower administration wanted to take credit for the 1957 Civil Rights Act but had not enforced the law. He accused President Eisenhower of a "hideous failure" in not following up with "effective leadership" the Supreme Court's desegregation decision of 1954. He urged the creation of a federal fair employment practices commission; revision of the Senate's rules to restrict filibusters; extension of the Civil Rights Commission; opposition to efforts to curb the power of the Supreme Court; and passage of a bill to offer technical and financial assistance to local school integration programs.[34]

Hart's political style still displayed the reticence that irritated some Democrats, but which others found refreshingly modest. "He literally apologizes for being alive," said an exasperated Democratic candidate as Hart characteristically thanked his audience for "suffering through this," or "letting me impose on you."

For the most part, though, by 1958 Hart was an effective, self-confident campaigner. Said an astute Republican in appraising Phil: "He's grown from a hesitant young officeholder in the shadow of Williams to an assured political figure in his own right." Hart's warmth and sincerity projected particularly well on television. "Unlike Williams, who's at his best striding into a roomful of strangers and grabbing for a hand," said an observer, "Hart is most effective in the relatively protected TV studio." His consistent friendliness was also a major asset. "While driving himself fiercely toward his goal of higher office," said a columnist, "Hart has never stopped smiling at the world. Opponents call him 'Friendly Phil.'" Yet Hart's style also gave the impression of firm determination and beliefs as hard as steel. While talking politics, he would stab the desk with his well-manicured fingertip to emphasize his points.[35]

Joe Rauh, one of the founders of Americans for Democratic Action and the general counsel for the United Auto Workers, first met Phil in 1958 at the UAW Convention in Atlantic City. At dinner with a small group Rauh tried to size up this unusual candidate. At first, Hart said little, a peculiar trait, Rauh thought, for a U.S. Senate aspirant. "I thought he was extremely quiet and reserved. I couldn't quite picture him as a fine politician. Everything he said I agreed with, but it was always very quiet-spoken." But by the end of the dinner Rauh had come to a fuller understanding. "You were immediately impressed by his sincerity," said Rauh. "He wasn't tooting his own horn. He was giving thoughtful and sensitive answers." Thereafter, Hart and Rauh became close friends.[36]

Maine's Democratic senator Edmund Muskie, first elected in the summer of 1958, flew into Michigan to campaign for Hart in October and, like Rauh, judged him as a clearly different stripe of candidate. "He was not one of the 'old pols' as we used to call [them] up in New England," said Muskie. "He was thoughtful [and] did not indulge in the hot political rhetoric typical of campaign . . . speeches. He was more like a college professor. So he stood out in my mind."[37]

In his campaign, Potter endorsed the "Republican system" of free enterprise and praised the Eisenhower foreign policy for keeping the

United States out of war. Organized labor was the special target of his scorn. He urged a twelve-point program of labor reform, including secret balloting for union officials and increased surveillance of union funds. Labor wanted to elect Democrats in order to secure a planned economy, he charged. Unless people voted for Republicans, "We face the wildest, most irresponsible spending spree in our history, and new license for labor abuses." Phil was a captive candidate because of the $19,000 labor had contributed to his campaign. Hart was owned lock, stock and barrel by the union bosses, Potter charged.

Hart responded indirectly. Noting Potter's description of himself as an unbossed candidate, he said his Republican opponent had stated that "business should quarterback all the plays in Washington." "Is that an unbossed candidate?" Hart asked. "If I go to Washington, I'm going to call everybody into the huddle, and then I'm going to call the plays."[38]

Most observers commented on the gentlemanly nature of the campaign, especially of Hart's campaign. "The campaign was one of the most polite in history," concluded the *Washington Post.* "It was a strange campaign," the *Detroit News* said, "strange in that the challenger made less noise than the incumbent."[39]

The candidates remained relatively gentle with each other until the last two weeks of the campaign, when Potter unleashed a barrage of charges that provoked Phil's angry rebuttal. Potter accused Hart of double talk on civil rights. "While I was fighting for President Eisenhower's civil rights bill, Hart and his leader, Governor Williams, were sitting on their hands, strangely silent at the most critical time of our nation's history." Williams and Hart were "millionaires," content to have Michigan be "half-slave and half-free." Potter also cited Janey Hart's $8,000 contribution to the campaign as evidence that Hart's candidacy was being bolstered by "sweatshop dollars from the Briggs factory."

Hart was incensed. He was proud of his support for civil rights and hated to be called a millionaire. Janey's contribution to his campaign was only a small portion of the $100,000 he would spend. He responded angrily that Potter had engaged in an "irresponsible smear" in a "desperate effort to rally a dying campaign." Instead of dropping to the level of attacking his wife in the campaign, Hart charged, Potter should be talking about the real issues—"the 4,000,000 unemployed, the failure of leadership that produced Little Rock, and the silence in the White House over integration."[40]

Editorial endorsement by the conservative *Detroit News*, ordinarily a supporter of Republican candidates, provided impetus to Hart's campaign. On the eve of the election, the newspaper described Potter as a decent man who had not been a bad senator, but who had shown little talent for leadership and had appeared to stand for both sides of the same issue. By contrast, Hart had excellent educational credentials and had "won the grudging respect of rural Republican legislators not used to giving anything to the Democratic, CIO-supported state administration." He had also shown a degree of independence from the "Reuther-Williams machine." For example, the *News* said, "We note his reiteration in union halls that, although workmen can expect his normal agreement with their aspirations, labor should not assume his automatic rubber-stamping of all they advocate."[41]

On 4 November 1958, Hart won the election, earning 53.5 percent of the vote and a 170,000-vote margin. Nationally, the Republicans suffered their worst defeat since the Depression. In both houses Democrats outnumbered Republicans almost two to one. The influx of northern Democrats into the Senate changed the composition of the party, allowing the northern wing to gain numerical superiority over southern Democrats. Furthermore, the nine new liberal senators, including Hart, swelled the ranks of progressivism among northern Democrats.

More than 300 Hart supporters gathered for an election party at the Sheraton-Cadillac Hotel in Detroit. At 3:15 A.M. Senator Potter called to concede defeat. Blushing and waving to the crowd to be quiet, Hart took the phone. Potter extended his congratulations and offered to assist in the transition.

"I know you're having difficulty making this call," Hart said. "For some time, I anticipated having to do the same thing. I naturally wanted to win—but yet I didn't want to beat anybody badly."

"In such aggressive campaigns," Potter responded, "some things are said that . . . "—then Potter's voice trailed off as Hart interrupted with assurances there would be no lingering bitterness.

"If I had to lose to a Democrat, I'm glad it was you," Potter said before hanging up.

After the concession by Potter, Hart addressed his own supporters: "I have wanted very much to be a senator. I hope I can come back here at the end of my six-year term and present a record which you will think has been good."

The morning after his victory, Hart returned to the same plant gates he had visited earlier in the campaign. "Why are you back here?" asked an incredulous worker, shocked by the appearance of a politician the morning after winning a victory. "To thank you," was Phil's soft-spoken reply.[42]

Hart's victory surprised everyone because he out-polled Williams, who won reelection as governor by only half the margin of his 1956 victory. What did Phil think about surpassing his mentor's vote-getting appeal? a reporter asked after the election. Hart seemed almost apologetic: "All I can say is that I am happy he has won."

Williams' glamour was wearing thin, his star fading. He had always been as repugnant to business as he was attractive to labor. The South had solidified against his presidential ambition because of his uncompromising support of civil rights legislation. With hindsight, Williams made the biggest mistake of his life when he decided to run for governor in 1958. His often tense relations with the Republican-controlled legislature reached a grim climax with a state financial crisis in 1959. Michigan had been suffering chronic budget deficits, and when a difference of opinion that arose over tax philosophy resulted in a stalemate between the governor and the legislature, the rivalry became bitter and often vicious. On 5 May 1959, Michigan could not pay its employees. The payless payday made national news, conveying the image of a bankrupt state and badly tarnishing Williams' image. "The state's financial embarrassments," said historians Dunbar and May, "whatever their origins, effectively destroyed any hopes Williams might have held for the presidency." Williams did not seek reelection in 1960. After John Kennedy's election as president, Michigan's Democrats were bitterly disappointed that Williams was not appointed to a major cabinet position. Instead, Kennedy selected him as Assistant Secretary of State for African Affairs, not a choice assignment or one that advanced Williams' career.[43]

So while Hart moved to Washington to build his senatorial career, his mentor's political stature was declining.

NOTES

1. Janey Hart, interview, Washington, D.C., 1 and 2 April 1989.
2. Ibid.
3. *Birmingham* [Michigan] *Eccentric*, 22 January 1970; Janey Hart, interview, Washington, D.C., 1 and 2 April 1989; Neil Staebler, telephone interview, 27 August 1987.

4. *Detroit Free Press*, 9 March 1969; Willis Dunbar and George May, *Michigan: A History of the Wolverine State*, rev. ed. (Grand Rapids: William B. Eerdmans Publishing Company, 1980), 629-32.

5. Dunbar and May, *Michigan*, 629-30; "G. Mennen Williams," in *Current Biography Yearbook 1963*, ed. Charles Moritz (New York: The H.W. Wilson Company, 1963), 468.

6. *New Republic*, 27 October 1958; Janey Hart, interview, Washington, D.C., 1 and 2 April 1989.

7. *Birmingham Eccentric*, 22 January 1970; *Lansing State Journal*, 17 April 1954; Janey Hart, interview, Washington, D.C., 1 and 2 April 1989.

8. Adelaide Hart, telephone interview, 2 March 1988; Janey Hart, interview, Washington, D.C., 1 and 2 April 1989; Joseph Rauh, interview, Washington, D.C., 29 March 1988; Neil Staebler, telephone interview, 27 August 1987; Sidney Woolner, telephone interview, 12 and 14 January and 5 July 1988.

9. Helen Berthelot, telephone interview, 23 May 1988; Carolyn Burns, telephone interview, 9 May 1989; Nancy Williams, telephone interview, 20 March 1989; Sidney Woolner, telephone interview, 12 and 14 January and 5 July 1988.

10. Janey Hart, interview, Washington, D.C., 1 and 2 April 1989; Sidney Woolner, telephone interview, 12 and 14 January and 5 July 1988.

11. *Detroit Free Press*, 9 March 1969; Janey Hart, interview, Washington, D.C., 1 and 2 April 1989; Sidney Woolner, telephone interview, 12 and 14 January and 5 July 1988.

12. *Detroit Free Press*, 9 February 1958; Basil Briggs, telephone interview, 15 March 1990; Janey Hart, interview, Washington, D.C., 1 and 2 April 1989.

13. Alfred Fitt to (?), 13 October 1976, unprocessed Alfred Fitt Papers, Washington, D.C.; clipping, Hart Scrapbook, Hart Papers, Bentley Library; *Detroit Free Press*, 9 March 1969; *Detroit News*, 4 August 1954; Alfred Fitt, telephone interview, 28 April 1989; Janey Hart, interview, Washington, D.C., 1 and 2 April 1989.

14. *Detroit News*, 3 November 1954; *Lansing State Journal*, 17 April 1954; *Pontiac Press*, 18 October 1954.

15. *Pontiac Press*, 18 October 1954.

16. Ibid; clipping, Hart Scrapbook, Hart Papers, Bentley Library; *Detroit News*, 4 August 1954; *The Detroit Times*, 9 November 1954; Mildred Jeffrey, telephone interview, 31 May 1988; Carolyn Burns, telephone interview, 9 May 1989.

17. Clippings, Hart Scrapbook, Hart Papers, Bentley Library; *Detroit News*, 3 November 1954, 27 December 1976; *The Detroit Times*, 9 November 1954; Carolyn Burns, telephone interview, 9 May 1989; Alfred Fitt, telephone interview, 28 April 1989; Janey Hart, interview, Washington, D.C., 1 and 2 April 1989.

18. Clippings, Hart Scrapbook, Hart Papers, Bentley Library; *Detroit News*, 3 November 1954; *The Detroit Times*, 9 November 1954.

19. *Detroit News*, 3 November 1954, 5 November 1958; Dunbar and May, *Michigan*, 630-31; Moritz, "Williams," 468; William Beckham, telephone interview, 9 May 1988; Adelaide Hart, telephone interview, 2 March 1988; Janey Hart, interview, Washington, D.C., 1 and 2 April 1989; Nancy Williams, telephone interview, 20 March 1989.

20. *Detroit Free Press*, 8 November 1954; *New Republic*, 27 October 1958; Adelaide Hart, telephone interview, 2 March 1988; John Feild, telephone interview, 20 March 1989; Jerald terHorst, telephone interview, 28 March 1989.

21. Clipping, Janey Hart Papers, Washington, D.C.; *Detroit Free Press*, 28 December 1976.

22. *Detroit Free Press*, 8 November 1954, 9 February 1958.

23. Clipping, Hart Scrapbook, Hart Papers, Bentley Library; *Detroit Free Press*, 9 February 1958; *Detroit News*, 7 November 1956; Janey Hart, interview, Washington, D.C., 1 and 2 April 1989.

24. *Detroit Free Press*, 9 February 1958; Jerald terHorst, telephone interview, 28 March 1989.

25. *Detroit Free Press*, 9 February 1958; Janey Hart, interview, Washington, D.C., 1 and 2 April 1989.

26. Dunbar and May, *Michigan*, 645-46; Neil Staebler, telephone interview, 27 August 1987.

27. *Detroit Free Press*, 9 February 1958, 9 March 1969; Adelaide Hart, telephone interview, 2 March 1988; Janey Hart, interview, Washington, D.C., 1 and 2 April 1989; Mildred Jeffrey, telephone interview, 31 May 1988.

28. *Detroit Free Press*, 9 March 1969; *Kalamazoo Gazette*, 12 February 1958; Dunbar and May, *Michigan*, 646; Adelaide Hart, telephone interview, 2 March 1988.

29. Robert Burk, *Dwight D. Eisenhower: Hero and Politician* (Boston: Twayne Publishers, 1986), 160; John Diggins, *The Proud Decades: America in War and in Peace, 1941-1960* (New York: W.W. Norton and Company, 1988), 324; David Horowitz, Peter Carroll, and David Lee, *On The Edge: A History of America Since World War II* (St. Paul: West Publishing Company, 1989), 136-40.

30. *Detroit News*, 11 March 1958, 21 October 1958, 22 October 1958, 27 October 1958, 5 November 1958, 27 December 1976; "Charles E. Potter," in *Current Biography: 1954*, ed. Marjorie Candee (New York: The H.W. Wilson Company, 1954), 513-14.

31. *Detroit News*, 27 December 1976.

32. *Detroit News*, 5 November 1958; Janey Hart, interview, Washington, D.C., 1 and 2 April 1989.

33. Clipping, Hart Scrapbook, Hart Papers, Bentley Library; *Detroit Free Press*, 9 February 1958; *Detroit News*, 22 October 1958, 27 October 1958, 5 November 1958; *Labor*, 25 October 1958; *Lansing State Journal*, 24 January

1958; *The Michigan Teacher*, 19 February 1958; Stephen Ambrose, *Eisenhower: The President*, vol. 2 (New York: Simon and Schuster, 1984), 487; James Sundquist, *Politics and Policy* (Washington, D.C.: The Brookings Institution, 1968), 458.

34. *Detroit News*, 27 October 1958; *Labor*, 25 October 1958; Ambrose, *Eisenhower*, 497; James Sundquist, *Dynamics of the Party System*, rev. ed. (Washington, D.C.: The Brookings Institution, 1983), 356-57.

35. Clipping, Hart Scrapbook, Hart Papers, Bentley Library; *Detroit Free Press*, 9 February 1958; *New Republic*, 27 October 1958.

36. Joseph Rauh, interview, Washington, D.C., 29 March 1988.

37. Edmund Muskie, telephone interview, 13 July 1988.

38. *Detroit News*, 21 October 1958, 28 October 1958, 1 November 1958, 2 November 1958, 3 November 1958.

39. *Detroit News*, 5 November 1958; *Washington Post*, 27 December 1976.

40. *Detroit News*, 23 October 1958, 1 November 1958, 5 November 1958.

41. *Detroit News*, 22 October 1958.

42. *Detroit News*, 5 November 1958, 27 December 1976; Ambrose, *Eisenhower*, 488; Michael Foley, *The New Senate: Liberal Influence on a Conservative Institution* (New Haven: Yale University Press, 1980), 26-27.

43. *Detroit News*, 8 November 1956, 5 November 1958; *Detroit Free Press*, 9 March 1969; *Kalamazoo Gazette*, 12 February 1958; *Washington Evening Star*, 7 November 1958; Dunbar and May, *Michigan*, 643-46; Vreeland, *Philip A. Hart*, 4.

CHAPTER 4

Gaining Respect, 1959-1970

In early January 1959, Phil Hart moved into the Hotel Raleigh, twelve blocks down Pennsylvania Avenue from Capitol Hill, and started preparing for his new senatorial duties. Janey arrived by train from Lansing with the six oldest children to witness Phil take the oath of office. The next day she returned to Lansing where the children finished the school year, leaving Hart to "bach it" at the hotel for six months. In the morning he walked to his office in the old Senate Office building. Not much of an office, it was on the first floor at the back where the level was partly underground. He was starting at the bottom in more ways than one.

His main concern was his committee assignments. Coming in with a large class of Democratic freshmen, he did not expect much. He had to be interviewed by the staff of the Democratic majority leader, Senator Lyndon B. Johnson of Texas. He was delighted to receive his first choice, the Judiciary Committee, but disappointed with his other appointment, the Agriculture Committee. A few years later he switched from the Agriculture Committee to the Commerce Committee.[1]

On an evening soon after his arrival in Washington, the new Democratic senators, class of 1958, and their wives were invited to the home of Senator Vance Hartke of Indiana. During the evening Hartke expansively picked up the telephone and contacted the powerful and imperious Johnson at the LBJ Ranch in Texas. "I've gathered the new boys here, Mr. Leader," Hartke said, fawning over Johnson, "because I thought you might want to say a few things to them." Janey Hart

79

recalled the event: "One by one, like little boys, they trooped to the phone to say 'Yes, Mr. Leader, No, Mr. Leader. Of course, Mr. Leader.' It was disgusting. I kept hoping that Phil wouldn't go to the phone. But he did. And I chewed him out all the way home."

"All I can say in my defense," Hart later joked, "is that I was the last to go to the phone." But, he added seriously, "Politicians are human, and people don't understand this. They are subject to the same pressures as anyone else, even more. But politicians, too, worry about their job, their houses, their paycheck. So they go to the phone—to be safe."[2]

Tradition dictated that the freshman senator be patient and respectfully observe his seniors. He was expected "to seek advice, ask questions, consult elder members, remain diffident in public, and generally be available and willing to assist the senior senators in their legislative duties." Some senators in the freshman class of 1958 bridled at the restraints on junior members and became more assertive and unruly.

Hart was somewhere in between. He sought advice, asked questions, consulted elder members, and was generally available and willing to assist senior senators in their legislative duties. Yet he was also independent and intended to fight for progressive changes.

Johnson tried to initiate Hart into becoming a loyal Democrat on the Senate floor, but this time, Phil bridled. In January 1959, Hart faced his first roll call vote, which was to be a test of Johnson's strength. "You're always supposed to vote with the leader when he wants to adjourn out of trouble," reflected Hart. "I wasn't ready to quit, so I voted against the leader's motion to adjourn." The next day Johnson came over to Hart's desk in the rear of the Senate chamber, towered over him, and drawled quietly: "Senator, let me tell you a little story. When Sam Rayburn first came to Congress, the Speaker told him: 'Young man, you vote against the leadership whenever your conscience or the interest of your state require it. But don't do it very often and don't do it on anything important.'" A little shaken, Hart told Johnson that he understood. But he really had not gotten the message because he added politely, "Don't count on me."[3]

Hart had little aptitude or interest in supervising his office staff. "He was probably a super legislative politician," said a staff member, "but would have been a disaster as an executive politician." He hated staff meetings and avoided them as often as possible. "Today is the day I have a staff meeting," he would say disgustedly to Janey. However, his administrative assistant effectively supervised the day-to-day management of the office, and his staff was considered one of the best in the Senate. During his years in the Senate, Hart had two administrative assistants: William Welsh (1959-1966) and Sidney Woolner (1966-1976). Among the other members of his personal staff were his press secretaries, Jerry Kabel and John Cornman; legislative assistants, Muriel Ferris and Burt Wides; and his personal secretary, Florence Roth.

Inevitably, there were disagreements among staff members, but Hart shied away from them because he hated to deal with conflict. After learning of an intense argument within his staff, he said wearily, "If Janey were let loose on this, she'd have it settled in thirty minutes and all the blood mopped up off the floor."

He rarely expressed anger at staff members and tended to be lenient in judging the quality of their work. "Work would come in late," recalled Woolner, but he "never dressed them down." During Hart's first year in the Senate, Welsh angrily chastised a staff member for sending out a sloppy letter, filled with typing errors, to thousands of constituents in Michigan. But Phil took a different perspective. After inspecting the letter, he said, "Obviously somebody who didn't know how to type thought that I wanted this to go out and worked overtime to get it out, and we have to really thank that person for going beyond the call of duty." The staff was shocked. "It amazed everybody," said Muriel Ferris. "You wouldn't have found another person who would have had that kind of reaction. . . . It was a prime example of his kindliness."[4]

Because he was kind, fair, patient, generous with praise, and listened to their opinions, staff members acquired deep respect and affection for their boss. When Ferris complained that her salary was much less than that of the men doing comparable work in the office, Hart immediately corrected the injustice by increasing her salary. "I was right up with the guys," she said.

Hart patiently moderated debate among staff members before making up his own mind. "He had none of the paranoia and jealousy that other members [of the Senate] have," said Mike Pertschuk of the Commerce Committee's staff, and he had "none of the pettiness. Many of the senators are very jealous of their own staffs. They feel threatened by them. They're jealous of their specialized knowledge. . . . They [become] defensive. There was nothing defensive about Hart. He welcomed staff as colleagues."

There was exceptional competition for his time. The staff, constituents, lobbyists, fellow senators, committee hearings, floor votes—all
demanded his time. So did his family. "Janey would call me up," said
Kabel, "and complain that Hart had been scheduled into Grand Rapids
on somebody's birthday. . . . He was always in the middle."[5]

Increasingly, Hart's voting record and positions on issues reflected
his belief that the federal government must respond to the needs of less
powerful people. With few exceptions he voted with the Kennedy-
Johnson administrations. He received high ratings from the liberal
Americans for Democratic Action for his support of liberal legislation
and low marks from the conservative Americans for Constitutional
Action. Farmers saw him as a friend; the Consumer Federation of
America viewed him as a complete success; but in the eyes of business
interest groups he was a failure.[6]

For the most part, Hart supported organized labor's position on
issues- civil rights, medicare, federal housing, social security. Being
solidly pro-labor was an advantage for Phil in Michigan where union-
ized labor was one of the strongest single political influences in the
state. He saw the best side of labor, the progressive side, represented
by the United Auto Workers. Like Walter Reuther, Hart wanted to
raise the dignity and the purchasing power of workers and to use the
power of the UAW for the public good. Stanley Smoyer, a law school
classmate, met Phil in Washington and quizzed him about his support
of organized labor. "I asked him if he really supported all of labor's
causes, considering the fact that he came from an affluent Philadelphia
conservative background, or whether he wasn't doing this for political
reasons. Without becoming indignant, he simply said that he really
believed in all the positions of the labor movement, without exception.
I smiled, but wasn't and am not now, prepared to question his
integrity." Actually, despite Hart's general support of the union's position, he was independent and, unlike G. Mennen Williams, escaped
having the political albatross of labor bossism successfully hung around
his neck.[7]

Hart upheld the law and the Constitution, but particularly upheld
the Bill of Rights. He consistently opposed police powers that might
infringe on civil liberties. In 1962, some in Congress sought to investigate the ultra-right John Birch Society, most of whose views and methods were light-years away from Hart's. But he spoke in opposition,
warning of the potential dangers of the investigation. "Liberals have to

be consistent," he said. Congressional inquiries may mean "that someone will fear to express a view that is unpopular."

Hart's strong endorsement of civil liberties sometimes placed him in
the middle of intense controversy, like that surrounding pornography. A
citizens' group against pornography in a Detroit suburb invited the senator to a public meeting to discuss a proposed antipornography ordi-
nance. One hundred and fifty persons attended and speaker after
speaker condemned the menace and demanded tough laws against it.
Robert Pisor, who covered the meeting for the *Detroit News*, reflected,
"If there was ever a perfect time for a politician to stand up and say, 'I
could not agree more. This is the most terrible material and should
never reach the hands of our children' and split, that was the time." But
when Hart took his turn to speak, he patiently, almost apologetically,
but firmly explained that while pornography was offensive to many people, it was impossible to design a law that did not tread on the Bill of
Rights. Then he advised them on the importance of maintaining the
freedom to speak, and write in a free country. Many in the audience
were unhappy with his remarks, but seemed to respect him anyway.
Reporter Pisor was impressed with Phil's reasoning, but "I was more
impressed at his timing and his daring, and his straightforwardness than
I was with the cogency of his argument."[8]

Hart rejected the charge that he was a knee-jerk liberal. He contended that unmet domestic needs should be given top priority. It was
much easier to solve technical problems than social problems. "Ten
years is enough time to build a spaceship, but it is only a blink of an eye
in the history of man's long ascent toward a just and humane society."
The threat to the country's survival was as great from domestic needs as
from Mao Tse-tung. "Which has priority if you're fighting for the dollar—the Pentagon or a neighborhood health center? When the day
comes that prayer and good luck will solve all problems, then we'd be
justified in thinking that money is not needed for schools and health
care. It shouldn't have taken a senate committee to remind us that there
are millions of children suffering from hunger. If that's knee-jerk liberalism, well . . . "[9]

Part of his legislative efforts naturally involved Michigan. He supported
measures to improve shipping on the St. Lawrence Seaway, to enhance
fishing on the Great Lakes, and to improve economic development in
northern Michigan. As reporter Saul Friedman put it, however, "Hart is
not a pork barreler." Although he sought some federal programs for

Michigan, most of his effort was aimed at overall federal programs from which Michigan might benefit.[10]

One legislative initiative for Michigan was particularly close to his heart, but completing it took ten years and caused him considerable anguish. In the late 1950s, the National Park Service identified Sleeping Bear Dunes in Michigan as an area suitable for a national lakeshore. Sleeping Bear Dunes was a region along the northwest coast of Michigan's Lower Peninsula where a succession of forces, natural and cultural, had contributed to a landscape of remarkable diversity. Its immensely captivating beauty included broad stretches of inland lakes, forests, shining dunes and Lake Michigan beyond. Preserving the region was important to Hart partly because he was disturbed that private overdevelopment on the New Jersey shore had ruined the natural beauty of the idyllic area he so loved as a youth. It was too late for the New Jersey shore, he said privately, but "we still have a chance" at Sleeping Bear Dunes.

Therefore, when the National Park Service suggested preserving the area as a national lakeshore, Hart and his staff jumped at the opportunity. "We thought it would be well for us to be the first to put in a bill," said Kabel. With only minimal research, on 27 June 1961, the senator naively introduced legislation, written by the Department of the Interior, for a 77,000-acre national lakeshore. Unfortunately, he underestimated the fears of residents in the region, specifically the owners of 1,600 cottages included within the proposal, and aroused the opposition of the Republican congressman in whose district the Sleeping Bear Dunes was located.

Because the Department of the Interior had been through difficult fights in other parts of the country, it wrote a very restrictive, harsh bill, knowing from experience that much of it would have to be compromised away. This was the legislation Hart introduced. "Not surprisingly," observed Kabel, "that bill met a hell of a lot of opposition from local groups. . . . And most of that was due to clumsiness on our part."

The legislation was poorly drafted, critics charged; property values would depreciate, and government condemnation policies would compensate owners at too low a price. At public hearings in Michigan the director of the National Park Service exasperated local residents with his arrogant attitude. "I'm a bureaucrat and proud of it," he said. "You have made a good showing, but we will vote you down." The large crowd responded with jeers and boos. Another factor, expressed privately, explained the furious opposition of local residents and cottage owners: the specter of hordes of blacks from Detroit and Chicago descending on them to use the alluring public recreation. Hart's staff often heard the lament. "We all knew it," said Ferris.[11]

As concern mounted, columnist Judd Arnett of the *Detroit Free Press* asked Hart to justify his support of the legislation. In late September 1961, he responded—too frankly as it turned out—and Arnett published the letter. The senator explained that his legislation was a necessary first step. Public hearings would listen to competing interests and evaluate them. The National Park Service would be authorized to acquire property and, "of course, payment [would] be made [to] the owner." Then he added unwisely: "I am with you that it takes a Philadelphia lawyer to figure out some of the language of the bill. To help here, the Department of the Interior prepared a memorandum which in simpler language gives their point of view on some of the recurring expressions of concern."

Hart's letter met withering criticism. He was a "visionary" in "Nebulous-Nebulous Land," Arnett charged in his column, because he endorsed a bill that he conceded was poorly drawn. "However," Arnett added sarcastically, Hart "hopes the people who may lose their homes will overlook this shortcoming because the Department of the Interior—which can guarantee nothing outside the letter of the act as passed by Congress—has issued a memorandum 'in simpler language.'" There was no guarantee, Arnett concluded, that the Secretary of the Interior would give owners fair market value. An editorial in the *Free Press* added to the senator's anguish. "The Sleeping Bear park proposal looks worse every day," the newspaper charged on 2 October 1961, as the National Park Service made unsupported claims for the legislation and Senator Hart "praised it highly" but "now agrees that he doesn't understand it."[12]

Critics called the project "Phil's Folly." Hart and Stewart Udall, secretary of the Department of the Interior, were burned in effigy at Traverse City. One protestor's sign proclaimed "Merry Christmas to you all—except for Phil and Stewart Udall." Some of the most vociferous hate mail Phil ever received emerged out of the controversy. Ferris worried that the intense opposition might imperil Hart's reelection in 1964.

The senator put on a confident, optimistic front. "Not all of the information has been accurate," he said on 1 November 1961, "and I am as much to blame as anyone." But he added that he was still proud to sponsor the measure. "Having done that, win, lose, or draw, my conscience is clear. I hope we win." Privately, though, he told Bill Welsh, "I think we ought to drop out of this." After Hart's staff polled Michigan residents and found extensive, quiet support for the national lakeshore, however, he was encouraged to persevere.[13]

Unlike his experience with the Sleeping Bear Dunes issue, Hart was initially more adept and more successful as a champion of the consumer. The old-fashioned butcher was often accused of weighing his thumb. "We want to be sure that today's consumer isn't still buying that thumb, but in a fancy package." With this explanation, in June 1961, Phil commenced three days of controversial hearings before the Senate Antitrust and Monopoly Subcommittee on deceptive practices in packaging, and in the process helped stimulate a major change in consumer awareness and government action to protect the rights of consumers.

The hearings made headlines as housewives, economists, and researchers charged manufacturers with misleading them with a bewildering jungle of claims—odd-sized packages, concealed content statements, reduction in content—while maintaining package size and price. High on the list of complaints were giant-size boxes that were not full and misleading terminology. What was a jumbo half-quart? Poet, critic, and housewife Marya Mannes testified, "We're paying enough for outer space not to have to pay for inner space too." She added that "most of us are too busy or too tired or too harassed to take a computer, a slide rule, and an MIT graduate to market to figure out what we're buying." Maurine Neuberger, Oregon's Democratic senator and also a witness, talked about her shopping experiences: "One box may contain fifteen and three-eighth ounces for forty-seven cents, while the adjacent box will have sixteen and one-half ounces for fifty-three cents. Which is the better buy?"

A manufacturer of a laundry soap sold his product in a twelve-and three-quarter ounce box for thirty-four cents. Seeking to prove the need for standardized weights, Phil inquired about the price per ounce:

HART: What is it, really?
MANUFACTURER: I don't have my cost sheets before me.
HART: Neither does she.
MANUFACTURER: If she wanted to know she would be smart enough to figure it out in her head or with a pencil.

HART: Tell me how much it is per ounce.

MANUFACTURER: Would I be out of order if I suggested we return to this point later?[14]

The free enterprise system presumed that given the information, the consumers would make rational choices. The premise was that they be given the information. If they were given little or misleading information, Hart argued, how could they make a rational choice in picking a product? "We [were] trying to make the free enterprise system work," said Jerry Cohen of the subcommittee's staff.

The old dogma "let the buyer beware" was an empty justification, Phil thought, obsolete and no longer adequate or tolerable. "You just can't justify the concept of 'let the buyer beware' when in an average supermarket, for example, the consumer is presented a choice among 6,000 different items." Too many businessmen seemed to feel that "What I can get away with" had replaced "Is it right or wrong, honest or dishonest." Too often a producer was penalized for a forthright declaration of package content, while his competitor gained a trade advantage by not being so forthright. The consumer, Hart declared, had a right to find out what he was buying, how much he was buying, and what the cost was on a per-unit basis.[15]

After Hart started stirring things up, executives of companies manufacturing products found in supermarkets loudly condemned his charges (while busily changing packaging to which he objected). Changes would force added cost that would be reflected in prices, would put marketing in a strait jacket, and would grant federal officials extraordinary powers to impose their preferences on the marketplace. Besides, said critics, Hart's charges insulted the housewife. "Senator Hart is trying to convey the idea that Mrs. Consumer is thoroughly confused and doesn't really know whether she is getting a good deal or not," said a manufacturer. "Senator Hart doesn't understand the consumer. You don't fool Mrs. Housewife as easily as he believes."[16]

"At the time you would have thought the world was coming to an end," reflected Cohen of the avalanche of criticism from manufacturers. "All it boiled down to," added Cohen of Hart's simple goal, was "letting the consumer know how much was in the damn package!" To those who worried that new legislation constituted undue government interference, the senator responded that the same argument was probably used with equal vigor when the government decided to monopolize coinage and enact child-labor laws. For five years (1961-1966) Hart struggled upstream against massed industry opposition to convince Congress to pass a truth in packaging law.[17]

The most burdensome and complex assignment Hart had in his entire senatorial career started in 1963 and lasted for thirteen years. On 10 August 1963, Senator Estes Kefauver died of a heart attack and Phil was in line, on the basis of seniority, to succeed him as chairman of the Senate Antitrust and Monopoly subcommittee. It was an exceptionally difficult assignment and a tough act to follow.

First elected Democratic senator from Tennessee in 1948, the big six-foot three-inch Kefauver had been a dogged, colorful crusader, a "cross between a bloodhound and a hawk." He had come tantalizingly close to realizing his boyhood dream of becoming president in 1952 when he led on the first two ballots at the Democratic Convention before losing to Adlai Stevenson. In 1956, he beat John Kennedy for the vice presidential nomination and ran with Stevenson.

The subcommittee's mission grew out of the Sherman Antitrust Act of 1890, but it was not until 1953 that the Senate established the Antitrust and Monopoly Subcommittee. And it was not until 1957, when Kefauver shed his national ambitions for the presidency to concentrate on the Senate, that the subcommittee developed a purpose. "Over the next six years the feisty Tennessee populist was able to use his subcommittee as a pulpit for exposure of antitrust practices," observed Mark Green in *The Progressive*.

Kefauver believed that because of the concentration of economic power, the few exploited the many, and this economic exploitation would eventually lead to political exploitation, a fear Hart came to share. A society that provided free competition between many producers was a prerequisite for a democratic political system.

Although little legislation emanated from Kefauver's Antitrust and Monopoly Subcommittee, during his six years as chairman, the Subcommittee held hearings that filled twenty-six volumes, issued comprehensive reports on administered prices, and conducted special investigations of monopolistic practices in the steel, auto, and drug industries.

Hart respected Kefauver's main goal—to improve the condition of ordinary people. "Common people everywhere—and perhaps not without some justification—have the feeling that there are great and powerful forces aligned against their better interests," he said, and "Kefauver . . . did a lot to relieve their feeling of helplessness."

Kefauver claimed that he was protecting the free market economy. He was not against profits—only the way they were made. "The best friend a businessman has are the antitrust laws," he stressed. Many critics, however, thought he was biased, charging that the subcommittee was a forum for attacking American business and that Kefauver often seemed to view bigness as evil and businessmen as knaves. By the time Kefauver died, the subcommittee was still a long way from framing comprehensive new legislation to deal with the monopolistic practices it had been documenting, partly because neither the Senate nor Presidents Eisenhower and Kennedy were interested.

Although Kefauver enjoyed a wide national following, he was a political loner, a maverick in the Senate, never accepted by its inner circle. After widely publicized hearings on high drug prices, Senator James Eastland, chairman of the Judiciary Committee, clipped Kefauver's wings by ignoring his recommendations for filling vacancies. Instead of liberal Democrats, Eastland appointed conservative Democrats so that by 1962 Kefauver found himself hamstrung by members of his own subcommittee. This was the situation Hart inherited.

Hart was as liberal and tenacious and probably more intelligent than Kefauver, but far less flamboyant and aggressive. "The difference between Kefauver and Hart," said an observer, "is that Keef was a born prosecutor who went after the jugular, and Phil is a judge." Kefauver opened a hearing by announcing that he already knew what he was going to discover; Hart waited to hear the evidence.

As Hart remembered, "There was only one Kefauver. He had style, a national constituency. He was a real populist, battling against the bosses and the bankers. He was a man who knew the value of publicity, knew how to attract it, and he welcomed it." Hart never pretended he could be like Kefauver. "My own temperament was different," Phil later said. "I knew it would be unwise to perform out of character. But Kefauver had created intense loyalties and antipathies. The subcommittee was at sixes and sevens. So I was compelled to simply be myself and do what I could."[18]

Some conservatives privately worried that Hart would be too liberal as chairman. Those who spoke publicly, though, praised him and his selection. "He is one of the most sincere and fair individuals it has ever been my privilege to meet," declared conservative Republican senator Roman Hruska of Nebraska. Even though "Senator Hart is a liberal," a Detroit businessman chimed in, "he's intellectually honest, and you can always get along with a fellow who is honest."

Hart's statements shortly after assuming the chairmanship were judicious and moderate. "When you get on the Monopoly Subcommittee," he said, "the feeling develops that you're out to change the economic system. That's not me." Most people were against monopolies and were also against the intrusion of government into private enterprise. This caused confusion, he said, and "darned little concentrated study to find out what the proper role of government is—to find a happy medium where the interests of both are safely guarded." Hart indicated that he would be alert to monopoly trends. "As concentration of capital develops, there is a danger of monopoly," he said. "There must be an agency, a party, capable of observing impartially the effect of this on all of society." Then he added with a grin, "I hope that this won't be taken to mean that I am going to become an ogre. I am not."

Former Kefauver staff members were disgusted with Hart's statements after he assumed the chairmanship, and were heard murmuring nicknames for Phil, like "chicken Hart" and "faint Hart." They assumed he was going to be too nice, stay out of trouble, and not make anyone mad. Many of them quit and moved to other committees, looking for more excitement. Some reporters agreed with the disillusioned Kefauver loyalists. Jerald terHorst remembered having the "feeling that one of the most important power bases in the Senate had just gone to a guy who doesn't intend to use it as a power base."

Although not as colorful or aggressive as Kefauver, Hart's perseverance, insistence on judiciousness and facts, and unwillingness to engage in unseemly brawls produced more long-term respect. It was a much better subcommittee under Phil, terHorst later conceded. "It was less inclined to look for momentary headlines, but produced more long-term results."[19]

No one in the Michigan Democratic party could ever be weak on civil rights. "We became, under Mennen [Williams], an integrated party," observed Neil Staebler. But Hart's belief in civil rights went far deeper than the political expectations of his state party. By the 1960s he had shed the remnants of prejudice he displayed in World War II. Possessing a concept of justice enlarged by several magnitudes, he fought for justice in the broadest sense, in all aspects of life—employment and economic opportunities, decent housing, education, voting. Justice was on his mind much of the time. Government must strive to assure that people were treated justly and, specifically, must rectify the worst case of injustice—the treatment of the blacks.

One of his favorite phrases was "Don't judge a person at fifty feet," meaning do not allow anything, especially race, to affect your judgment of an individual until you come to know the person. He would not let a cab driver get away with a racial slur, even if he could finish his ride in comfortable silence.[20]

Racism offended Hart's Christian principles. He never publicly discussed his religious beliefs except in the context of civil rights. In an address at Georgetown University on racial housing restrictions he asked pointedly, "What would Mary and Joseph have done if a stranger had moved in next door?" Shortly before the 1964 election, Jerry Cohen, worried that Hart's reelection might be imperiled by his highly visible leadership in the civil rights field, urged him to slow down and become less visible on the issue. "Jerry, I understand," Phil replied; "I'd like to be accommodating, but I've got a little problem." "What's that?" asked Cohen. "I really believe that Jesus Christ lives in every human being," replied Hart. Cohen was astonished by the simplicity of the reply: "It was so profound . . . so fundamental."

Others, besides Cohen, questioned the political wisdom of Hart's high visibility on civil rights. "Politically," observed a Michigan newspaper early in 1964, "Senator Hart's specialization in equal rights contains little to gain and something to lose. His extreme activity appeals to the Negro voters and to those who are equally ardent on the subject. But he and his party in Michigan have most of those votes anyway. On the other hand, there are votes to be lost among those who take a different view of some aspects of racial equality now. Lifelong Democrats might be hesitant about a senator who presses with such emphasis in a civil rights movement promising to threaten their own way of life." Such arguments did not phase Hart, whose views on civil rights transcended politics.[21]

To William Beckham, a young black student intern in Hart's senate office, Phil acted as a father or older brother. They often chatted and Hart advised Beckham on his future. He wanted Beckham to learn during his internship, not shuffle paper. "Don't worry about all the work in this office," he told Beckham. "You need to worry about how much you can learn, how much you can see, how much you can hear in the years you are here."

Hart read extensively about race relations. Reviewing two books on race problems for *The Progressive* magazine, he observed that "Northerners delude themselves that racial and religious discrimination is confined to the 'backward' South while at the same time aiding and abetting the growth of restrictive racial covenants in property deeds" in the North.

In his first term Hart endorsed the advanced positions recommended by the U.S. Civil Rights Commission and became a leading spokesman for a law that would appoint federal referees to pass on voter qualifications, expedite voting cases in the courts, and require southern election officials to use the same standards to judge all who applied to vote, black or white. The senator also advocated cutting off federal funds to any state for programs that engaged in racial discrimination.

By 1964, southern Jim Crow laws had become a national disgrace. Liberal legislators and civil rights, labor, and religious groups, created a powerful coalition to push for new federal civil rights legislation.

The assassination of President Kennedy stimulated a more favorable climate for civil rights. "No memorial or eulogy," President Johnson told Congress, "could more eloquently honor Kennedy's memory than the earliest possible passage of the civil rights bill for which he fought so long." Johnson refused to compromise its major provisions, and with extraordinary skill he persuaded Republican leaders that civil rights was an idea whose time had come. (Phil observed gratefully that the "Hand of the White House" was being felt more forcefully in Congress under President Johnson than during the Kennedy administration.)

The major obstacle to civil rights reform was Senate Rule XXII, which protected the right to unlimited debate—the filibuster. Until 1959 the rule stipulated that two-thirds of all senators were needed to curtail debate. Then it was modified slightly so that two-thirds of senators *present and voting* met the requirement. (Phil urged that a simple majority of the members or of those present and voting be able to limit debate.) The rule was formidable because the filibuster allowed an intransigent minority of southern senators to block all civil rights bills. In the 1950s civil rights forces could barely muster thirty votes for cloture (limiting debate to one hour for each senator).

Without the votes for cloture southern senators could hold the senate in session round the clock. They divided into teams, scheduling eight-hour shifts for each team. "That," reflected Senator Hubert Humphrey, "left proponents up all night to answer quorum calls, having to produce fifty-one bodies whenever, in Senate jargon, someone said, 'I suggest the absence of a quorum.' Unless a quorum could be produced, the Senate would be forced to adjourn."

Inevitably, civil rights forces and those opposed to the filibuster wore down first. "Most senators were not ready to see pet projects or other important legislation blocked," Humphrey observed. "No other matters could come up so long as the filibuster was in progress."

Southern Democrats jealously insisted that all civil rights proposals be sent to the Senate Judiciary Committee, headed by powerful chairman James Eastland of Mississippi, a segregationist without peer. Hart was a member of the Senate Judiciary Committee, but Eastland had used his iron control of the committee to bury civil rights bills. (During the previous decade only one out of 121 civil rights bills had emerged from Eastland's protective custody.)[22]

The civil rights bill was moved for consideration on 9 March 1964, commencing one of the longest filibusters in the Senate's history. Southerners organized themselves into teams, but Senate supporters were better organized than they had been in the past.

Majority leader Mike Mansfield of Montana selected Hart as one of four floor managers for the bill. (Democrat Hubert Humphrey of Minnesota led the Senate's civil rights forces.) Senate supporters were assigned to master particular sections of the bill and to defend them in Senate debate. Strategy sessions were held in the morning and afternoon; a daily information bulletin kept supporters up to date. "We kept a good spirit throughout, even on the most difficult days," reflected Humphrey of the Senate's civil rights forces. "There was little acrimony and few signs of temper."

Hart played a key role in keeping the bill away from the Dixie-led Judiciary Committee. When some senators argued that the bill should not be debated in the Senate until after it had been discussed in the Judiciary Committee, Hart dissented. "Nonsense," he told his colleagues on 26 March 1964. "I'm on the Judiciary Committee. I serve with mixed emotions. We have to face the facts of life about that committee." To send the bill to the Judiciary Committee after seventeen days of southern filibuster on the motion to take up the bill, Phil said, "would be a hideous setback in the eyes of the American people. This is not time for ritualistic referral." Recalling the long debate in the House Judiciary Committee and on the House floor before the bill passed, he added: "We have been guaranteed more, indeed much more—a hundred times more of the same—here in the Senate by our southern colleagues. Is it possible to believe that before the close of debate in this body, a single comma will be left unchallenged by opponents of this bill, or a single phrase unexplained?" Hart's position won: the vote against returning the bill to Eastland's committee was 50-34.

During a critical stage of the Senate's maneuvering, influential Republican minority leader Everett Dirksen offered amendments to the bill. Liberal senators had to decide whether Dirksen's proposals amounted to an acceptable compromise. At a Democratic caucus Phil responded in a unique and increasingly characteristic manner. He suggested that the basic question to be asked was, "Can I, in all good conscience, support these changes?" Hart answered that he could.

On 10 June, for only the second time in twenty-nine years, the Senate voted cloture (71-29). Shortly after the bill passed in the Senate, President Johnson signed it on—2 July 1964. The landmark law forbade discrimination in the use of federal funds; mandated equal access to all public accommodations and government facilities; provided tough controls on voting rights; granted assistance to local school districts but also provided penalties for continued discrimination; and, finally, forbade discrimination in employment and established the Equal Employment Opportunities Commission (EEOC). "Philip Hart worked long and well on this bill," Humphrey reflected.[23]

While Hart wrestled with the problems of civil rights, consumers, antitrust, and Sleeping Bear Dunes, he was also suffering privately from a debilitating personal crisis. He seemed to be a natural-born worrier. He worried about coping with cantankerous fellow senators, about the progress of civil rights, and about effectively presenting his ideas. "He worried about everything," said John Feild, a staff member in the early 1960s. "He worried about his kids, about his wife . . . about the world." Because he set extremely high standards for himself, he felt vulnerable and helpless when he did not meet them. Yet he attempted to keep his worrying private, not wanting to burden others.

In 1959, when Janey became ill with what was initially diagnosed as leukemia, Phil became enormously distressed. "He went completely to pieces," said Janey. Subsequently, though, when Janey was discovered to have mononucleosis, a much less severe illness, he recovered and felt better.[24]

But in the early 1960s Phil fell seriously ill with depression, debilitating him more severely than his bout with the illness after World War II. His exaggerated reaction to an influence-peddling scheme involving a supporter in Detroit triggered his depression. During Hart's early years in the Senate he did not have a full-time, paid staff in Michigan and therefore welcomed assistance from volunteers. In about 1960 a man from Detroit volunteered to pick him up at the airport and drive him to appearances throughout the state. Because of his services, the man ingratiated himself with Hart and with Fred Burke of his staff. Proffering his services further, the man offered to act as Hart's intermediary in meeting with the Veterans' Administration in the state. All he needed, he said, was a letter of introduction, signed by Hart, indicating that he was his representative to the VA. Busy with Senate work, the senator lost track of the Detroit man.

However, Fred Burke obliged and arranged for the letter of introduction and for the senator's signature from an automatic signature machine. Unbeknown to Hart, Burke, or anyone else on the staff, though, the Detroit man was actually a hustler with sinister motives. Employed by private builders, he was scheming to acquire lucrative building contracts from the VA. The man approached key officials at the VA in Michigan, showed them Phil's letter, portrayed himself as Senator Hart's agent, and demanded they cooperate with him on all building contracts or face the wrath of Senator Hart.

Incensed by the man's threats and intimidation, the VA contacted officials in the Justice Department in Washington who dispatched FBI agents to Hart's office. The agents showed the senator the letter, explained the threats and intimidation, and demanded an explanation. Hart was horrified—"absolutely off the wall," recalled Welsh. His staff scrambled to uncover the details. Some insisted that Hart fire Burke for inadequately supervising the Detroit man, but he quickly rejected the suggestion. This was his responsibility, he insisted, and he would not foist it off on someone else.

Hart was totally innocent. "If he was guilty of anything, it was naiveté," said Kabel. "Yet he was so sensitive about his reputation that he apparently convinced himself that this was going to drag him to the depths of scandal." Although not guilty of anything, the senator expected the incident to become public at any moment and died a million deaths every day for almost a year and a-half, waiting for the shoe to fall.[25]

The Detroit incident started Hart's descent into serious illness. For about eighteen months in 1962 and 1963, he displayed the symptoms of unipolar depression: sadness, guilt, hopelessness, pessimism, low self-esteem, loss of gratification, inability to sleep, difficulty in concentration, and reluctance to approach people. For the most part his illness did not directly affect his work in the Senate. Except for his friend, Senator Eugene McCarthy, no other senator seems to have known about Hart's problem. His staff effectively covered for him. He understood votes and issues and functioned in the committee room and on the floor of the Senate, but as soon as his mind was not engaged in Senate business, he reverted to self-destructive thoughts.

He began seeing a psychiatrist in Washington who counseled him and prescribed antidepression drugs, but neither approach lifted Hart out of his doldrums. Both Janey and the psychiatrist worried that Phil might attempt suicide. "If he wasn't a senator, I'd have him in the hospital," the psychiatrist told Janey.

Frequently Hart would disappear and no one knew where he was. Sometimes he would sit in a corner of the Senate cafeteria, hold a newspaper in front of his face, eat his grilled cheese sandwich and buttermilk, and hope nobody would notice him.

One day Hart got off the elevator near his office, spotted Florence Roth, and, in deep distress, immediately launched into a lament on how the Detroit incident was going to ruin his reputation. "He was exceptionally upset that particular day," recalled Roth. "He was such an innocent. He was so afraid people would not believe that he wasn't involved."

Hart's staff thought his fears and reactions were grotesquely exaggerated. "Just for the life of us," recalled Kabel, "we could not fathom what the hell was causing this exaggerated reaction." "Nobody could do anything with him," said another staff member.[26]

Janey Hart was surprised by his sudden descent into depression, for although she had weathered the same illness after World War II, it never occurred to her that it might happen again. The illness placed a terrible strain on the Hart family. "It was difficult for the children," said Janey; "They didn't understand." When Phil drove his son Michael to school, he would stop at a series of churches to pray. "If you read something terrible about me in the newspaper, would you still love me?" Hart asked his daughter Ann. But the atmosphere at home was not always gloomy. "He definitely had a lot of bouts with depression," observed Phil's son Walter. "But even at those times, at moments, there was elation and laughter with him."

At his worst Hart came to the point where he almost convicted himself of fraud. Janey wearied of the same lament. "I knew what was going on in his head, and I didn't want to hear him." Usually Phil was quiet at home, but occasionally he would start telling Janey all the things he had done "wrong." "I don't want to hear it anymore!" Janey shouted at him. "If that's what you want to talk about, I'm not going to listen anymore!"

Both Janey and Ann Hart speculated that Phil's depression stemmed in part from his Catholic upbringing. "He aspired to sainthood," said Ann and when the Detroit incident exposed his imperfections, he became self-abusive and depressed. "As far as I'm concerned," added Janey, "the Catholic Church had so guilt-woven him it was ruining him."[27]

Hart felt a compulsion to "confess" his "sins" to someone, and in 1962 he selected Martin Hayden, editor-in-chief of the conservative Republican *Detroit News*. The senator may have imagined that the *News* was about to "expose" the influence-peddling scheme and ruin his reputation. "He came in to see me," recalled Hayden, whose newspaper knew nothing about the incident. "He was just lower than low. He was very, very serious and very sad." Hart outlined the problem for Hayden. When he finished, Hayden laughed. He told Phil the incident was insignificant and nothing to worry about. "Nobody would believe you were colluding on this kind of deal!" Hayden said to him. "I told him to forget it," reflected Hayden. But Hart could not forget it and left Hayden's office still very sad.[28]

By 1963 the Detroit man had disappeared, and when the incident did not attract publicity, Hart started feeling better. Another factor may have contributed to his depression, and its solution coincided with his recovery. While Phil was depressed, Janey became pregnant again (with what would have been the Harts' tenth child), but she suffered a miscarriage. She did not want any more children, had lost faith in the Catholic Church's rhythm method of birth control, and had expressed her anxieties to her husband. "He, being sensitive," Janey later speculated, "I may have projected my concern in a way that I wasn't the most enthusiastic partner." Before she adopted a more effective method of birth control, she consulted Phil's psychiatrist to inquire if the alternative method would make his illness worse. On the contrary, the doctor told her, a better birth control method would probably make Phil feel better. "I think he may have been concerned about me having another pregnancy," Janey recalled.

About two weeks later, Hart's depression ended. "He never was depressed again," said Janey, "*ever.*" Although Janey never noticed any subsequent depression, some staff members did, but the bouts were shorter and milder than his horrible ordeal in the early 1960s.[29]

By the time his reelection campaign in 1964 began, Hart showed no signs of depression and the strong national tide for the Democrats bolstered his campaign. Lyndon Johnson's reelection was scarcely in doubt from the moment the Republican convention selected Senator Barry Goldwater as the GOP's nominee. The Arizona conservative proved to be the weakest possible candidate to oppose the centrist Johnson. Goldwater's "ideologically tinged speeches, his radicalism and extremism, and his seeming proclivity for a direct confrontation with Communist forces in Vietnam and elsewhere alienated most modern Republicans," observed Paul Conkin, Johnson's biographer. Having captured the large middle bloc of voters, Johnson had built broad coalitions for his legislation—a tax cut, the Civil Rights Act of 1964, and his antipoverty program. So far he seemed cautious on Vietnam, yet had used the Tonkin Gulf incident to demonstrate his firm defense of U.S. interests and honor. Even the aftermath of John Kennedy's death seemed to bless his candidacy.[30]

Hart's opponent in the 1964 election was Elly Peterson, forty-nine, a lively Republican party activist in Michigan for many years. She had served as vice chair of the state party since 1961 and was vice chair of the Republican National Committee. In 1962 she led an army of 150 women in the Women's Advisory Council to help make George Romney the first Republican governor of Michigan in fourteen years.

During the 1964 campaign, Peterson kept pointing out that Hart had loyally supported nearly every major liberal program of the Kennedy-Johnson administrations, and charged him with being a rubber stamp for Johnson, rather than a senator for Michigan. Hart was an ineffective senator, a weak man who had gotten where he was because of a wealthy wife.[31]

Hart avoided returning any abuse and said he was interested only in discussing issues, not personalities. He made an exception, though, in the case of Barry Goldwater, saying he was terrified of the radical supporters who were rallying behind the Republican nominee. "We had hoped this element was put down by Americans following President Kennedy's assassination," he charged. "It would be disastrous to give them public approval now by adopting the causes their candidate espouses."

Hart successfully projected a statesmanlike image. Holding a commanding lead, he campaigned as a thoughtful, prudent and moderate public servant. He did not soft-peddle his views or his voting record.

Almost every day of the campaign he praised civil rights, medicare, area redevelopment, accelerated public works, and the antipoverty programs. "The reason I believe in the war on poverty is simply this: it puts a heavy emphasis on education. It fights school dropouts. It will train youngsters who otherwise would remain unskilled. It will help get college degrees for youngsters who otherwise would never be able to finish." Hart disagreed with skeptics who dismissed the antipoverty program "as an impractical idea, as a vote-getting gimmick, as a do-gooder project that will fall apart of its own weight." The senator thought that Sargent Shriver, director of the antipoverty program, would make it work as well as the Peace Corps, which he had also directed.

Issues were neither black nor white, Hart often said; no party had a monopoly on wisdom. Among sincere people there could be honest disagreement. Typical of his soft-sell approach was his speech to college students in Flint. After discussing the Johnson administration's proposals, Hart said: "Now I happen to strongly favor all of these issues. But let's face facts. The civil rights bill may inconvenience some who don't deserve it. There will be some waste—however careful we are—in foreign aid. And there will be those whom the poverty program can't help. But on balance, I strongly believe all these measures are good ones—although you are certainly not obligated to share that belief. If you judge these issues and others on the basis of thoughtfulness and reason, then—regardless of how you decide—you have done your job."[32]

"How do you manage a landslide?" reflected a Hart campaign organizer of his overwhelming lead throughout the campaign. A poll in October 1964, showed Hart with a 64 percent to 28 percent lead. The senator knew he had the election wrapped up. He joked privately to a reporter: "Gee whiz. God, Jerry! Elly Peterson is one heck of a nice woman. I don't want to go out there and run against her. Why don't they give me somebody I can get my teeth into!" Ironically, that was actually one of Peterson's problems—she could not get her teeth into Hart.[33]

Hart's popularity and Johnson's impending landslide in Michigan were enough to doom Peterson's candidacy, but allegations of a scandal involving her husband dealt a fatal blow. On 8 October, Governor Romney fired two generals and a lieutenant colonel from their jobs with the Michigan National Guard because, without authorization, they had sold state land at the Guard's summer training headquarters to private individuals including many members of the military. Peterson's name surfaced when it was discovered that she and her husband had been among several hundred persons who bought parcels of the land. Colonel W. Merritt Peterson was U.S. Property and Fiscal Officer at Michigan's National Guard headquarters. It became a volatile political issue when Michigan's Democratic chairman, Zolton Ferency, asked for an investigation to determine whether or not the Petersons had received special treatment in purchasing their twenty-three lots. Ferency raised the question that possibly Colonel Peterson had inside information about the land sale because files on the case showed the Petersons paid $17.40 a lot, while twenty-seven other lots in the same block sold for $35 each.

At a news conference on 12 October, Mrs. Peterson defended her husband's purchase and denounced the "orgy of character assassination on behalf of my opponent." Then she switched her attack to Hart, who she wrongly assumed had helped coordinate the barrage against her and her husband. "One thing I have avoided injecting into this campaign," she said, "has been the personality of my opponent or his wife's money. I married a man who had to work for a living. I did not inherit the resources to protect and shelter my husband and to foster his career by private wealth." Mrs. Peterson continued, "I believe the smear tactics of Senator Hart and his Democratic henchmen are a poor excuse for a campaign. . . . Only a man with such a pitiful record of accomplishment as his would need to resort to such repugnant tactics."

Hart's immediate reaction was to deny having anything to do with Ferency's attack on the Petersons. "Certainly I haven't and don't intend to make the Peterson lot purchase an issue in the campaign," he said after Mrs. Peterson's press conference. "I have said nothing about it because—except for what I have read in the papers—I know nothing about it." Later he held a press conference in which he declared that the scandal should have no bearing on the election. There was no evidence that a crime had been committed or even an indiscretion. More importantly, he added, Mrs. Peterson had nothing to do with the investigation. Despite Hart's refusal to exploit the alleged scandal, media coverage of it damaged Peterson's campaign.[34]

Hart defeated Peterson by 900,000 votes (1,996,912 to 1,096,272). None of the accusations thrown around in the campaign poisoned their future relationship. Several years after the election, when Peterson retired as vice chair of the Republican National Committee, she invited

Hart to her farewell party at a Washington hotel. He attended, the only Democrat to do so, and when Mrs. Peterson spotted him, she rushed to him and the two embraced, more like two long-lost relatives than former political rivals.[35]

After his victory in the 1964 election, Hart resumed his efforts on behalf of civil rights, consumers, and antitrust, and wrestled with new issues and problems, all the while increasing the respect with which he was held by colleagues and political observers.

After passage of the 1964 Civil Rights Act, intimidation and discrimination continued against blacks who attempted to register to vote in the South. In March 1965, when voting rights demonstrators were brutally beaten in Selma, Alabama, millions watched the horror on national television, spurring Congress to consider more forceful federal legislation allowing blacks to register to vote.

The measure fashioned by the Johnson administration provided an automatic formula to wipe out discrimination. An openly regional measure, it singled out seven southern states where literacy tests were used. It sought to register voters, not like in the past—through tedious and cumbersome lawsuits—but by using federal examiners appointed by the executive branch, an approach Hart had urged for several years.

Hart was the chief Senate strategist and floor manager for the historic Voting Rights Act. He memorized the bill, line by line, so he could answer every question thrown at him and every amendment proposed by opponents who intended to kill it. Above all he was reasonable. "Even after the bill passed," observed a Senate colleague, "some members of the opposition came up to congratulate him on the way he handled it."

The bill passed in only five months. From March to August 1965, the civil rights forces maintained their momentum. On 25 May, seventy senators successfully imposed cloture, breaking a desultory southern filibuster, and the following day the Senate passed the bill. By early August it had become law. "They came in darkness and they came in chains," said President Johnson on signing the bill. "Today we strike away the last major shackle of those fierce and ancient bonds."

The law was extraordinarily effective, bringing the majority of blacks in the South into the mainstream of southern politics. In Mississippi, for example, the number of black voters increased from 29,000 in 1964 to 325,000 in 1978. The law succeeded so well, said historian Steven Lawson, "because it automatically suspended discriminatory voting qualifications and gave the president the authority to send examiners to register Negroes directly."

Hart always pointed to the Voting Rights Act as the most fulfilling legislative achievement in his senatorial career. A few years later, he and two of his sons drove through the South en route to a family vacation in Mexico. He wanted to drive rather than fly because he wanted to see the results of his civil rights efforts, particularly the results of the Voting Rights Act. "He wanted to stop and see the black sheriff," said Janey.[36]

The high-water mark for liberal success occurred in the mid-1960s with the Great Society programs of Lyndon Johnson. By the late 1960s liberal influence was declining in the Senate and opinion polls found Americans increasingly skeptical of government policies and more cynical about the federal government. People wanted more order and security and were tired of hearing about America's obligations to the poor and the minorities. The skyrocketing costs of federal programs caused concern. "The innocuous $33 million allocated to the food stamp program in 1965, for example, had burgeoned to $550 million by 1970," observed Michael Foley, an expert on the U.S. Senate. The public was becoming skeptical that social welfare projects were aggravating problems and not living up to President Johnson's optimistic assurances.

A Louis Harris poll in August 1966 showed that 46 percent of whites would object to having a Negro family live next door, and 70 percent thought Negroes were trying to move too fast. In the summer of 1965 a major riot occurred in the Watts ghetto in Los Angeles, and there were forty-three additional disturbances nationwide the following summer. Then in July 1967, rioting erupted in Detroit and by the time the uprising had been quelled at least 43 people were dead, 1,700 stores looted, and 1,383 buildings burned. "The image of the Negro . . . was no longer that of the praying, long-suffering, nonviolent victim of southern sheriffs," reflected the scholar James Sundquist; "It was of a defiant young hoodlum shouting 'black power' and hurling Molotov cocktails in an urban slum."

Riots, black militancy, and a white backlash hindered passage of new civil rights legislation. In 1966 an aide to President Johnson complained "that it would have been hard to pass the Emancipation Proclamation in the atmosphere prevailing this summer." Said columnist Mary McGrory, "The music has gone out of the movement."

But Hart kept pressing for additional civil rights laws. In the three years following passage of the 1965 Voting Rights Act, he fought for additional Senate legislation providing for nondiscriminatory juries, equal job opportunities, protection for civil rights workers, and renewal of the Civil Rights Commission. But his primary goal was to enact an open housing law. The recent civil rights acts had eliminated most forms of racial discrimination in jobs, services, public facilities, education, and voting but had hardly touched the problems of the northern cities. Having failed to outlaw segregation in housing, residential segregation and all-white suburbs were still the norm throughout the country. But open housing was an exceptionally sensitive issue for white voters.

The senator wanted a national commitment that a person would not be judged by religion, color, or national origin when seeking housing. Testifying on behalf of open housing at a Senate hearing, Hart observed, "I want to be judged as an individual whose habits and conduct are good or bad, not as an Irish Catholic or a Scotch Presbyterian. . . . That is the way I want to be judged, and I have an obligation to judge everybody else that way, too. We cannot make that judgment if the only test is skin color."

"Tragically, I think, we never hear from the most persuasive witness. . . . I would suspect that the best witness in support of this bill is a Negro father who has worked hard all his life . . . and has saved some money, and wants to give his children a setting removed from the squalor which might have surrounded him, so he goes out and he tries to buy a house, and he is denied, and he has to explain that denial to his son and daughter. I would like to hear it from that father."

Because state and local ordinances were often ineffective, federal legislation was needed to secure open housing for blacks. Hart used the District of Columbia as a prime example. The District had a fair housing law, and Maryland and some of its subdivisions provided some legal coverage. But Virginia had none and was unlikely to enact an open housing law in the near future. Therefore, he pointed out, "Real estate operators have a golden opportunity to manipulate the market in this area on the basis of prejudice and fears and rumors that they create and further."

The public seemed in no mood to "reward" the Detroit rioters of 1967 with new civil rights laws. But Hart disagreed. The urban riots suggested that more—not less—civil rights legislation was needed. "I am neither so foolhardy nor so lacking in logic as to suggest that the Negro in the ghetto, sniping from a rooftop or propelling a Molotov cocktail, is motivated by congressional failure to pass adequate civil rights legislation. . . . But I do say that the failure of Congress to enact legislation directed toward the goal of building a just and equal society is part and parcel of the climate of despair and hopelessness that has contributed to the riots. . . . And I do say, too, that those who obstruct and hinder civil rights legislation are contributing to the very disorder and violence in our lives that they so loudly decry."

Few people expected any progress on civil rights in 1968. It seemed that the congressional coalition of northern Democrats and moderate and liberal Republicans—the key to passing the 1964 and 1965 civil rights acts—was in disarray. Nonetheless, on 6 February 1968, Senator Walter Mondale (D-Minn.) proposed a major open housing amendment to a House bill intended to protect civil rights workers. Hart assumed leadership of the liberal group fighting for the measure. With an impending filibuster by southern senators, few thought it would pass. On 19 February the *Wall Street Journal* referred to "the almost certainly doomed bill banning racial discrimination in housing." The following day, though, the open housing bill received a surprisingly close cloture vote, indicating that Republican senators supported the measure in larger numbers than expected.

Initially, Hart's low-keyed approach to the legislation caused some reservations among fellow liberals. At the beginning of debate some grumbled about the indecisive leadership he provided as floor manager. But his strategy was to take the bill through the Senate "in our stocking feet." For eight weeks the senator sat in the majority leader's chair, patiently listening to southern objections, occasionally responding with low-keyed rebuttals. All the while he kept pressing Majority Leader Mike Mansfield for cloture votes to cut off southern debate. "It was largely out of personal respect for Senator Hart," observed the *New York Times*, "that Mr. Mansfield permitted four different attempts at cloture—something that had never been done before on a single bill."

On 4 March the Senate successfully voted cloture by precisely the two-thirds requirement (65-32) and on 11 March, after a lively debate and amending process, the Senate passed the bill (71-20). During debate on the bill in the House, Martin Luther King was assassinated on 4 April, creating a national mood of remorse, helping to stimulate passage of the law on 10 April. President Johnson signed the bill the next day.

Despite the lack of assistance from party leaders, the absence of mobilized mass support, and an unfavorable political climate, Hart and his colleagues succeeded in reawakening the northern Democratic-Republican coalition. They passed a measure that most regarded as lost. "It was an astonishing turnaround," observed a historian of civil rights legislation. "In no issue was Hart's prestige more evident than in the fight for open housing legislation in 1968," concluded Michael Foley.

What is commonly called the Open Housing Act of 1968 had three components: protection for civil rights workers, nondiscrimination in housing, and punishment for perpetrators of riots. The open housing portion prohibited discrimination in the advertising, financing, sale, and rental of most homes and charged the executive branch with acting affirmatively to achieve integrated housing.

Afterward, integration in housing still came at a snail's pace. Nonetheless, the bill established a moral standard and provided a legal basis for blacks who were willing to defy local conventions and demand access to white suburbs.

Hart's leadership in the fight aroused the ire of suburban whites in Michigan, but he met the fears head-on by addressing the issue in speeches in the white suburbs surrounding Detroit. Before all-white audiences of the Knights of Columbus and Kiwanis, he devoted his entire speech to open housing, carefully explaining the reasons for his support. "Everybody in the audience would be opposed to it to a person," said an observer, but they listened politely. In 1969 even some Michigan Democratic activists were upset with Phil because they worried that blacks would move next door.[37]

After the 1964 election, Hart kept pushing his Truth in Packaging legislation. He modified the bill, softened some of its provisions, accepted amendments from colleagues, and compromised. Most important, he pried it away from the hostile Senate Judiciary Committee to place it into the more friendly hands of the Senate Commerce Committee. In 1965 the Johnson administration threw the weight of its support behind the proposal.

Finally, in 1966 Congress passed the Truth in Packaging Act, which encompassed most of Hart's original goals. Its major provisions established standards and regulations for package information and identification and encouraged the voluntary development of package size standards by manufacturers. "It protects the honest manufacturer against dishonest competition," said President Johnson as he signed the law. "It encourages fair competition, competition based on quality, value, and price. It reflects our strong belief that American producers can meet—and want to meet—the test of truth." Shortly after the bill was enacted, the *Louisville Courier Journal* praised Hart for being a "spokesman for the great, amorphous mass of consumers in this country, poking around in shadowy corners of the domestic scene for the enlightenment of the public. . . . He is a valuable man to have in the Senate."[38]

Passage of the Truth in Packaging Act inspired Hart to philosophize about truth in a broader sense. In an article in the *Nation* in October 1967, he highlighted the revealing testimony of Dr. Ernest Dichter, a motivational researcher. Dr. Dichter had been hired by a co-op with a number of marketing problems. The co-op was buying the same canned peaches as a competing supermarket, except the competitor labeled the peaches as "gorgeous," while the co-op more modestly labeled theirs as "reasonably good." The competing supermarket sold many more peaches. Dr. Dichter reasoned that the housewife bought the "gorgeous" peaches because she had been trained for decades to apply the same psychological disbelief to both statements. She figured that the supermarket peaches were probably fairly good while the co-op peaches were probably poor. The doctor went on to estimate that citizens automatically discounted 40 or 50 percent of statements made by advertisers.

Hart thought that Dr. Dichter's insights probably carried over to politicians and to society, generally with very damaging results. "When it comes to exaggeration, politicians are not without a certain susceptibility. The politician who makes the papers is the one who 'condemns' an idea or 'blasts' an opponent. A balanced and reasonable political statement—after that automatic 40 percent discount has been applied to it—is bland indeed. So with a public conditioned to exaggeration, no politician is likely to describe his peach of an idea as 'reasonably good.'"

Exaggeration fed on itself, Hart mused. "Hyperbole has never been uncommon with us, but with the growth of mass media in the past twenty-five years, it comes at us constantly and from all sides. Where fifty years ago a citizen might have entertained himself by reading a mystery novel about one murder, now he may watch a dozen victims fall in a single half-hour show. Television heroes are certainly more often 'gorgeous' than 'reasonably good.' The watcher of the heralded 'grand TV spectacular' settles himself down to watch mediocre vaudeville. The modern man finds himself applying the automatic 40 percent discount a hundred times a day."

Hart had no intention of examining who was exaggerating too much and who was discounting too much, but he worried that the "exaggeration-discount syndrome" was beginning to play a significant role in political affairs and social intercourse. "I wonder if Gresham's Law on coinage might not apply to philosophy, with exaggeration and skepticism driving out the reasoned statement and the balanced view." A society that found it necessary to discount everything was not a trustful society. "And without trust," he concluded, "a civilized nation will find it difficult to endure."[39]

Hart was not an expert in foreign policy and his committee assignments gave him little opportunity to improve his understanding. "I don't think [foreign policy] was his interest," said Welsh. "He was a baby lamb in terms of foreign policy," added his daughter, Ann. Like other leading liberal Democrats who came out of the era of the late 1940s and early 1950s—Hubert Humphrey, Mike Mansfield, Gale McGee, Henry Jackson—Hart was a zealous anticommunist in the Cold War. In 1959 he said he would be willing to have the United States use force to prevent a communist takeover in Cuba if it turned out that Fidel Castro was a communist.[40]

Hart lagged behind in the growing national debate over the Vietnam War. In August 1964, the Senate passed the Gulf of Tonkin Resolution, allowing President Johnson "to take all necessary measures" to repel any armed attack in Vietnam. Johnson refused to submit his Vietnam policies to legislative debate, partly because many in his administration believed that foreign policy issues were too complex and too important to be left to a divided, unwieldy Congress. "Johnson thus took the nation into war in Vietnam by indirection and dissimulation," observed George Herring, a historian of the Vietnam War. Many members of Congress, including Hart, found it impossible to vote against funds for the war while American forces were in the field. Indebted to President Johnson for his effective assistance on domestic issues, Democrats were reluctant to challenge him directly.

In 1966 Hart argued that the United States should put "unremitting pressure in a carefully measured response to the aggression of the enemy." The following year he was still saying little publicly about Vietnam, but when pressed he gave tacit, if reluctant, support to the president's policies. Perhaps sensing the Senate's restiveness on the war issue and the increasing number of antiwar senators, Hart decided to educate himself. He immersed himself in books and articles about

Vietnam. In late May 1967, he toured Southeast Asian countries—including Vietnam—for three weeks, visited his old unit, the 4th Infantry Division, but returned still a supporter of the war. The United States must fulfill its initial commitment to the South Vietnamese. "We should not have gotten into Vietnam in the first place," he said, "but, now that we're there, we can't leave or the rest of Southeast Asian countries will feel we won't uphold our commitments. Call it face-saving or what you will, but the Oriental culture puts a lot of emphasis on whether someone keeps his word."

By the end of 1967, a few senators from both parties were openly critical of the war, but they operated on the fringes of the party leadership structures. Almost everyone assumed that President Johnson would be renominated by the Democrats in 1968. When Hart's friend, Senator Eugene McCarthy of Minnesota, decided to challenge Johnson for the nomination, hardly anyone thought the back-bench senator would have any success.

Then on 30 January 1968 at 2:45 A.M., Vietcong sappers attacked the U.S. embassy in Saigon. The attack was a small part of the Tet offensive, a major Vietcong assault against urban areas in Vietnam. Eventually the offensive would be interpreted as a defeat for the Vietcong, who suffered far more casualities than U.S. or South Vietnamese forces. At the time, though, almost everyone in the United States perceived the offensive as a defeat for the American cause. Tet was unique because the enemy, which lost completely in the tactical sense, came away with an overwhelming psychological and political victory.

The assault sent shock waves throughout the United States, eroding public support for the war. George Herring noted that "Televised accounts of the bloody fighting in Saigon and Hue made a mockery of Johnson and of [General William] Westmoreland's optimistic year-end reports, widening the credibility gap, and cynical journalists openly mocked Westmoreland's claims of victory."

In a New Hampshire campaign speech, Senator McCarthy acidly summarized the prevailing liberal reaction to Tet:

> In 1963, we were told that we were winning the war. . . . In 1964, we were told the corner was being turned. In 1965, we were told the enemy was being brought to its knees. In 1966, in 1967, and now again in 1968, we hear the same hollow claims of programs and victory. For

the fact is that the enemy is bolder than ever, while we must steadily enlarge our own commitment.

After the Tet offensive, more of Hart's Senate colleagues questioned President Johnson's policy of widening the war and deploying over 500,000 U.S. troops without adequate consultation with Congress. The senators wanted a strong voice in future decisions. In early March 1968, prominent senators vented their frustrations. Senate Foreign Relations Committee chairman J. William Fulbright argued that the chief issue "is the authority of the Administration to expand the war without the consent of Congress and without any debate or consideration by Congress." This view was echoed by his colleagues. "I think we must insist upon that," stated Senator Clifford Case. "I think we cannot any longer evade a responsibility of a share in the decision." Senate Majority Leader Mike Mansfield also expressed concern. "We are in the wrong place and we are fighting the wrong kind of war," he stated, at the same time crediting President Johnson with having "tried hard and vigorously and consistently to find a way to the negotiating table." During the Senate debate, Hart's voice remained quiet.[41]

Actually, though, in 1968 Hart was privately agonizing over the war. "I think he thought he wasn't doing enough," said Eugene McCarthy. He often discussed the issue with his friend Edmund Muskie. "We shared the same torture," recalled Muskie. They both wanted President Johnson to change his policy, but "We both found it difficult to break from the president."

Pressure not to break with Johnson on Vietnam may have been more than just a problem of party loyalty. "There were some practical reasons too," said Jerry Kabel. The staff had important legislation it wanted passed (particularly revised legislation on Sleeping Bear Dunes) that needed Johnson's support. "I remember reminding Hart of these things," Kabel observed. Hart received the reminders without much comment.

The Tet offensive boosted McCarthy's campaign. His audacious challenge to President Johnson produced surprising success in the New Hampshire primary on 12 March 1968. By winning 42 percent of the vote, McCarthy embarrassed the president and transformed his campaign into a major political challenge. Thereafter, tumultuous political changes occurred rapidly. On 16 March Senator Robert Kennedy of New York entered the Democratic presidential contest, and on 31

March President Johnson announced he would not seek reelection, opening the door for his vice president, Hubert Humphrey, to challenge for the Democratic nomination.

Although Hart remained mostly quiet during the raging debate about Johnson's war policy, he did address related issues. In November 1967, after Selective Service director Lieutenant General Lewis B. Hershey had proposed that student protesters who interfered with the draft or military recruiting be subjected to immediate induction, Hart denounced the suggestion. He did not want to condone illegal or irresponsible behavior, but Hershey's proposal "short-circuits the judicial process." At a news conference Hart charged that "Apparently General Hershey makes a judgment that the laws have been violated, a judgment usually reserved to our court system, and then takes punitive action." Hershey's action would violate the due process guarantee and curtail the rights of free speech and petition.

Hart also lectured draft boards for wrongly reclassifying deferred students who took part in draft board sit-ins. Such action put draft officials in the position of being both judge and jury. Local draft boards should remember that "the right to protest in our society is a very basic one."

Hart worried about the attitude of antiwar protesters. "He cautioned us against arrogance and self-righteousness," observed Phil's son Walter. When the senator was asked to speak to students at the University of Michigan in February 1969, instead of a harangue against the Vietnam War, which the students would have preferred, he taught a different lesson.

Speaking to several hundred students, Hart gently needled his own generation, but also cautioned the students against arrogance. "Everywhere we turn." he said in his speech, reprinted in the *New York Times*, "we see students who are losing faith in a society that we middle-aged politicians have labored so hard to make perfect."

"Students are upset," Hart continued, "because they live in a society that talks peace but drops napalm. Their youthful and inexperienced eyes seem to see an inconsistency in that. I've met young people who are irritated because our system can build luxury apartment buildings so high that they can be seen from slums miles away. And there are even some students who wondered how our system could send men to the moon on Christmas day while on earth thousands of homes went unvisited by a kindlier astronaut, Santa Claus."

He cautioned the students, though, not to fall into the trap of believing they were in sole possession of the truth. One mark of a nonarrogant person was a willingness to suggest positive alternatives. "It is not enough in my mind for students to rule out workable alternatives by simply saying, 'That's not our job.' Be loud and vocal, but also be creative. The politics of harassment—in and of itself—is neither an end nor is it the substance of meaningful change. Somewhere, somehow, the machine needs new parts. And someone needs to design them, build them, make them work, and keep them running."

"So I guess my message in my homily would be the very old one: get involved. Dissent but remember that arrogance only diminishes effectiveness. Find failings in the system, but remember that there are some problems that are nobody's fault—and that alternatives are welcomed."[42]

Hart spent most of his time as chairman of the Antitrust and Monopoly Subcommittee. There his primary assistant was Jerry Cohen, the subcommittee's able and energetic staff director and chief counsel. Howard "Buck" O'Leary succeeded Cohen in 1969. Other key staff members were attorneys Charles Bangert and Donald Randall and press aide Patricia Bario. When legislative proposals coming out of the subcommittee and the full Senate Judiciary Committee faced insurmountable roadblocks from conservatives, Hart sidestepped, moving his legislation over to the Senate Commerce Committee. There he worked closely with staff members Mike Pertschuk and Lynn Sutcliffe.

Hart faced insurmountable problems and limitations with the subcommittee. "In many ways it was a thankless job," observed Woolner. Because the issues were so technical and complex, Hart had to spend an inordinate amount of time studying, compared to the chairs of other committees. Part of his problem with the subcommittee was the political limitation of his mission. Antitrust was seldom a subject of household discussion, nor did it launch hopeful candidates into the presidency.

Antitrust lacked a constituency. "Conservatives are for big business, and liberals are for federal regulation," observed Kabel. "Antitrust is in the middle and hard to explain." There were times when Hart and like-minded associates felt that liberals had forsaken them to join conservatives in arguing that giantism in business was fine.

Hart's hearings on monopolistic practices attracted little public attention partly because the complex, technical data presented by experts involved little drama and therefore attracted minimal press and television coverage. "Is anybody listening?" asked a reporter for the *St. Louis Post-Dispatch* of the senator's hearings on economic concentration.[43]

Public interest advocates respected Hart but were disappointed with the results of his antitrust efforts. Mark Green, director of Ralph Nader's Corporate Accountability Research Group, said that, "for all his admirable qualities, Hart ultimately fails as an advocate." Hart was too deliberate and shy, Green charged, and his militant speeches were written by his staff and delivered without vigor or passion. A Senate colleague agreed: "He likes everyone and can understand everyone's problems and arguments, which makes him a lousy advocate."

Staff members on the subcommittee were often frustrated with Hart as well. Some were zealots who wanted all-out war against the abuses of big business. But the senator would restrain them. "Well, now," he would retort, "let's try to see this from the other side." The zealots didn't want to see the other side. "Lots of days we thought he was wishy-washy," recalled Pat Bario. The staff would sit around and gripe, some saying, "If he would just come in one Monday morning and say, 'Damn it. I want you to go out and investigate these guys!'" But he never did. Of the huge volume of antitrust activity, observed Bario, "None of it was initiated by Phil Hart. But he hired good people and he trusted them, and he had the courage to let them go ahead."[44]

Hart once told an interviewer, "You could do a lot of things, if you had the votes." But he did not have the votes. The majority of the subcommittee's senators were alternately apathetic or antagonistic. By 1967 Democrats outnumbered Republicans six to three on Hart's panel, but he could count on only two of them—Thomas Dodd of Connecticut and Edward Kennedy of Massachusetts. The largest block of four senators were conservative. Led by Everett Dirksen (R.-Ill.), the group included one more Republican, Roman Hruska of Nebraska, and two southern Democrats, John McClellan of Arkansas and Sam Erwin of North Carolina. The subcommittee was rigged so that Dirksen could command more votes than Hart. Also, because of conservative objections, Hart was usually unable to issue subpoenas on large companies. Therefore, no significant antitrust legislation was passed.

"Those guys can stop us from getting legislation," said a staff member of obstructionist senators, "but they can't stop us from holding hearings." Since legislative efforts for antitrust mostly failed, Hart and the subcommittee's staff conducted hundreds of days of hearings in an attempt to establish facts and inform the public. They studied industrial concentration, the growth of conglomerates, the negative correlation between bigness and innovation, and the relation of corporate size to the maintenance of competition.[45]

To prepare Hart, the staff compiled a large notebook that he took home to study the night before a hearing. By the next morning he had digested the information. Staff members also prepared carefully, doing extensive research, considering issues from different angles. Yet, often the first question Hart asked stumped them. "He always managed to ask the question we didn't know the answer to," recalled Bario. "It was a great question. He went to the heart of [the issue] so quickly." Phil gave his staff wide latitude, took many risks with them, and allowed them to present speeches throughout the country.

Hearings started at 9:00 A.M. and sometimes ran until 7:00 P.M. Often Hart was the only senator present. Other senators would drop by briefly and then leave, content to allow staff members to question witnesses. Reluctant to do that himself, Hart thought it was important for a senator to listen to the witness and provide a presence. He issued many press releases, but they were designed to inform and to educate, not to gain personal publicity. Contrary to his critics' claims, Phil expertly edited speeches written for him by his staff, and the speeches reflected his own thoughts.

Gentle with all witnesses, if Hart thought a question prepared for him was too harsh, he toned it down. "I have a hunch," he often said at hearings, which was his method of saying something softly that otherwise might appear abrasive. He made it clear to staff members that they could disagree with a witness on an issue, but they could never attack the person. He cut off an aide's hard-hitting cross-examination of a witness because, he said, "it sounded too much like Kefauver." "That is the way he conducted himself," said Donald Randall, "and we knew we had to do the same thing."

Hart often took the opposition's viewpoint and argued against his own staff. He made them prove, beyond a shadow of a doubt, that they had the evidence. He sat more like a judge than an advocate. "We had to make the case to him," observed Chuck Bangert; often they had to make the case during the course of the hearings. "He was right in the way he made us [work hard]," observed Randall. "We had greater credibility as a result. . . . We were right because he made us be right."[46]

Despite objections by the conservative majority of his subcommittee, Hart pushed ahead with an impressive series of hearings that exposed the seamy practices of big business. In July 1964, the sub-committee began hearings on concentration in American industry. "We are not opposed to bigness as such," the chairman said in his opening statement. Nonetheless, because knowledge of economic concentration was limited, "To understand fully its dimensions we need to know the underlying structural aspects, the level, trend and causes of concentration."[47]

For six years the subcommittee gathered evidence showing that corporations were getting bigger and bigger and fewer and fewer and that the consequences of the trend were something about which Americans should be alarmed. As the years passed, Hart felt more comfortable with the complex problems of antitrust, making himself as knowledgeable as anyone in the country on the issues.

In 1968, after four years of hearings, Hart began to state publicly his position on economic concentration. The hearings had led him to a very harsh indictment. Morton Mintz, a reporter for the *Washington Post*, contrasted the gentle manner and low-keyed style of Hart's speeches with the hard content of his message. "We tend to forget what antitrust is all about," Phil said. "It is about power—political, social and economic power. We seek diffusion of political power, and the antitrust laws are aimed at restraining its concentration."

"When Congress wrote the antitrust laws," he said, "it was concerned with human values. Somewhere, we lost sight of this goal." He often expressed his concern for the future of competition. "Antitrust today is sick and nobody seems greatly concerned. What our corporate executives desire is not competition but security; not the discipline of the marketplace, but the anarchy of unrestrained pricing. . . . [In] the federal government, I fear they have found an accomplice."

Often critical of the federal regulatory agencies, Hart urged investigation into the desirability of outright abolition of the Interstate Commerce Commission for interfering with market forces in the transportation industries. He criticized the way the Justice Department and the Federal Trade Commission handled the merger problems in the Kennedy and Johnson administrations. Enforcement "unfortunately . . . has been spotty," he said, and marked by "a lack of inspiration and enthusiasm."[48]

On 2 December 1968, in an address to the National Council of Salesmen's Organization, Inc., in New York, Hart presented a wide-ranging indictment of conglomerate corporations, and in the course of his address brought up another problem not easily measured: the effect of economic concentration on individualism.

There was an ever-growing paradox:

Free enterprise—long idolized as the last bastion of rugged individualism—may be leading to the greatest institutionalized thwarting of individualism in the country: Big, Big Business. As you know, until now Big Business has been spelled only with initial capitals. Now, if we want to give the comparative picture, it should be in all caps—BIG BUSINESS. For business has gotten to the point where "big" is really too small an adjective. Soon we may have to borrow a Hollywood word—such as gigantic or the old reliable, fantastic.

Our top companies are staggeringly big at home—where we are told 200 will soon hold two-thirds of all the nation's manufacturing assets. And they are big on the world scene—the top five U.S. companies' sales exceed the top companies in the European Common Market. Sales of General Motors alone—the world's No. 1 giant—exceed the gross national product of all but ten nations of the free world.

The Senate Antitrust and Monopoly Subcommittee had tried to measure the power of the huge companies, Hart said. "But we have not measured what to me—as a so-called liberal—is an equally distressing thing: their 'people power.'" There were no charts or graphs, no thoughtful statements, no acknowledgment as to the effect "company-eating contests" had on the desire for individualism.

Unfortunately, Hart contended, too often they meant that individualism was mummified:

Social scientists tell us that essential to an individual developing a sense of his own worth is recognition. Traditionally—and wonderfully—the free enterprise system has offered just that. Under it, each man took his ideas, his efforts, his determination and put them together into a marketable product. And, if he and his product—be it talent or something more material—were good, he would rise to the top.

But a second-grader could figure out that if what today are 100 companies and eighteen years ago used to be 500 companies, less and less is "there always room at the top." The man who years ago might have been a "big man in the community" because he headed a large local company now finds himself No. 1 in Company Z, which is a subsidiary of Company Y, which in turn, is a subsidiary of Company X. This is frustrating to anyone concerned with his individuality.

A sense of identity was also frustrated "by the mobility the giant insists on if a man is to move up the ranks." As a consequence of the moves came "lack of identity" with a community—not only for the man but his family. The giant frustrated not only the individual who worked for it, but each consumer as well. Big business to a large extent determined the prices, qualities, and quantity of the goods purchased.

> Local economies rise and fall on its decisions of where to open and where to close plants. And there is no voting box for those who don't like the way things are being run. In short, giant industry has begun to gather the barnacles of bureaucracy that it has always decried in the federal government. But it lacks the most saving grace government has—it doesn't have to stand for election.

One of Hart's solutions was to dust off proposals made sixty years earlier by President Theodore Roosevelt: federal corporate charters.

> This seems to me a conservative approach—when contrasted to other alternatives such as pervasive government regulation—which has been tested in the banking and credit union fields, for instance, and proved both successful and popular.
>
> Today we see massive international corporations doing business under ground rules and under the authority of charters granted by states only a fraction of their size. The plural "states" may be misleading. For all the states must accept the charters (which establish the purpose and authority of corporations) of the least stringent among them. The interstate corporation can shop the states and incorporate where it can get the best terms for incorporation. This is precisely what is done. The result is the lowest common denominator becomes the standard.

Unchecked giantism—whether it be political, religious or economic—had never been compatible with individualism, Hart concluded. "The lesson has been spelled out over and over in history. Surely this democracy of ours should be a most apt pupil."[49]

A particularly sensitive political subject Hart tackled was monopolistic practices in the communications and newspaper industry. In May

1968, he called for aggressive antitrust action against the mergers and the predatory practices in the communications industry. "What is involved here," he said, "is power—political and economic." A democratic society could not survive the concentration of ownership in industries dealing with communication of ideas, Hart argued. A cobweb of ownership and partnership was growing between newspapers, broadcasting, book publishing, and cable television. "In the top twenty-five markets with a total of ninety-seven TV stations," he pointed out, "fifteen are owned by networks and thirty-four—more than a third—are owned by newspapers."[50]

Hart was incensed when Congress passed the Newspaper Preservation Act in 1970, giving an exemption from the antitrust laws to competing newspapers that merged their business operations and fixed prices on advertising rates. The bill passed the House and Senate overwhelmingly with Hart being one of the few dissenting votes in the Senate. The move for antitrust exemption began when two Tucson, Arizona newspapers entered into a joint operating agreement that the courts objected to because its monopolistic price fixing eliminated competition for advertisers. The Newspaper Preservation Act was introduced in the Senate shortly after to overcome the legal troubles. Hart realized that sound arguments could be made for the bill—that newspapers, pressed by television and radio competition, needed the exemption for financial survival—but he thought there were even stronger arguments against it. He was particularly upset with the red-carpet treatment the powerful newspaper publishers received from his Senate colleagues. The bill had harmful effects on the publishers of small weeklies and suburban dailies, he pointed out. At a hearing before Hart's subcommittee, the editor of a small San Francisco area newspaper testified, "If you plant a flower in the University of California property or loose an expletive on Vietnam, the cops are out of the chutes like broncos. But if you're a big publisher and you violate antitrust laws for years and you emasculate your competition with predatory practices and you drive hundreds of newspapers out of business, then you're treated as one of nature's noblemen."

Many senators did, indeed, treat the important publishers like nature's noblemen. When publishers appeared at hearings to praise the merits of the bill, Hart noted with veiled disgust, each was courteously accompanied into the hearing room by one or both of his home-state senators. "How many other classes of citizens," Phil observed, "found guilty of legal transgressions by the courts, could hope to find an energetic Congress ready to reverse the decision within sixteen months?" He added, "Swift Congressional rescue of the publishers must make fascinating reading for the blacks, who until the 1964 Civil Rights Act, had waited decades for relief from court convictions for eating in certain restaurants and hotels."[51]

The complex issues of antitrust never excited Hart as much as civil rights, except when he could see that his work ultimately benefited the consumer. In addressing the concerns of consumers, Hart thought he was on the side of business even if spokesmen for business did not agree. Unless business met the legitimate needs of consumers, their industries would decline. "Very early on [he] articulated the kind of 'Search for Excellence' philosophy that the consumer is No. 1 . . . for value received," said Lynn Sutcliffe. His subcommittee investigated sports monopolies, the rising price of quinine, the cost of television advertising, and price fixing of children's library books. Two important investigations focused on the expense of auto repair and doctor ownership of pharmacies and drug companies.

"Senator Hart's most recent battle won't make him the Prince Charming of Michigan's thriving robust automotive industry," wrote columnist Drew Pearson in December 1968. Hart had just started lengthy hearings on the skyrocketing repair bills consumers received when they took their cars to garages. The nation's auto repair bill ran to between $20 and $25 billion a year and the price of auto parts had increased 52 percent from 1960 to 1967, and another 10 percent in 1968, far beyond the general increase in the cost of living.

Within a year after the subcommittee began its hearings, thousands of angry car owners, disgruntled mechanics, and automotive specialists testified about shoddy repairs and ballooning costs in the auto repair business. Testimony showed that some repair shops considered women "fair game" and a good source of revenue, because it was easy to convince them that their cars were on the verge of breakdown.

The most revealing insights came from Glenn Kriegel, owner of a car repair diagnostic center in Denver, who testified that tests on 5,000 cars in his shop showed that only one auto out of 100 was being repaired properly. Many cars bore no evidence of repairs at all, even though the owners had paid for them. "There is a certain amount of cancer in the industry that needs correction," said Kriegel. "I am somewhat ashamed that I am part of the automobile industry because of what we see in our

Philip Hart (on right) with his mother, father, and younger brother Clyde.

Janey and Philip Hart on their wedding day, 19 June 1943.

Philip Hart during World War II.

Janey and Lt. Governor Phil Hart in Lansing, Michigan.

Philip Hart in April 1950 with Ann, 2, Cammie, 1, and Walter, one week.

Playing checkers with his children about 1959.

1958, with Phil about to enter the U.S. Senate.

Janey and Phil Hart at the White House during John Kennedy's presidency.

Phil Hart in discussion with Lyndon Johnson.

At a bill signing ceremony with colleagues and President Lyndon Johnson.

Reading the newspaper aboard the ferry to Mackinac Island.

Phil Hart at the 522-feet level above the Straits of Mackinac with Lawrence A. Rubin, executive secretary, Mackinac Bridge Authority.

In the early 1970s, posing with his beard.

With son Michael in 1971.

Phil with his son Michael and daughter Mary in November 1976, shortly before his death from cancer.

day-to-day efforts. It is very frustrating. I am depressed almost every day."

"And for a good reason," Hart interjected. "To be otherwise, I think, would be to ignore unpleasant reality. It is not just additional cost to automobile owners, but it is the additional exposure to injury and death."[52]

A survey by the National Auto Dealers Association revealed that 36 percent of auto owners were dissatisfied with repair work. "Some of those people admittedly would be the kind that nobody could satisfy," Hart said. "Give them a brand-new car, and they still might not be satisfied, but it is my impression that only a small percentage would be dissatisfied if the repair work were done correctly. If you take 36 percent of the 25 billion dollars that is spent annually on repairs and then discount it a little for the people who are unreasonable, you'd still come up with a lot of money spent on unsatisfactory or wasted repairs."

The subcommittee's staff pointed part of the blame at Detroit's automakers, where styling instead of repairability seemed to encourage replacement, rather than repair, of parts. Not only was the consumer forced to buy more new parts, but he had to pay a ballooning price for them. Hart criticized the U.S. auto industry for its inefficiency and for not investing more in research and development. "They were lethargic," reflected Randall; "They were stodgy; they were not innovative; they were not concerned with competition because they were an oligopoly [and] didn't have foreign competition to any extent in those days." When auto executives and others accused Hart of being overly critical of the U.S. auto industry, he rejected the charge. "I'm trying to strengthen it," he said.

An outgrowth of Hart's hearings on auto repairs was the Motor Vehicle Information and Cost Savings Act (the so-called "bumper bill"), which specified fragility standards for auto construction. "Senator Hart is a man of courage," said *Motor Trend* magazine. "To attack a problem as large and politically explosive as automotive repair, especially for the senator from Michigan, the home of the auto industry, is no small undertaking."[53]

Another major consumer-oriented series of hearings involved the incestuous relationship of physicians, pharmacies and drug companies. Hearings disclosed that in 1966 about 10,500 physicians (of the nation's 225,000 practicing doctors) employed unethical means of making extra money out of the prescriptions they wrote for their patients.

The main abuses stemmed from doctors with an interest in drug stores who overprescribed for patients so their store profits would soar. One study presented at the hearings showed that physician-owned drug stores filled three to five times more prescriptions on the average than did other pharmacies. Free samples manufacturers sent to doctors were not given away but were used to fill prescriptions in the pharmacies the doctors owned, with the patients being charged the standard prices. Doctors' profits from drugs led to a sharp increase in spending for public welfare funds. A California doctor had been writing $10,000 worth of welfare prescriptions a year, but when he decided to open his own pharmacy, the amount of his welfare prescriptions soared to $55,000 a year.

The subcommittee also took a hard look at doctor-controlled drug firms that bought pills from drug manufacturers, put on their own labels, and sold the drugs at prices much higher than the manufacturers' prices. Hart sponsored legislation that bluntly forbade physicians to profit from the medications they prescribed, and clamped down on eye doctors who prescribed and also made eyeglasses for patients.

"Clearly, a doctor's participation in the ownership and profits of pharmacies and drug companies in his geographic area puts a financial decision in front of him each time he picks up a pen to write a prescription," Hart charged. "Apparently there are doctors—and I emphasize that they are a tiny minority—who use monopoly prescription power, which was given by law to protect the patient, in order to exploit that patient, to damage independent businessmen, and to enrich their own bank balance."[54]

These practices had been declared unethical by the American Medical Association's Judicial Council, but they still flourished because the council lacked the necessary power to enforce its principles. Hart criticized the medical profession for not policing itself. "What amazes me," he said, "is that a great and noble calling such as medicine has members who apparently are willing to besmirch the public image of the great majority of dedicated doctors for the possible extra financial rewards involved." He added: "What further amazes me is that this same overwhelming majority of dedicated physicians let their colleagues get away with it." Apprehensive that a minority of their ranks might besmirch the honor of an entire profession, and worried about Hart's legislative proposals, the American Medical Association held its first National Congress on Medical Ethics in 1966.[55]

Until 1968 Hart had not taken a decisive stand on the sensitive issue of gun control, but the assassination of Robert Kennedy in June 1968 deeply disturbed him. After the assassination, President Johnson appointed Hart to the National Commission on the Causes and Prevention of Violence, and during his eighteen months on the commission the senator carved out a controversial position against the sale of handguns. Good people were safer if they did not have handguns, even if the bad ones have them, Hart argued. In eight out of ten cases it was the good people who were shot—the husband of an angry wife, the child who found the gun in a drawer, and the neighbor who was mistaken for a burglar. He particularly worried about the danger caused to policemen by the unrestricted ownership of handguns.

"It was a touchy political issue," said Jerry Kabel of Phil's support of handgun control. The National Rifle Association (NRA) began urging its members in Michigan to express their views to Hart. Michigan had one million of the 15 million hunting licenses sold in the nation, the NRA pointed out; license fees added millions of dollars to Michigan's program of resources management, and deer and small-game hunters, with their trips to Michigan's Upper Peninsula, pumped $70 million a year into the state's economy.

Before the senator's speech in northern Michigan, reporter Saul Friedman had to act as Hart's bodyguard as pro-gun forces berated and screamed at Phil. Yet the crowd settled down and listened to his speech. Before another group of hunters, Hart clearly outlined all the arguments in favor of handguns. But, he said, those arguments must be weighed on a scale alongside other considerations—the reasons for regulating guns. "Most people found it difficult to get angry with him," Kabel observed, "because he always expounded his views with such sincerity and a good deal of logic."[56]

In 1968 Hart was almost nominated for chief justice of the Supreme Court and probably could have been confirmed had he agreed to accept the appointment. In 1968, Chief Justice Earl Warren told President Johnson of his intention to retire and Johnson selected Abe Fortas as his choice to replace Warren as chief justice. Fortas, a brilliantly successful lawyer and close advisor to Johnson, had been appointed to the court by Johnson in 1965. He quickly established himself as a member of the dominant liberal bloc. Under the leadership of Chief Justice Warren, the court was in the midst of a historic expansion of individual rights and Justice Fortas had participated in those decisions.

The Senate Judiciary Committee grappled with the Fortas nomination in the summer of 1968, and in September, with the presidential election campaign in full swing, debate began on the Senate floor. Republicans and conservative Democrats severely criticized Fortas for his outside activities, his liberal judicial philosophy, and his participation in the alleged excesses of the Warren court. Opponents were determined to fill the Warren vacancy with a strict constructionist who would break the controversial "leftward drift" of the court. Partisan politics also played a role. Republicans hoped to keep the seat open so that the new president to be elected that November—presumably Republican Richard Nixon—could fill the vacancy.

Hart supported Fortas. In fact, Fortas' biographer credits him with being the Johnson administration's "selfless point man" in the confirmation fight: "There was little question . . . that the senator from Michigan deserved the major credit for carrying the fight for Fortas in the Senate." The senator fought ably, but on 2 October 1968, after supporters failed to end a filibuster on the Senate floor, Fortas asked Johnson to withdraw his name from consideration. Jubilant Republicans and conservatives gloated.[57]

Just before the end of the 90th Congress, Johnson, smarting from the Senate's rejection of Fortas, came up with a clever idea for sweet revenge. Rather than let the chief justice nomination fall to his successor, Johnson decided to send to the Senate the name of a man the Senate could not refuse, one of its own members who held the esteem and respect of everybody: Phil Hart. Johnson sent out the appropriate feelers.

Janey Hart heard on the radio that Johnson was considering Phil. When he returned home that evening, she said, "Well, I hear you are going to be on the Supreme Court." Phil replied, "Chief justice, no less!" Hart briefly considered the informal offer; the honor tugged at him. But he rejected it for several reasons. At the moment he was happy with his Senate work and was good at it, and he feared he might not be effective on the Supreme Court. Besides, he felt awkward benefiting from Fortas' misfortune. Finally, there was not enough time in the legislative session to push his nomination and the idea died. "I sent back word—thanks, but no thanks," Hart later said. "So there never was a formal offer. I said I was comfortable in the Senate."

Johnson's idea might have succeeded had there been a few more weeks in the session and had Hart agreed to the nomination. Senator

Eastland quietly told Phil that he would not oppose him. Senator Sam Erwin, a constitutional conservative, later said that even he might have supported Hart despite their opposite views on recent Supreme Court decisions. "The nomination of Hart . . . would have been ironic," observed Saul Friedman. "Johnson, who once wondered if Hart would ever become his kind of senator, was ready to elevate him to the Supreme Court, partly out of gratitude for his fight in the Senate on Fortas' behalf."

In 1969 Fortas was pressured into resigning from the court after allegations that he had acted improperly in his financial relationship with Louis E. Wolfson. (Phil agreed that Fortas had acted improperly.) Subsequently, President Nixon nominated first Clement Haynsworth and then G. Harrold Carswell to the vacancy, but both nominations failed in the Senate, with Hart playing a major role in opposition.[58]

Before March 1968, Hart reluctantly supported Lyndon Johnson for reelection, but in March he declared he would remain neutral in the Democratic presidential race between Johnson, Eugene McCarthy and Robert Kennedy. The party's best hope for unity, he said, lay in an "open convention [where] everyone is free to express any view." But the senator's family was needling him about the Vietnam War and wanted him to distance himself from President Johnson and his war policies.

Janey Hart and the older children opposed U.S. intervention in Vietnam, and eventually the intense debate within the Hart household about the war affected him. The rest of the Hart family did not have the loyalty to the Democratic party and to the Johnson administration that Phil had, making it easier for them to condemn the president and the war. With Ann a major youth coordinator for Eugene McCarthy, and Walter and James working in primary states for the Minnesota senator, the family began to wear Phil down. In any case, he was becoming disillusioned by the lying of the government (and later by the U.S. incursion into Cambodia). "Yes, he did change," said Janey. "It was gradual. Our government was lying and that began to bother him."[59]

By the summer, Robert Kennedy had been assassinated, Johnson had bowed out, and Hubert Humphrey was challenging McCarthy. Hart had reservations about both Humphrey and McCarthy. Humphrey had not detached himself enough from Johnson's disastrous Vietnam policy. Although McCarthy was a friend whose mind, insight, and humor Hart appreciated, he was disturbed with McCarthy's indolence and his undependability when embattled liberals had needed another voice and another vote. But Hart appreciated McCarthy's role as the herald of opposition to the war, confessing, "Gene McCarthy turned my children around. He gave them hope." Gradually, Hart leaned toward McCarthy. He had no illusions that McCarthy would be a great president, but he hoped his friend would select an excellent staff and assumed McCarthy would be the candidate most likely to disengage the United States from the war.[60]

The tumultuous convention in Chicago in the summer of 1968 upset many Democrats, including Hart. He agonized over the police riot, Mayor Richard Daley's dictatorial control of the convention, his decision to endorse McCarthy, and rumors that he might be considered for vice president.

At the convention, before a caucus of the Michigan delegation, mostly strong Humphrey supporters, Hart dramatically endorsed McCarthy. He talked of the feelings of his wife and children and the need to stop the war. At times he choked up and dabbed at his eyes. Then, after hearing a rumor that McCarthy was about to bow out of the race, he rushed out of the meeting and the convention hall to look for his daughter, Ann, assuming she would be distraught. "He cared that much about her," recalled Mildred Jeffrey, "and he thought this might be very devastating." As he left the caucus, a television newsman asked, "Senator Hart, can you tell us what is going on in there?" Phil brushed past him. "I can't answer you now," he said. "I just need to find my daughter." He found Ann in her hotel room where they discussed the rumor and Phil's endorsement of McCarthy. He apologized to her for the awful chaos of the convention. "He was profoundly distressed," Ann recalled.[61]

Before both the Democratic conventions of 1964 and 1968, Hart had been mentioned as a possible candidate for vice president. However, he quickly threw cold water on all the suggestions; he did not even want to be asked. The thought of being vice president appealed to him, he admitted, but he added with a twinkle in his eyes, "only if they could give me iron-clad assurances that I'd never be promoted. My temperament would make me the worst president this country has ever had." In another interview he discussed his concerns more explicitly: "I'm the sort of person who has difficulty going to sleep at night if I have an unresolved problem on my mind. You can see what that would mean in terms of the White House. I would be a basket case in three months."

The primary argument advanced by Hart's admirers for putting him on the ticket with Humphrey in 1968 was Humphrey's need to unite the party and bring the liberal faithful back under his banner. But Phil was adamant. At the Chicago convention, William Welsh, Hart's former administrative assistant, worked as a key aide to Humphrey, and when Hart learned that the Humphrey forces were still mentioning him as a possible running mate, he was enormously upset. He sought out Welsh on the convention floor and said, with intense feeling, "You've got to promise me that I won't be considered as a vice presidential candidate on the ticket. I can't be. You know my problems. That is something I could never cope with."

Later, during the demonstration for Humphrey after his nomination, the Michigan delegates were on their feet, wildly waving and cheering. All except Hart. He was the only one still sitting, leaning forward, his head in his hands. When a television cameraman tried to film him, Sidney Woolner stood in the cameraman's way, leaving Hart to contemplate alone.[62]

Happier news arrived for Hart just before the 1970 election, when he finally secured passage of a cherished piece of legislation. Despite the political difficulties he had with the Sleeping Bear Dunes issue in the early 1960s, he persevered with revised proposals throughout the rest of the decade. The national lakeshore was "near and dear to his heart," observed Woolner. The 1964 election had encouraged him because of the strong support he received in Leelanau and Benzie counties where the proposed park was located. Subsequently, he and his staff consulted with Michigan politicians of both parties, arranged public hearings to iron out problems, provided better protection for existing home owners and commercial properties within the boundaries, and constantly modified his legislation to win passage in Congress. In the final deliberations in the House, for the first time the entire nineteen-member Michigan delegation joined in voting for the measure. On 21 October 1970, almost ten years after Hart initiated the proposal, President Richard Nixon signed legislation designating Sleeping Bear Dunes as a national lakeshore, and 61,000 acres came under federal park control. Completing the project was a "great achievement," concluded Kabel, "because we had so many obstacles to overcome. We kept persevering with it."[63]

NOTES

1. *Jackson Citizen-Patriot*, 4 January 1959.
2. *Detroit Free Press*, 9 March 1969; Janey Hart, interview, Washington, D.C., 1 and 2 April 1989.
3. *Detroit Free Press*, 9 March 1969; Foley, *The New Senate*, 120-21.
4. John Cornman, interview, Washington, D.C., 26 March 1988; Muriel Ferris, interview, McLean, Virginia, 26 March 1988; Janey Hart, interview, Washington, D.C., 1 and 2 April 1989; Barbara Kincaid, telephone interview, 23 May 1988; Sidney Woolner, telephone interview, 12 and 14 January and 5 July 1988.
5. Muriel Ferris, interview, McLean, Virginia, 26 March 1988; Jerry Kabel, telephone interview, 24 February 1988; Leila McKnight, interview, Washington, D.C., 25 March 1988; Michael Pertschuk, telephone interview, 13 April 1988.
6. *Bay City Times*, 30 October 1964; Vreeland, *Philip A. Hart*, 10-22.
7. Stanley Smoyer to author, 7 February 1989; *Ann Arbor News*, 3 June 1961; *Chicago Tribune*, 29 September 1968; Vreeland, *Philip A. Hart*, 5; William Beckham, telephone interview, 9 May 1988; Joseph Rauh, interview, Washington, D.C., 29 March 1988.
8. *Detroit News*, 27 December 1976; William Beckham, telephone interview, 9 May 1988; Robert Pisor, telephone interview, 21 March 1989.
9. *Washington Post*, 15 February 1970, 5 November 1986.
10. *New York Times*, 7 November 1963, 14 November 1963, 31 March 1964, 24 September 1964; Vreeland, *Philip A. Hart*, 6.
11. Philip A. Hart, "The Total Landscape of Sleeping Bear Dunes," *American Forests*, January 1969, 36-37, 48; Stephen Maddock, "An Analysis of Local Opposition to the Sleeping Bear Dunes National Lakeshore" (Ph.D. diss., The University of Michigan, 1971), 31, 38, 42; Muriel Ferris, interview, McLean, Virginia, 26 March 1988; Jerry Kabel, telephone interview, 24 February 1988; William Welsh, telephone interview, 23 April 1988.
12. *Detroit Free Press*, 26 September, 2 October 1961.
13. *Detroit News*, 2 November 1961; Ann Anderson, interview, Washington, D.C., 26 March 1988; Muriel Ferris, interview, McLean, Virginia, 26 March 1988; Janey Hart, interview, Washington, D.C., 1 and 2 April 1989; William Welsh, telephone interview, 23 April 1988.
14. *Washington Star*, 7 April 1966; *Newsweek*, 10 July 1961, 52.
15. *New York Times*, 15 June 1961; *Washington Post*, 28 June 1961; Jerry Cohen, interview, Washington, D.C., 30 March 1988.
16. *Business Week*, 23 November 1963, 47; *Business Week*, 8 May 1965, 34.
17. *Business Week*, 8 May 1965, 34; *The Nation*, 29 June 1963, 543; Jerry Cohen, interview, Washington, D.C., 30 March 1988.
18. *Detroit Free Press*, 6 June 1966; *Newsweek*, 19 April 1963, 18-19; *Newsweek*, 2 September 1963, 65; *The Progressive*, July 1975, 24; *Time*, 30 August 1963,

17; Charles Fontenay, *Estes Kefauver: A Biography* (Knoxville: The University of Tennessee Press, 1980), 369; Joseph Bruce Gorman, *Kefauver: A Political Biography* (New York: Oxford University Press, 1971), 300-6; Vreeland, *Philip A. Hart*, 16.

19. *Detroit Free Press*, 6 June 1966; *New York Times*, August 20, 1963; *Newsweek*, 2 September 1963, 65; *Time*, 30 August 1963; Jerald terHorst, telephone interview, 28 March 1989.

20. *Jackson Citizen-Patriot*, 20 February 1964; Alfred Fitt, telephone interview, 28 April 1989; Janey Hart, interview, Washington, D.C., 1 and 2 April 1989; Muriel Ferris, interview, McLean, Virginia, 26 March 1988; Neil Staebler, telephone interview, 27 August 1987.

21. *The Catholic Standard*, 20 February 1959; *Jackson Citizen-Patriot*, 20 February 1964; *The Progressive*, May 1961, 42-43; William Beckham, telephone interview, 9 May 1988; Jerry Cohen, interview, Washington, D.C., 30 March 1988; Mildred Jeffrey, telephone interview, 31 May 1988.

22. Clipping, Box 551, Hart Papers, Bentley Library; *New York Times*, 10 January 1960, 28 March 1960, 6 April 1960, 13 March 1962, 10 April 1963, 19 April 1963; Hugh Graham, *The Civil Rights Era* (New York: Oxford University Press, 1990), 144-45; Hubert Humphrey, *The Education of a Public Man* (Garden City, New York: Doubleday and Company, Inc., 1976), 269-70, 281; Steven Lawson, *Running for Freedom* (Philadelphia: Temple University Press, 1991), 99.

23. *Detroit News*, 27 March 1964; *Jackson Citizen-Patriot*, 20 February 1964; Humphrey, *The Education of a Public Man*, 281, 479; Lawson, *Running for Freedom*, 99; Sundquist, *Politics and Policy*, 267-70; Charles and Barbara Whalen, *The Longest Debate* (New York: New American Library, 1985), 187.

24. John Feild, telephone interview, 20 March 1989; Janey Hart, interview, Washington, D.C., 1 and 2 April 1989.

25. Patricia Bario, interview, Washington, D.C., 28 March 1988; Janey Hart, interview, Washington, D.C., 1 and 2 April 1989; Jerry Kabel, telephone interview, 24 February 1988; William Welsh, telephone interview, 23 April 1988.

26. David Rosenhan and Martin Seligman, *Abnormal Psychology* (New York: W.W. Norton and Company, 1984), 309-12; Patricia Bario, interview, Washington, D.C., 28 March 1988; Janey Hart, interview, Washington, D.C., 1 and 2 April 1989; Jerry Kabel, telephone interview, 24 February 1988; Florence Roth, interview, Washington, D.C., 29 March 1988.

27. Ann Anderson, interview, Washington, D.C., 26 March 1988; Janey Hart, interview, Washington, D.C., 1 and 2 April 1989; Walter Hart, telephone interview, 30 April 1988.

28. Jerry Kabel, telephone interview, 24 February 1988; Martin Hayden, telephone interview, 13 May 1988.

29. Janey Hart, interview, Washington, D.C., 1 and 2 April 1989; Jerry Kabel, telephone interview, 24 February 1988.

30. Paul Conkin, *Big Daddy From the Pedernales: Lyndon Baines Johnson* (Boston: Twayne Publishers, 1986), 189.
31. *New York Times*, 10 March 1964, 1 November 1964; *Washington Post*, 23 March 1964.
32. *Bay City Times*, 30 October 1964; *Kalamazoo Gazette*, 28 October 1964; *Marshall Evening Chronicle*, 15 October 1964; *New York Times*, 1 November 1964.
33. *New York Times*, 1 November 1964; William Beckham, telephone interview, 9 May 1988; Jerald terHorst, telephone interview, 28 March 1989.
34. *Christian Science Monitor*, 21 October 1964; *Detroit News*, 27 December 1976.
35. *Detroit News*, 27 December 1976.
36. *Detroit Free Press*, 6 June 1966; Graham, *Civil Rights Era*, 171; Steven Lawson, *Black Ballots* (New York: Columbia University Press, 1976), 312-13, 318, 339-43; Sundquist, *Dynamics of the Party System*, 362-63; Sundquist, *Politics and Policy*, 273-74; Janey Hart, interview, Washington, D.C., 1 and 2 April 1989.
37. *Chicago Tribune*, 29 September 1968; *New York Times*, 23 November 1966, 20 May 1968; Conkin, *Lyndon Baines Johnson*, 218; Dunbar and May, *Michigan*, 664-65; Foley, *The New Senate*, 142-43, 196-98; Graham, *Civil Rights Era*, 270-72; Lawson, *Running for Freedom*, 133; Sundquist, *Politics and Policy*, 278-81; Senate Committee on the Judiciary, *Civil Rights Act of 1967*, Hearings before the Subcommittee on Constitutional Rights (Washington, D.C.: U.S. Government Printing Office, 1967), 71, 476-80; William Beckham, telephone interview, 9 May 1988; Mildred Jeffrey, telephone interview, 31 May 1988.
38. *Detroit Free Press*, 9 March 1969; *Business Week*, 8 May 1965, 34; *Congressional Quarterly Almanac*, 89th Cong., 2d sess., 1966, vol. 22, 355, 362.
39. *The Nation*, 23 October 1967, 400-1.
40. *Detroit Free Press*, 27 December 1976; Ann Anderson, interview, Washington, D.C., 26 March 1988; William Welsh, telephone interview, 23 April 1988.
41. *Detroit Free Press*, 22 May 1967; *Detroit News*, 27 December 1976; Todd Gitlin, *The Sixties: Years of Hope and Days of Rage* (New York: Bantam Books, 1987) 299; George Herring, *America's Longest War: The United States and Vietnam, 1950-1975*, 2d ed. (New York: Alfred A. Knopf, 1986), 132-33, 175, 186-87, 191; Sundquist, *Dynamics of the Party System*, 380; Herbert Schandler, *The Unmaking of a President: Lyndon Johnson and Vietnam* (Princeton, New Jersey: Princeton University Press, 1977), 206-7; Irwin and Debi Unger, *Turning Point 1968* (New York: Charles Scribner's Sons, 1988), 102-3; Janey Hart, interview, Washington, D.C., 1 and 2 April 1989.
42. *New York Times*, 15 November 1967, 23 February 1969; *Washington Post*, 16 December 1965; Herring, *Longest War*, 202; Walter Hart, telephone inter-

view, 30 April 1988; Jerry Kabel, telephone interview, 24 February 1988; Eugene McCarthy, telephone interview, 7 June 1988; Edmund Muskie, telephone interview, 13 July 1988.

43. *St. Louis Post-Dispatch*, 22 January 1967; *The Progressive*, July 1975, 24; Vreeland, *Philip A. Hart*, 2; Donald Randall, interview, Washington, D.C., 28 March 1988; Sidney Woolner, telephone interview, 12 and 14 January and 5 July 1988.

44. *The Progressive*, July 1975, 24-25; Patricia Bario, interview, Washington, D.C., 28 March 1988.

45. *St. Louis Post-Dispatch*, 22 January 1967; *The Progressive*, July 1975, 25-27; Vreeland, *Philip A. Hart*, 17.

46. Charles Bangert, interview, Washington, D.C., 28 March 1988; Patricia Bario, interview, Washington, D.C., 28 March 1988; Donald Randall, interview, Washington, D.C., 28 March 1988; Lynn Sutcliffe, telephone interview, 22 April 1988; Sidney Woolner, telephone interview, 12 and 14 January and 5 July 1988.

47. *Detroit Free Press*, 9 March 1969; *New York Times*, 2 July 1964.

48. *St. Louis Post-Dispatch*, 22 January 1967; *Washington Post*, 5 April 1968, 8 April 1968, 6 January 1969, 31 January 1969, 11 August 1970; William Welsh, telephone interview, 23 April 1988.

49. Clipping, Box 551, Hart Papers, Bentley Library; *Washington Post*, 6 January 1969.

50. *New York Times*, 30 May 1968; *Washington Post*, 30 May 1968.

51. *Playboy*, August 1972, 156.

52. Clipping, Box 551, Hart Papers, Bentley Library; *Detroit Free Press*, 6 June 1966; *Reader's Digest*, September 1969, 58, 60; Lynn Sutcliffe, telephone interview, 22 April 1988; Burton Wides, interview, Washington, D.C., 29 March 1988.

53. *Motor Trend*, April 1970, 92; *Popular Science*, June 1969, 64-65; Vreeland, *Philip A. Hart*, 18; John Cornman, interview, Washington, D.C., 26 March 1988; Donald Randall, interview, Washington, D.C., 28 March 1988.

54. *Labor*, 24 October 1964; *Washington News*, 21 January 1967; *Life*, 24 June 1966, 87; Morton Mintz, *The Therapeutic Nightmare* (Boston: Houghton Mifflin, 1965), 312-17.

55. *Life*, 24 June 1966, 87-88, 92; Mintz, *Therapeutic Nightmare*, 312-17.

56. *Daily Press* [Escanaba, Michigan], 14 July 1975; *New York Times*, 21 June 1968; Vreeland, *Philip A. Hart*, 10; Saul Friedman, telephone interview, 17 May 1988; Janey Hart, interview, Washington, D.C., 1 and 2 April 1989; Jerry Kabel, telephone interview, 24 February 1988.

57. *Detroit News*, 18 June 1975; *New York Times*, 7 April 1982; Bruce Murphy, *Fortas: The Rise and Ruin of a Supreme Court Justice* (New York: William Morrow and Company, Inc., 1988), 411, 478.

58. *Detroit Free Press*, 9 March 1969; *Detroit News*, 18 June 1975; *Los Angeles Times*, 20 June 1975; *New York Times*, 7 April 1982; *Washington Post*, 6 June 1975.

59. Ann Anderson, interview, Washington, D.C., 26 March 1988; James Hart, telephone interview, 31 May 1989; Janey Hart, interview, Washington, D.C., 1 and 2 April 1989; Walter Hart, telephone interview, 30 April 1988.

60. *Detroit Free Press*, 9 March 1969; *Washington Post*, 29 December 1976; Ross Baker, *Friend and Foe in the U.S. Senate* (New York: The Free Press, 1980), 164-65; Janey Hart, interview, Washington, D.C., 1 and 2 April 1989; Sidney Woolner, telephone interview, 12 and 14 January and 5 July 1988.

61. Ann Anderson, interview, Washington, D.C., 26 March 1988; Mildred Jeffrey, telephone interview, 31 May 1988; Sidney Woolner, telephone interview, 12 and 14 January and 5 July 1988.

62. *Chicago Tribune*, 29 September 1968; *Daily Eagle* [Wayne, Michigan], 19 February 1975; *Detroit Free Press*, 12 August 1968; William Welsh, telephone interview, 23 April 1988; Sidney Woolner, telephone interview, 12 and 14 January and 5 July 1988.

63. Clipping, Box 551, Hart Papers, Bentley Library; *Detroit News*, 13 October 1970, 22 October 1970; *Lansing Labor News*, 28 February 1964; Maddock, "Sleeping Bear Dunes," 78; Sidney Woolner, telephone interview, 12 and 14 January and 5 July 1988.

CHAPTER 5

Profile: Personality, Character, Family

"Doesn't everyone want to be liked?" Phil Hart once said to William Welsh. Hart tried hard to be liked, had great capacity to be liked, and consequently almost everyone liked him. He had a host of traits that others found admirable and that earned him widespread affection. "Phil was very difficult to dislike," said Saul Friedman, "because he was a genuinely reasonable man, a genuinely civilized man."

Those who knew Hart differed sharply on whether he was shy. "I don't think he was shy," insisted Janey Hart. But the *Washington Post* thought Phil blushed "easier than anyone else in the Senate." Others thought Hart's body language and demeanor suggested almost painful shyness in a crowd. "With people he did not know well," said Burt Wides, "he was at the other end of gregarious." All agree, though, that Hart was reserved. "If you reached out to him in a more personal way," said a staff member, "he would shrink back a little because he was so intensely private." After a political meeting or a day on the campaign trail, reporter Robert Pisor of the *Detroit News* often met politicians in the bar for informal evening conversation. But Hart went to bed. "There was a reserve about him," concluded Pisor, "that didn't invite easy conversation."[1]

That Hart was shy in some circumstances and usually reserved handicapped him in making a favorable initial impression on people and seriously limited his ability to assert himself aggressively. Nonetheless, because he was kind, modest, witty, honest, and a gentleman, people grew to like him.

131

Hart did not try to score political points back home in Michigan by personally attacking others. "I never heard him speak harshly of anybody," observed Edmund Muskie. When Hart became angry or frustrated, he would not strike out, careful never to turn his personal frustration on somebody else who did not deserve it.

"He was kind," said Janey Hart, "and he was *never* unkind." He was not a liberal who cared about humanity but not human beings. "He cared very much and foremost about humans," said Wides. "There was no contradiction in his character," added Harrison Wellford, a member of Hart's staff, "no meanness, no pettiness." If he were racing through the halls to get to a meeting, an appointment, or a speech, and someone stopped to talk to him in the hall, he would not say, "Sorry, I haven't got the time now." He would stand and just listen. "The poorer they were, the blacker they were, the more inarticulate they were, the harder he would listen," observed Florence Roth.[2]

He was fatherly with young senate pages and his staff members. Occasionally he drove the pages home in the evening because he worried about their safety in Washington, D.C. After Wides pressured Hart to stay late at the office to phone fellow senators concerning extension of the Voting Rights Act, the senator went home and wrote a personal note to Wides' wife apologizing for keeping Burt in the office so late. "People look at me," recalled Wides, "as if I'm talking about a man on the moon when I talk about a senator like this."[3]

Hart took an intense interest in condolence letters to relatives of Michigan soldiers killed in Vietnam, carefully inspecting casualty reports issued by the Pentagon and personally signing the condolence letters. When the son of a Michigan friend was wounded in Vietnam, Phil was distressed. "What have we heard?" he inquired of a staff member. "What can we do?" Hart took the same personal interest in the problems of his staff. After the newborn baby of a staff member suffered health problems, every morning the senator inquired about the infant's progress.[4]

When Richard Ryan began his job as the Washington correspondent of the *Detroit News*, he made an appointment to interview Hart at his senate office. However, Ryan was stalled in rush-hour traffic and missed their meeting. Embarrassed, he phoned Phil to apologize. "Dick, don't worry about it," the senator replied. "I'm the one who should be interested in meeting you. You're more important to me than I am to you." They arranged another meeting the following day. "He was so kind," recalled Ryan, and "totally sincere."

When fellow senators were in trouble—either Democrat or Republican—sooner or later it was discovered they had talked to Phil Hart about what they should or should not do. Some colleagues called him "Father Phil" because he was a sympathetic hand-holder with senate colleagues suffering personal problems or wanting advice.[5]

In hundreds of handwritten notes he personally thanked people for a service or a kindness. Some contained a strong dose of self-effacement. "For the hard cash in this campaign, thank you," he wrote Welsh near the end of the 1964 campaign. "But for far more, wisdom, patience, loyalty, acceptance of limitations of mine which must frustrate you and disappoint you too, I am grateful. Whatever the result of this election, whatever may lie ahead, all these kindnesses will comfort and sustain."[6]

Hart's modesty and self-effacement also won him affection. Deep down he must have had his vanities and his need for self-identification and reward. He was proud of his ideas, his abilities, his accomplishments, and he took special pride in being an effective politician. "I have an ego," he told reporter Friedman. "Don't sell me short, Saul, because I'm a decent fellow. I have as much ego as any man."

If he had as much ego as any man, however, he rarely displayed it. Modesty was a hallmark of his personality. "Among politicians," observed Joe Rauh, Phil "would get an awful high rating on selflessness. . . . He wasn't always seeking credit. In fact, I don't know that he sought credit at all." Senator Paul Douglas (D-Ill.) agreed, describing Hart as one of the saints of the Senate. Douglas was particularly impressed with Hart's modesty. "Politics produces few saints," Douglas observed. "At best, it requires a large degree of personal striving to arrive and survive, and this encourages egotism. Modesty is one of the first virtues eroded and is an especial handicap in large states, where it is hard for a man to become known." But Hart was a notable exception to the rule, concluded Douglas. He was "an effective senator who had consistently sought to conceal his many virtues."[7]

Hart was not possessive of his ideas or his legislation. Although his Antitrust and Monopoly Subcommittee was the first to take up issues such as truth in packaging, no-fault auto insurance, and auto repair rip-offs, he was content to deliver the stalled legislation from his conservative-dominated subcommittee to the more friendly control of Senator Warren Magnuson's Commerce Committee where his legislation could be passed. In the process, he usually did not get the credit he deserved, but he was content as long as the legislation progressed. Phil left "the glamour and glory to others as long as the result was right," Senate Majority Leader Mike Mansfield remarked. "He literally shunned the limelight when other people elbowed each other aside to seize it," added Wellford.

Hart never allowed staff members to begin a letter, an article, or a speech with the personal pronoun "I," making it necessary for them to write convoluted sentences. He never issued a press release in which he hailed himself as the originator of a successfully passed bill. Politicians often issued self-admiring biographies at the request of the news media or for speaking engagements. "I never had one," said Jerry Kabel, "because I couldn't clear it!" The problem was to compose a biography that would make mention of Hart's accomplishments while satisfying his distaste for self-congratulatory political documents. For years his staff limped along with a biographical sketch that merely listed the offices he held and the years he held them. The arrangement satisfied the senator's sense of truth but was clearly unsatisfactory to anyone who wanted to understand his accomplishments.

When Hart was finally convinced that such nonsense was a necessity, he agreed, on two conditions: that the biography be clearly labeled as a product of his staff ("That way no one need take it too seriously," he said) and that he be allowed to insert parenthetical comments. With those stipulations, "We finally composed one," said Kabel. But every time Kabel attempted to praise his boss, Hart gently deflated him. In one paragraph Kabel praised the senator's efforts on behalf of civil rights legislation and quoted Senators Mike Mansfield, Edward Kennedy and Edward Brooke to excess ("Your dedication and energy, your sure grasp of the legislative process . . . "). Hart intervened, writing in the margin: "The reader would do well to remember that the Senate is sometimes guilty of a certain exaggerated courtliness." The biography was laced with Hart's self-deprecating parenthetical comments.[8]

Pat Bario, who wrote speeches for Hart, said the staff joked that the "first thing Phil Hart did when he started a speech was to apologize for showing up." Bario actually wrote a speech that began with the apology and Hart delivered it. Whenever he was given applause for a speech, Hart rejected the credit, saying, "I didn't do this myself." After receiving an award for fighting for the consumer, he introduced staff members sitting at a nearby table and said he could not have been successful without them. "He really meant it," said Florence Roth.

It did not occur to Hart to ask for special privileges. Usually when a senator rang for the elevator in the Capitol, other passengers waited as the elevator whisked the senator to his destination. But when he entered the elevator, Hart always said, "Take these people to the floors they were going to first." He would not assert himself to secure an airline ticket ahead of others. When he took his family to the Washington Monument, instead of identifying himself as a U.S. senator, he stood in a long line and waited. Unlike some senators, who sent their "girl" to fetch coffee from the cafeteria, Hart fetched the coffee himself and stood in the carry-out line. He insisted on carrying his own suitcases. "You couldn't help him, but he would help you," said Woolner.

Hart's Michigan constituents, the media, and fellow senators grew to appreciate his modesty. "That was one of his charms," said a campaign supporter. Hart's modesty "happens to be good politics," said Jack Cornman, "as well as the Hart style."[9]

Hart's humor was gentle, observant, quick, and usually understated. He enjoyed a joke or a funny story but never one that embarrassed or humiliated. Often he aimed his humor at the foibles of politicians. He took gentle, private amusement at the fears and ambitions of his senate colleagues. A fellow senator told Hart that he admired his stand in favor of regulating handguns and found his arguments compelling. But when Hart asked his colleague to co-sponsor a controversial handgun bill, the senator quickly shied away. Chuckling, with his eyes twinkling, Hart said to an aide: "Burt, higher ambitions are the curse of this joint!"

In the early 1960s, like most legislators', Hart's office was deluged with mail containing arguments on the wisdom and cost of landing a man on the moon. "I have heard arguments," Hart said, "that if we can go to the moon why can't we also (1) eliminate poverty and hunger in the nation or (2) make our cities more livable or (3) wipe out water pollution or (4) develop a silent politician. Why not, indeed? At least on the first three items, where there is some possibility of success."[10]

Hart hoped to impress his colleagues and opponents with the rightness of his own position and with the integrity of the process by which he took the position. He never approached his colleagues in terms of logrolling, or trading votes, or using a friendship as the basis for asking for something. Fellow senators trusted him because they knew that whatever he proposed was done for the highest motives. It was pleasant to work for Hart because whenever he proposed something and an aide called other senators to join him, nobody suspected his motives. He was not asking support because he was in trouble with an interest group, or wanted to move up in the Senate's leadership, or wanted to get publicity on the evening news. As Wides observed: "It was never a question, 'What was his angle?' It was a given fact he didn't have one." Therefore, while others might disagree with his idea, they did not have to overcome the first hurdle of wondering what Hart's motives were. "Mr. Hart is one of the rare politicians, senate colleagues say, whose stated reasons are his real reasons," wrote a reporter for the *New York Times*.[11]

Hart remained alert to any situation that might damage his credibility. Early in his tenure on the Antitrust and Monopoly Subcommittee, the staff prepared a long report in galley form on an investigation of the insurance industry. The report was supposed to be confidential. A reporter came to the senator's office, asked to see the report, and Welsh gave him permission, providing the reporter did not quote from the document. When Hart saw the reporter studying the document, he called Welsh into his office and said, "You can't do that. This has not been released yet. This is a breach of confidence." He ordered Welsh to stop the reporter from reading further. Then he personally went to the senator who had given him the document and explained the breach of confidence. "I can't have senators thinking they give me something with a degree of trust [and] confidentiality, and we let someone unauthorized look at it," he told Welsh. He built up such deep credibility that fellow senators sought to have him on their side. "Everybody would have liked to use Hart's credibility for their own issue and would have been happy to have him give up some of his credibility on their particular issue," said Cornman.[12]

Hart was extremely candid and open with himself and with others about his uncertainties, regrets, and errors. He admitted he was wrong—"not in off-the-record, dinner-party murmurings," observed columnist Mary McGrory, "or from the privileged sanctuary of memoirs long after the fact, but at the time, and in public." He publicly apologized for having supported a federal housing program that attempted to move low-income people into their own private residences. Many developers built shabby homes, which soon deteriorated, leading to massive complaints and major scandal.

Hart also tried to accept responsibility for the errors of others. When Florence Roth made a mistake, Phil took the blame. "I didn't make myself clear, Florence," he would say. Actually, he had made himself perfectly clear. "*I* [had] made a mistake," recalled Roth.[13]

Partly because of tradition and partly because of the floating coalitions in the Senate, fellow senators treated each other in a courtly manner, but Hart went the extra mile. "A gentleman to the core," said the *Washington Post*, "it is hopeless to try to get him engaged in name-calling of opponents or even enemies." Hart understood the norms of the Senate and always played by the rules. Although a strong advocate of his positions, he was never a belligerent advocate. "Some folks around here," said Senator Sam Erwin, "believe that if you entertain views hostile to their own, there must also be a personal hostility. Senator Hart is unfailingly a fine gentleman."

One of his most disarming gestures was to inform opponents of his intimate strategy in order to create an environment for rational debate. When Hart was floor leader of the 1968 Open Housing Act, he and others mapped out strategy on opening debate and moving for cloture. At the same time, a group of southern opponents met in the office of Georgia senator Richard Russell to discuss their own strategy. They were uncertain about how to proceed because they did not know Hart's plans. During their discussion a letter arrived from Hart, addressed to Russell, and in it the senator precisely explained his strategy. After he read the letter, Russell tossed it to his colleagues and said, "Now, *there* is a real gentleman."[14]

Hart had other important traits that won him deep and widespread respect. A conscientious senator, he was absent for votes less often than the average for senators and went on record for most of the votes he missed; committee staff members also praised his dutiful attendance at hearings. Being conscientious was a manifestation of Hart's idealistic view of the politician. "Politics is the noble art of governing," he often said. For some politicians, running for office was fun and exciting; for him, running for office was something one had to do to have the opportunity to govern nobly.[15]

"I remember the expression that the politician is the lay priest of society," Hart said. "The corporal works of mercy are part of the business of how the government runs. A solid case can be made that whatever the venality that attaches to the profession, politics is still a high vocation. I have regarded it as an opportunity to make a more humane life for everybody." To talk in terms of the "corporal works of mercy" showed that Hart was uniquely out of his time, thought Eugene McCarthy. "Phil was still using language and concepts that would have been current and understood at the time of Thomas More." Added McCarthy: "It was a good quality."

Hart preferred to speak at high schools and universities because he enjoyed inspiring young people to go into government service and to share his vision of the politician. William Simpson, an aide to Senator James Eastland, closely observed Hart and was most impressed with the depth of his concern for public service. "Senator Hart . . . really cared, *really* cared—didn't talk about it—*cared*, in his heart, about what was going on in the country and in the world. . . . That quality, that real concern, *real* caring, just sort of shined through Hart's career."

Hart's conception of the politician influenced those who worked closely with him. "There was a kind of spirit of goodness about Phil Hart that tended to elicit a more noble response from other people," said Wellford. "You were ashamed to be narrow and polemical and partisan in his presence because he gave you the impression that he was so much more than that himself."[16]

Even opposing partisan audiences were often charmed by Hart's approach to politics. G. Mennen Williams once half-jokingly complained about Hart's knack for selling the Democratic philosophy to non-Democrats. "I can make a speech about liberal beliefs and goals and get nothing but objections," Williams was quoted as saying. "But Phil Hart can present the same beliefs to the same audience and be cheered as a statesman."[17]

By listening to his constituents, avidly reading newspapers (particularly editorials) and monitoring radio and television news broadcasts, Hart stayed carefully attuned to politics and current events. "He was not above politics," said Cornman of the practical side of the senator as a politician. He combined determined idealism with practical realism. Without lowering his final sights, he framed compromises, accepted half a loaf, because for him compromise was part of the noble art of governing. He often sensed in advance the direction of public opinion and had exceptional political acumen, instinctively sensing the importance and potential of an issue. When Muriel Ferris approached him with an arcane idea, Hart responded, "Well, that's a good idea, but it sure won't sell any newspapers on the streets of Detroit."

Although Hart seemed to be substantially to the left of Michigan's public opinion on social and political issues, the beauty of his character and his gentleness were so attractive that many voters supported him not because of his stands on issues, but simply because they trusted him. "If I was a cynical politician," observed Cornman, "and I wanted to be successful, I would *fake* myself as Phil Hart."

"He had a core of personal integrity and professional integrity which I seldom observed in anybody," said Jerry Cohen. "He was probably one of the most honest people I ever saw in politics," Martin Hayden observed. "He would be honest on things that really were not that much of a test of integrity. . . . He would *always* do what he thought was the honest thing and then so frequently worry about it." When a staff member suggested manipulating the dates for meetings of the Antitrust and Monopoly Subcommittee in order to put pressure on a recalcitrant industry, Hart immediately rejected the idea. "No. I am not going to do that. That isn't right." He saw it as a matter of integrity— one did not manipulate the scheduling of meetings once they were scheduled. "That was so out of keeping with the way everyone else behaved," said the staff member. "I ended up shaking my head, but respecting him at the same time."[18]

The Detroit influence-peddling incident led Hart to adopt extraordinary methods to avoid even the hint of another scandal. Beginning in the early 1960s, he, along with a few other senators, made voluntary, annual disclosure of all his financial holdings and income. His 1969 disclosure indicated he had earned $42,500 in salary, plus $10,176 income from stocks and bonds and $1,933 from his veteran's disability pension. (Although he revealed his own assets, he refused to divulge Janey's, arguing that since her money derived from a trust fund, disclosing her income would also divulge the income of other members of her family who benefited from the trust.) He did not accept gifts from constituents or lobbyists and refused to accept honoraria or lecture fees for his speeches, because he feared being placed in the awkward ethical position of having an individual or an organization that paid him later ask for a favor.[19]

To be honest in politics was not enough; one should also avoid the appearance of dishonesty. When his campaign staff inadvertently erred in not reporting $10,000 in campaign contributions, Hart and his staff agonized about how to handle the problem. Worried that the error might damage his credibility, Hart said to Cornman, "Jack, the kids think they have an honest man in me and they do. And I want to make sure they know that." Finally, the senator and his staff settled on the most straightforward solution: they simply explained the error to the media and no criticism resulted.

In 1964 Hart testified before the Senate Rules Committee in support of full annual disclosure of all income and assets by all top federal officeholders. Although his idea was rejected by the Senate, he continued to press the plan. "I will continue to urge disclosure, not because there are a lot of dishonest men in Congress—there aren't—but because I think that disclosure would have a beneficial effect on the public's opinion of Congress."

Hart favored increasing the salaries of members of Congress and requiring that they receive no outside income, except for adequate provision to reimburse them for necessary expenses. When he told his aide, Barbara Kincaid, that he was going to propose raising the salaries of legislators, she told him it was going to be very unpopular. "You are going to take some flak." He reflected on her remarks for a few moments, then returned to her office, unusually angry. Thumping the back of her chair, he said: "That really makes me mad because I have always believed that legislators ought to be paid well!" Yes, he was wealthy, he told her, but most legislators were not.[20]

Despite his precautions and his openness, the problem of money and influence and their effect on his credibility and the perception of his character plagued him for years. During his 1964 campaign, he received contributions from some corporate executives (including executives of General Electric) whose companies had interests before his Senate Antitrust and Monopoly Subcommittee. Campaign reporting qualifications in 1964 were lenient; Hart had no legal responsibilities to report the contributions. But he thought he had a moral obligation to report everything. He worried about the problem throughout 1965 and 1966, finally resolving it by filing his entire list of contributors with the clerk's office in the Senate. "He insisted it be on the public record, for his own conscience, for his own integrity," said Welsh.[21]

A student of history, politics, philosophy, and current events, he developed a questioning, probing mind. He considered issues and problems from many angles, using the test of reason. Hart was a "man of a thousand whys," and each major issue ignited analytical questions in his mind. How would the private interest benefit? How would the public interest benefit? What was the proper equation? He wanted the private interest to be treated fairly and to advance, but not at the expense of the public interest.

He grasped complex issues quickly. Typically, after his staff had prepared a report, he quickly studied it en route to the Senate floor where he would deliver articulate, intelligent comments. "He usually had mastered whatever the subject was," said Woolner. Hart defended his position with such compelling arguments that his colleagues knew he deeply believed them himself, and he forced his Senate colleagues to deal with the central issue, not tangents, making it more difficult for them to deal with his arguments. "Any senator who had the misfortune to find himself on the opposite side of an issue knew he would face a worthy adversary in Phil Hart," said Senator Herman Talmadge (D-Ga.). "On many occasions, I had this experience firsthand. And, as many of us know, it is not the most comfortable feeling in the world."[22]

He had an unadorned way of piercing to the heart of a matter and of posing a stark question. At a hearing he asked segregationist Governor George Wallace, "Governor, do you think that heaven is segregated?" In 1962 conservative senators were upset with a Supreme Court decision that ruled that officially prescribed prayers in the public schools were unconstitutional. Shortly after the decision, a group of senators appeared as witnesses at a hearing of the Senate Judiciary Committee on a variety of proposals, including constitutional amendments, to counter the court's ruling. Hart supported the court's decision. He asked Senator A. Willis Robertson (D-Va.), a fundamentalist Protestant, what he thought would happen if a prayer used in the public schools was the Catholic Hail Mary. Confused, Robertson at first indicated that the prayer would be fine. Later, though, Robertson phoned Hart's office and indicated that he did not think his fundamentalist Virginia constituents would want their children to say the Hail Mary.

Hart observed that a constitutional amendment proposed by Senator John Stennis (D-Miss.) would permit the recital of nondenominational and noncompulsory prayers in the public schools. Who would determine that a prayer was nondenominational? he asked. When Stennis replied that it would be a legal question to be decided by the courts, Hart questioned the wisdom of making members of the Supreme Court "theologians as well as justices."[23]

Hart's judiciousness generated much soul-searching. When a staff member worried about a personal problem, he would gently inquire, "Have you made your peace?" meaning, "Have you resolved your inner dilemmas?" Before he took stands on complex or important issues, Hart needed time to make his own peace, to solve his own inner dilemmas.

Fellow liberals sometimes described him, a little enviously, as a true liberal—a reflective man with convictions who understood the side he was arguing against, almost to a fault. He put himself in other people's shoes and understood their feelings and thoughts. When staff members criticized a high Pentagon budget, Hart tried to make them understand the Pentagon's point of view.

> You shouldn't get sore at those guys in the Pentagon. You should examine it from the standpoint of their assignment. Their assignment is to protect the nation from all threat. Now, if you had that assignment, you'd want everything. You'd want all the bombers, missiles and troops because that's how you'd see . . . your assignment. It's our assignment to make the final judgment, [to find] the balance between the needs of the rest of society and the needs of the military.[24]

Another example of his judiciousness was the thinking process he went through in trying to end sophisticated forms of discrimination in housing, such as zoning ordinances. "One method," he argued, "would be to withhold all federal funds for any purposes unless the potential recipient has a land-use plan which affirmatively provides for low- and moderate-income housing. But that might be unconstitutional since it can be argued that land usage is a function of local government. Besides," Hart continued, debating himself, "when you cut off federal aid for education, you penalize the school child, or federal aid for hospitals, the sick. The same thing applies to many federal aid programs." Yet "how do you visualize ever busting up the ghettos unless you open the suburbs? Maybe the urgency of opening up housing would justify [cutting off federal aid], but you'd have to be damn sure that it would have the proper effect before you did it."

Hart was so judicious, hesitant, and modest that his staff wrote a mock version of him introducing a bill: "I have a bill I would like to introduce on auto repair. I'm sure it is not a very good bill. I know most of my colleagues could write a better bill. Here are the main arguments *against* it that a reasonable person could make. . . ." After one of Hart's speeches, a member of Senator John McClellan's staff said, "We don't have to give our speech. He gave our arguments too."[25]

It was easy to joke about Hart's extremely judicious approach to issues and legislation, but when he made up his mind or formed his legislation, his senate colleagues knew the end result was fine-tuned. "When a piece of Phil Hart's legislation came to the senate floor, everyone knew that it would be expertly drafted and vigorously defended by a man who had studied the subject matter thoroughly," said Senator Robert Dole. "He apologized for introducing patently defective bills,"

Senator Edward Kennedy later joked, "but he thought it best, he said, to make his *fifteenth draft* available for study."[26]

By the 1960s Hart had corrected his earlier tendency to verbosity and delivered clear, concise, and usually brief speeches. "Brevity was a key to much that he did," Woolner observed. The senator's speaking style did not generate electricity. "His style was . . . well, different," said Douglas Fraser of the United Auto Workers. "He didn't exactly *excite* people." Nonetheless, most listeners were impressed with his eloquence and reasonableness. Usually his speeches were topical as he related current events to his activities in the Senate. He seldom rehearsed his speeches; instead, he thought as he spoke. "It was never a kind of performance," said Eugene McCarthy.

Hart's arrival for a speech at a Democratic party meeting in Michigan was the same as it had been earlier in his political career. Instead of walking into the room like he owned it, he would sidestep around the door frame, slide along the back wall, and wait until he was noticed. He did not want to offend the most humble of county chairs who was directing the meeting. "Please go ahead," he would say, always deferential to the local power who presided.

He was soft-spoken in all settings, even when paired with a rousing speaker. Using a few notes on a small piece of paper, he used excellent language in the service of inquiry. Partly because his quiet tones required people to listen carefully and partly because his audience respected him and his ideas, he would still the room. "It was as though the people in the audience [knew they] were with someone really remarkable," observed Donald Tucker, a campaign supporter from Michigan, "and were almost honored to have him there. He would always bring the crowd to a sense of quietude. Everyone strained to hear him."[27]

Hart was not given to dramatic floor speeches or histrionics on the senate floor, but his colleagues also strained to hear him. When he spoke, fellow senators carefully listened. "Oh, they definitely did," said Edmund Muskie. "He had a knack," said Muskie, "in the midst of a controversial debate, of standing quietly and, with his eloquent rhetoric, saying why he was voting as he was voting, not trying to influence others, that had a noticeable effect on the senators on the floor. I suspect it often changed votes." Hart did not have to be dynamic, said Muskie. In Phil's case, "understatement was often more eloquent than the most thundering orator." Rather than tell his Senate colleagues, "I know what's right," or "This is what the Senate should do," Hart was inclined to make his personal concerns public. "It was a different approach," observed Eugene McCarthy. "At times," Wides remarked of Hart's speeches to his Senate colleagues, "that quiet, steady voice would begin to attract attention, and he would sway votes . . . because they knew he had something to say; they knew he had no angle."[28]

A Michigan reporter commented,

> Phil Hart talking with a small group of people is a remarkable experience. Groping for just the right word, listening to others with his hands pyramided and then gently working up a point with long fingers, hesitating, making his case with care and precision, saying he doesn't know when he doesn't . . . Phil Hart is one of the few politicians with whom you can have a conversation rather than listen to a monologue.[29]

Television continued to be Phil's most effective medium. "He did superbly well on television," said Kabel. He often appeared on thirty- and sixty-second spots for Michigan television stations. Never using a teleprompter, he stationed a clock near the camera, thought through his material, and then ad-libbed his talk, usually in only one take. He was able to make the viewers believe he was talking to them personally in their living room. Neil Staebler thought the senator was the most believable politician he had ever seen on television. "He was so obviously hunting for an honest, direct answer," said Staebler.[30]

The major criticism of Hart was that he lacked assertiveness. Some claimed he did not take full advantage of his power; others complained about his indecisiveness and his penchant for worrying before and after decisions. Much of the criticism was accurate. His exceptional modesty may have partially undermined his ability to mobilize support for issues for which he had been the Senate's point man. At times he could have moved a particular bill or issue further by being more aggressive or insistent. He took things to heart and was excessively concerned that he do absolutely the right thing. "We used to say," said Wellford, "that we didn't think Phil could ever be president because he just could not handle the sense of responsibility to make decisions that had such fundamental impact on large numbers of human beings."

He frustrated ideologues and sometimes looked tentative because he was not always certain of his positions. Ralph Nader and other public interest lobbyists felt that Hart was so patient and gentle with opponents that in the areas of consumer protection and economic crime he was less effective than he could have been. They wanted a more hard-hitting, flamboyant, Kefauver-style attack on the corporations. Hart was not dramatic enough. He did not make headlines. He was *too* fair, *too* judicious. Critics would have preferred that he twist arms, lean on colleagues, and strike back sharply with a stinging rebuttal. A *New York Times* reporter thought the senator was "constitutionally unable to overstate his case, grab a headline or show personal anger."[31]

When asked about the criticism, Hart conceded his limitations while also gently putting down detractors. "It's probably true," he said. "There's always the need for someone who can dramatize an issue and galvanize public opinion. I'm not a charger." But he added, "I sometimes envy the man who thinks he knows the answers for everything. . . . The problems that confront us are so complex that the sane man can't be that decisive." For Hart, being liberal meant never being too sure you were right. He doubted that he would have changed his style, even if he could. "There's no telling if I could have been more effective or, in fact, less so, because it wouldn't be me. It would show through as a fake."

Had Hart been more assertive and aggressive he probably would have damaged his overall credibility and effectiveness in the Senate. Actually, he was not as indecisive as some of his critics charged. Often he refused to provide a simple and immediate response to a question or a problem when time was available for reflection. "He studied and reflected," insisted Eugene McCarthy, "and when ready he drew the line and marked the threshold."[32]

Hart often "drew the line and marked the threshold." Sitting on his desk was a plaque with a quotation from Edmund Burke: "Your representative owes you, not his industry only, but his judgment; and he betrays you instead of serves you if he sacrifices it to your opinion." He believed he was elected primarily to use his best judgment. At the beginning of his first term, he said privately that he intended to vote as if he were *not* going to run for reelection, an attitude which frightened members of his staff. A story circulated that reporters had asked Senator Everett Dirksen for the reason he had changed his mind on an issue. Dirksen responded, "You don't understand the senator from Illinois. He is a man of deep principles, and his first deep principle is electability." When a reporter related the story to Hart, he quietly responded, "I guess I'll never be an Ev Dirksen."[33]

"The one quality in him that stands out in my mind," said Jerry Cohen, "was his toughness." Hart did not enjoy being tough and often had to be prodded by his staff to start hearings on a difficult subject. But once he got into the hearings, added Cohen, "he was a quiet but very effective tiger." Hart often took tough, courageous stands. When the Antitrust and Monopoly Subcommittee held hearings on a bill to allow newspapers to enter into joint operating agreements, Cohen subpoenaed documents of the Associated Press. The AP's attorney angrily showed up in Cohen's office.

"You can't subpoena us now!" said the attorney.

"Why not?" Cohen replied.

"Hart's running for reelection. The newspaper industry is not going to take kindly to this!"

Cohen bristled at the threat. The attorney said he would complain directly to Hart. But the intimidation had no effect on the senator. Two weeks later the AP's attorney phoned Cohen. "Where do you want me to deliver the documents?" asked the lawyer. Hart had backed up his staff director and had insisted on following through with the subpoena. "This is one tough son of a bitch," Cohen thought.

In the late 1960s, the staff of the subcommittee suggested holding hearings on oil shale. When some senators from states with oil shale learned of the possible hearings, they were livid. A senator from the Interior Committee privately threatened to retaliate by blocking Hart's pet legislation on Sleeping Bear Dunes, intending to hurt his chances for reelection.

"Why should I hold the hearings?" Hart asked Cohen in the presence of the threatening senator.

"Because no one else will," replied Cohen.

"Well, that seems like a good reason," said Hart.

The subcommittee proceeded to hold the hearings on oil shale.[34]

In late 1968 Donald Randall proposed to Cohen that the subcommittee investigate the auto industry. Cohen related the proposal to Hart. Later, Hart met Randall in the hallway.

"Don, I understand you're recommending we go into investigation of the automobile business," Hart observed.

"Yes, sir," said Randall.

"Do you know that I'm running for reelection next year?"

"Yes, sir," said Randall.

"Do you know I'm from Michigan?"

"Yes, sir."

"You know that the biggest business in my state is the auto industry, don't you?"

"Yes, sir."

"And do you know that if I lose, you lose?"

"Yes, sir."

"Do you still want to do it?" Hart asked.

"Yes, sir," said Randall.

"Well," Hart advised, "go do it."

Randall later reflected on their conversation: "I had held him in high esteem, but, boy, at that moment he went off like a rocket."[35]

During John Kennedy's administration, Joe Rauh, the influential labor and civil rights attorney, came to Hart's senate office to state the UAW's position on complex legislation concerning monopoly in the communications industry. Hart had already committed himself on the issue, and Rauh informed him that the UAW objected to his position. Distressed to learn that he differed with his normal ally, Hart said to Rauh, "Joe, I have given my word. Maybe I made a mistake, but I cannot change." Only one argument might change Phil's mind. "If I thought this was a moral issue," Hart told Rauh, "I could go . . . and ask to be released from my commitment. Would you be able to say that it was a moral issue?" Embarrassed, Rauh conceded it was a technical issue, not a moral one. "Then I'm going to stick by it," Phil concluded. Rauh reflected, "It was almost beautiful. Phil drew the best out of the people he was talking to."[36]

Hart stood firm when a union official came to his senate office with a devious scheme to save the union money by cleaning its mailing list. The union had a "dirty" list, one with deceased persons and wrong addresses, and was losing thousands of dollars in postage costs. After a senator sent out a newsletter, the federal government cleaned up the senator's mailing list by removing all the returns from the list. The union's scheme proposed to have liberal, prolabor senators use their franking privileges to send a newsletter to all union members in their state. When the returns arrived and the federal government eliminated them from the list, the senator would convey the "clean" list to the union, saving the wasteful postage costs.

Hart asked the labor official what his attitude would be if conservative Republican senator Roman Hruska cleaned up the mailing list for General Motors.

"Would you think that was all right?" Hart asked.
"That was different," mumbled the labor official.
"How was it different?" Hart shot back.

The official responded that the union was the "good guy" and General Motors was the "bad guy." Hart quickly dismissed the rationale and refused to cooperate, irritating the union. However, other senators did cooperate.[37]

Privately, Hart joked about the tough decisions he made. "What every politician needs is a safe crusade," he said laughing; then it was easy to be courageous. An example was Senator Frank Moss, who could vigorously oppose cigarette smoking because he represented Utah, a state strongly influenced by the antismoking Mormons. "I want you to find me an issue," Hart joked to Cornman, "which will do for me in Michigan [what] being against smoking does for Frank Moss in Utah."[38]

"Phil Hart was one of the kindest men in the world," observed Senator Jacob Javits (R-N.Y.), "but beneath his soft manner lay a flint-and-steel dedication to principle. Everyone in the Senate understood that he was a man of his word who would carry out any obligation he undertook." Javits continued: "I never saw Phil influenced by what you might call *political* factors. Even if it meant closing a defense base in Michigan or having an adverse effect on a trade union that supported him, he stuck to his principles." "When you talked to Phil about his convictions," said Edmund Muskie, "you knew they were his convictions and not subject to compromise."[39]

Hart made life easy for the media. He was accessible and returned their phone calls. Once a week he met with about nine members of the Michigan press corps in his office. Rarely did he refuse to answer a question; occasionally he spoke off the record because he thought his comment might injure a colleague. Usually, though, he furnished candid, honest, and intelligent answers. He often posed probing questions to the reporters and asked their advice. "What is your opinion?" he would say. Both Hart and the reporters enjoyed the give-and-take.

He did not complain about media criticism. The conservative *Detroit News* often blasted his liberal positions, but he never recriminated. "I don't think he ever complained a single time about a story that I wrote," said Saul Friedman who published several critical articles in the *Detroit Free Press*.

Consequently, reporters unanimously liked and respected Hart. "I thought he was a wonderful person," said Ray Courage. "Everyone could trust him," Richard Ryan observed. "My admiration for him is based on his personal style rather than solely on his politics," said Wylie Gerdes of the Farmington, Michigan *Observer and Eccentric*. "It's not often a man can rise to be a U.S. senator and still be a decent human being."[40]

Hart did not want a formal leadership role in the Senate. He had no taste for the political warring and the wheeling and dealing that a leadership job required. He was content being a senator and did not want to be more than a senator. "Unlike most others in this business," he told a friend, "I have no craving for power." Often he played a supporting role, much like his support of General Barton in World War II and Governor Williams in the 1950s. Rather than being a leader, Hart preferred to be a person who exemplified right thinking, ethics, and justice.

Nonetheless, whether he wanted to or not, Hart was thrust into becoming an *informal* leader in the Senate and one with extensive, behind-the-scenes influence. His influence came partly because of his immersion in legislative duties, his commitment to senate traditions, and his ability to work quietly and effectively with his Republican and Democratic colleagues. Even though he was not a dramatic debater, held no powerful Senate position, and did not lean on colleagues or swap credits, he still influenced people because his colleagues knew he was always fair and that his positions were judiciously thought through and in the public interest.[41]

"He was a very persuasive person," said Cornman. In a calm, non-threatening manner, Hart told his colleagues at a Democratic caucus, "Gentlemen, this might get us through the problem today, but we all have history to worry about and . . . when historians begin to probe into this action, we're not going to look very good. However, if we arrange our affairs and do it this way, we might achieve very much the same result, while improving our chances to look good in history."

By 1968 Hart had become a leader of the fifteen to twenty senators in the liberal block. Senate liberals had recently lost their standard-bearers. Estes Kefauver was dead; Paul Douglas had been defeated for reelection; and Hubert Humphrey was vice president.

As Hart approached the end of his second term, by the unwritten rules he had been initiated into the inner club of the Senate. "He gets along well with others; his word's good—that's what makes him a member of the club," said a Republican senator. "Phil is a man we can respect and work with," commented an influential southern conservative. "When I need the liberals' votes, I now look to Phil," added a moderate leader.

When Hart was described as a leader or a spokesman for northern Democratic liberals, he rejected the labels, saying, "it means nothing" because the "hallmark of liberals is to march in nine different directions at the same time."[42]

Hart had many friends in the Senate but was closest to Mike Mansfield, Eugene McCarthy, Edmund Muskie, Edward Kennedy and James Eastland. Like Hart, Mansfield was smart, logical, understated, trustworthy, and not flamboyant. After Hart had congratulated Mansfield for an accomplishment, the Montana senator privately and with deep sincerity replied: "[If] I were to pick out the man for whom I had the greatest respect in this body, the list would be headed by one Phil Hart who in his quiet and persistent way and his courteous and understanding manner has a way of making his views known, getting them across and whether or not accepted, making an impression which is accepted by all." Mansfield concluded, "You are one of the truly best, Phil, and I want you to know that off the floor I am pretty sparse with my compliments."[43]

Hart, Muskie, McCarthy, and Edward Kennedy were seat mates in the back row of the Senate chamber. With seniority, the four could have moved toward the front, but they declined. "We decided to make the back row a row of distinction," said Muskie. "So we stayed there." The four discussed legislation and shared cloakroom gossip. McCarthy and Muskie became Hart's closest friends. Catholics, Democrats, liberals, nearly the same age, all three had arrived in the Senate in 1958. During their first year, with their families not in Washington, the three chummed around together and dined at restaurants on Connecticut Avenue.[44]

Hart liked both John and Robert Kennedy but developed a special affection for Edward Kennedy, who was first elected to the Senate in 1962. "I'm just amazed at what this Kennedy family has produced in this man," Hart said in 1968. "He's as fine a Kennedy as America has known and that includes John and Bob." They chatted in the back row of the Senate, dined together and became political allies. More important, Phil became Ted's teacher and mentor.

After Robert Kennedy's death in 1968, Ted Kennedy became depressed and drank heavily. Hart tried to help him. "Phil simply took him in hand," said an observer. When Kennedy sought advice on whether to run for the position of majority whip, he called on Hart first, and Phil helped him secure the post early in 1969. After Kennedy's terrible ordeal on Martha's Vineyard in July 1969, in which he drove his car off the Chappaquiddick Bridge in a late-night accident drowning his passenger, Mary Jo Kopechne, Kennedy became persona non grata in the Senate and lost his leadership post in 1971. Hart privately said that Kennedy had behaved badly at Chappaquiddick, but continued to mentor him. Shortly after the accident, Kennedy came to his office for a long discussion. "Phil was the kind of a guy you could unburden yourself to and not a word would ever get out," said a close observer of the Kennedy family. "Hart was very kind with him and very understanding," said Florence Roth of Hart's counseling. "I'm sure Ted Kennedy found him a source of comfort."[45]

Nothing more epitomized the quality of Hart's relations with his colleagues than his friendship with Senator James Eastland, a man whose views were more alien to Hart than anyone else's in the Senate. James Eastland, Democrat from Mississippi, wealthy owner of a 5,800-acre Delta cotton plantation, had been in the Senate since 1942. As chairman of the Senate Judiciary Committee, the tall, round-faced, cigar-chomping southerner ruled with an iron hand. Best known nationally as a symbol of southern resistance to racial integration, Eastland complained on the Senate floor about possible "mongrelization" of the races and often spoke of blacks as an inferior race. He railed against communism in government, schools, newspapers, and the arts, and suggested that all nine justices of the Supreme Court be impeached for "pro-communism decisions."

To northern liberals Eastland was the archetype of the southern racist, more inclined philosophically toward slavery than civil rights. But Hart saw a human side of Eastland, a compassionate and caring side, which few northern liberals ever saw. "Phil liked any person who had distinctive character," said Eugene McCarthy of Hart's friendship with Eastland. He trusted Eastland, telling friends that he had better dealings with the conservative Mississippi senator than he did with some liberal senators who did not always keep their word. Eastland was the only senator whose picture Hart hung in his office.

Perhaps by his personal example and discussion Hart hoped to convert Eastland into a more reasonable person. Occasionally in the afternoon he went to Eastland's office for a drink and free-wheeling, uninhibited discussion on a wide range of issues, including civil rights. They joked and teased. When Hart was up for reelection, Eastland said to him: "I'll campaign for you or against you, whichever would do you the most good."

When Hart met Eastland's aide, William Simpson, at the Dirksen Senate Building, he inquired about Eastland.

> "He's a little bit worried right now," responded Simpson.
> "Oh? What about?" asked Hart.
> "He is worried about his cotton crop," said Simpson.
> "Hmm. I sure would like to see him," said Hart.
> "Well, he's down in Mississippi, but we can go to your office or upstairs to our office, and I'll get him on the phone for you in two minutes," Simpson helpfully suggested.

But Hart did not want to phone Eastland.

> "No. I've known him for twenty years," said Hart, "and I've never seen him worried about a damn thing. I just wanted to *look* at him while he was *worried*."

Simpson closely observed the relationship between the two senators. "It was originally based on mutual respect," he said. "From that original respect grew this feeling of real friendship, of real trust in each other, a rare closeness between two men who . . . could not have been further apart as far as philosophy and section of the country. If you want to make a list of differences, it would sure be a long one."[46]

There were also practical and political reasons for their relationship. Because Hart chaired the Antitrust and Monopoly Subcommittee of the Judiciary Committee and Eastland chaired the full Judiciary Committee, they needed and wanted to trust each other. Eastland had such confidence in Hart that he seldom—if ever—interfered with his subcommittee hearings and staffing. There was iron-bound trust between the two, observed Simpson. "No cute little tricks; no blind siding; straight up front; straight on top of the table at all times."

Eastland's bombastic racism was partly concocted for the folks back home. When Hart consulted with him about the appointment of a Michigan black to a federal judgeship, Eastland said, "Don't you worry about your boy. He'll get through all right, but you [must] understand we got to put on a little bit of a show."

Eastland's crucial power position in the Senate was a terrible burden to bear for northern Democrats. In the 1960s, civil rights advocates, through adroit maneuvering, bypassed Eastland's Judiciary Committee and proceeded to write into law the landmark civil rights acts. Eastland seemed to hold life and death power over the Voting Rights Act of 1965. He could have bottled up the bill, but he did not. "Phil Hart was our bridge to Eastland," said Clarence Mitchell of the NAACP. "He was indispensable. Somehow he was able to talk to Eastland and got him to lift the roadblocks. I don't know how he did it. He was such an honest, such a fair man, that Eastland probably felt an *obligation* to act responsibly with him."

The most bizarre and devious speech Hart ever delivered in the Senate involved Eastland. In 1966, while Eastland faced reelection in Mississippi, Hart rose in the Senate chamber and denounced him as an obstructionist enemy of civil rights legislation. Because his language was unusually harsh, one of Eastland's allies, Senator Sam Erwin, surprised by Hart's broadside, rose to defend his colleague. But as Erwin started speaking, Eastland whispered loudly to him, "Damn it, Sam, sit down and shut up. You're ruining the whole thing." Erwin had not been in on the secret. Hart's speech had been delivered with Eastland's complete knowledge and total endorsement and was intended for circulation in Mississippi to help Eastland's reelection against a challenger who charged him with being too soft on the race issue. Hart's critical remarks were widely publicized in Mississippi. For Eastland to be under attack by a recognized liberal member of the Senate effectively served his political interest. It was "beneficial to Eastland," conceded Kabel, "because it made him look like an effective opponent of civil rights."

It was uncharacteristic of Hart to take part in a dishonest charade to assist the reelection of a southern racist, but his friendship with Eastland distorted his judgment. Moreover, the speech had some practical benefits for Hart and the cause of civil rights because it made Eastland slightly more beholden to him. In the next few years Eastland placed few obstacles in front of Hart's civil rights efforts and provided little opposition to getting federal judicial appointments in Michigan through the Judiciary Committee.

"I have never known a man I have been more apart from philosophically, but close to personally," Eastland said of Hart. "He is a man of principle, courage, and intellectual honesty. . . . But while he is invariably fair, I can tell you that on occasion he can be tough, firm, and, where deeply held principles are involved, unbending."[47]

In a 1970 interview for the *Washington Post*, the reporter mentioned that little was known about Hart off duty. Phil beamed and said, "Good," and then proceeded to do very little enlightening. He tried to keep his private life private. He avoided the Washington cocktail circuit—except for a few functions of Michigan constituents—and much preferred to be home for dinner. His family was a pillar that helped sustain him. "He was very close to the kids, very close to Janey," Woolner observed.

The Harts lived at 2812 Calvert Street NW in Washington. Janey was usually home with the children, and she had assistance from several black servants. "Assistant mother" Oner Lee, who had worked for the family since 1950, cooked, helped maintain discipline, took responsibility, and mothered the children. Her husband also occasionally worked for the family; a day worker came in several times a week to do laundry and the heavy cleaning; and an elderly black man did the gardening for the Harts and for others in the neighborhood.[48]

Phil glowed when he talked about Janey. "Color her vivid," he said. "There is nothing pastel about Janey." In the 1960s, Janey resumed her education at George Washington University, where she zipped around the campus on a yellow Honda motorcycle and earned her degree in anthropology in 1970. Diminutive and dynamic, intelligent and irrepressible, Janey had become a militant liberal activist by the late 1960s, labeled by Washington pundits as the "Martha Mitchell of the liberals." (Martha Mitchell was the outspoken conservative wife of President Nixon's attorney general, John Mitchell.)

The contrast between her own patrician upbringing and the plight of the poor pricked her conscience and partly led her to abandon the conservative Republicanism of her family. She remembered the shock she felt as a youth in the Depression as she saw long lines of hungry people. "I was not one of them. I remember the contrast." Her marriage to Phil heightened her desire to become involved in liberal causes.[49]

In late May 1967, Janey presided at the founding meeting of the Washington, D.C. chapter of the National Organization for Women (NOW). Several years earlier she had been one of the first to urge NASA to select women as astronauts. (She took the physical tests for astronauts and passed.) "Why must we handicap ourselves with the idea that every woman's place is in the kitchen despite what her talent and capabilities might be?" she said. Phil also supported the women's liberation movement. ("With a wife like mine, what can you expect?" he joked.) "If anyone doesn't understand that this culture, if that's what it is, has lost enormously in contributions of women, he's hopeless," he said.

To gain insight into the plight of the poor, Janey put the Hart family on a welfare budget for a week in 1969. The family spent twenty-five cents per person per meal each day. The children went to bed hungry every night. She grimly admitted there was a psychological difference between the real and the experimental poor: "At least we knew it would end in a week."[50]

Although Phil endorsed Janey's support of the women's movement, he remained silent about her criticism of the hierarchy of the Catholic church. "I get letters excommunicating me quite often," she said in 1970. In recent years she had charged publicly that the Catholic church was run by "authoritarian robots," and had prominently supported a married clergy, women for the priesthood, and birth control. In 1968 she became chair of the Center for Christian Renewal, which occupied a three-story row house on Kenyon Street in Washington and served as a home for priests who had been told to leave their rectories because they disagreed with Washington's Cardinal Patrick O'Boyle on the issue of birth control. In June 1969, in an open letter to Cardinal O'Boyle and Washington area Catholics printed prominently in the *Washington Post*, she condemned the archdiocese of Washington for discriminating against blacks.[51]

On 13 November 1969, Janey and 185 others were arrested on charges stemming from an antiwar ecumenical religious service in the concourse of the Pentagon. The group had celebrated a Mass to show that "the means of nonviolence are open to those who would change our society through nonviolent methods." The violation carried a possible $50 fine and thirty days in jail, and, for awhile, the media conveyed the impression that the wife of Senator Philip Hart might spend time in jail.

On 7 April 1970, Judge Stanley King imposed a $25 fine on a small group of defendants including Janey. "By their singing and hand clapping," King said, "the demonstrators created loud and unusual noise. By their conduct in placing themselves in that area of the concourse . . . they obstructed the usual use of such entrances and the concourse itself." (The defendants appealed and a federal judge later overturned their conviction.)[52]

Michigan Democrats differed sharply in their opinion of Janey. "She was a great activist in the peace movement," said Mildred Jeffrey, "and I think that helped Phil." More often, though, Janey's activities disturbed leading Democrats in Michigan, who worried about her effect on the upcoming 1970 election. Some wanted Hart to discipline her. "I'd get all kinds of complaints about [her]," said Carolyn Burns, a leader in the senator's reelection campaign in 1970; "I would get the feedback from the party people." Helen Berthelot thought she spoke for many Democrats when she said, "We were very unhappy with her."

As the 1970 election approached, Sidney Woolner also worried about Janey. "Having the wife of the senator in the jug was not the kind of picture we wanted to paint." But when Woolner asked Janey to tone down her antiwar activities, Janey firmly replied, "You take care of your problems, and I'll take care of mine!" Most likely, Janey's activities were more of a political liability than an asset for Phil, but since he had little trouble being reelected, Janey's impact was minimal.[53]

Did Janey worry about the effects of her activities on her husband's career? "There are times when I've helped, times when I've hurt," she said in September 1970. Then she added fiercely, "I expect to tell the truth as I see it. The truth, as close as humans can come to it, is not a political disadvantage."

Although he did not always agree with her, Phil staunchly defended Janey's independence and never interfered with her. Where did he stand in regard to the Pentagon incident? "With my wife," he responded. He knew some people would be offended by her. "But I hope not," he said. "I've always tried to encourage her and the children to be true to themselves. I'd be disappointed if the members of my family felt they had to gear their lives and their beliefs to suit my career." In private, when he heard complaints he simply said, "That's Janey! Janey is going to do what Janey wants to do!"[54]

"What I liked about their relationship," Ann said of her parents, "[was] the liveliness of the dialogue, the fecundity, the stimulation that they provided each other over issues." Janey described the political dimension of their marriage more succinctly: "Bedfellows make strange politics." While Phil nodded in agreement, Janey told a columnist, "We have beautiful fights. We have fights about whether the whole system has survivability built into it. I read the weekly news magazines and I say, "'Ye Gods, we're not giving anything to the kids—anything they can even correct.' Then I scream that it's all his fault. He's the institution and he should fix it." To which the senator added affectionately, "By tomorrow."⁵⁵

In February 1968, a reporter captured some of the political debate in the Hart household:

> "I know I will not vote for Johnson, that's all I know," said Ann Hart.
> It was too early to know who to vote for in November, Phil retorted.
> "I see [Johnson] as ruining our country, destroying the nation and the Democratic Party, by involving us in Vietnam," replied Janey. "I see the Republicans as not much better, but less dangerous."
> Johnson was an honorable man who did want to end the war, said Phil, but the consequences in the balance of power precluded immediate abandonment of the U.S. presence in Vietnam.
> "If wise old heads can't find the answer, it's time to change," Janey said. "We haven't made the first step away." She disputed Phil's contention that the United States had shown restraint in prosecuting the war. "Continued escalation isn't restraint. We're in the process of wiping out the whole population of Vietnam."

Phil thought that Janey and Ann could not see the forest for the trees. Vietnam would be a "footnote or a cruel chapter in history" before the nation's domestic problems were solved, and the Democrats, led by President Johnson, had proven their superiority over the GOP in coping with domestic problems.⁵⁶

When Janey would lose her temper and yell, Phil maintained his position, but sometimes, unable to contain himself, he broke out laughing and would clap and applaud the intensity of her fury. "He could barely contain himself around her," observed Walter Hart. "He would bubble over with enthusiasm."

Janey thought she seldom changed her husband's mind. "I don't influence him," she said. "It's more the other way. He's more reasonable than I am. He has a lot more information to work with. He is certainly more persuasive. He encourages me to be more optimistic."

Phil took pleasure in Janey's wide-ranging travels. She took trips to Europe, the Caribbean, and Central America, and since the senator was usually too busy to accompany her, they discussed her trip at length after she returned. That way, Janey said, "He would go on the trip with me." He often teased her. As they were leaving his office to go to dinner, Hart said to a staff member, "We're going out to dinner. What am I saying? Janey is taking me out to dinner!" Doubling up with laughter, he added: "*She's* the one with the money!" After Janey used a large amount of her income to purchase a piece of property, she unexpectedly suffered a shortage of cash and asked to borrow $700 from her husband. Howling with laughter, Phil teased her about having to borrow from *him*. "He just loved it!" recalled Janey. "That he had to lend money to me. He thought that was just wonderful."[57]

Hart was often away from his family—working on legislative matters late into the evening, delivering speeches, campaigning for reelection, and meeting with constituents in Michigan. He worried that he spent too much time at work and not enough at home. "He would have loved to spend a lot more time with [the family]," said Janey. "We had to share him a lot with the rest of the world and that was tough, and tough for him too," observed Walter. Nonetheless, added Walter, "We understood . . . he was doing this work because he loved us, and that made it much easier to accept."[58]

The arrival of a new baby always made Hart nervous because he did not understand babies. He changed a diaper only once—and it was a disaster. He never bottle-fed the babies and seldom held them in his arms when they were little. He was also absent-minded about the children. After two girls, Ann and Cammie, Janey gave birth to Walter. With Walter only a few days old, Janey left the infant in Phil's care while she shopped.

"How did it go?" Janey asked after she returned.

"Just great," said Hart. "I took the girls out to the drug store and we had ice cream."

"What?" said Janey. "What about Walter?"

"Oh, my God!" said Phil, hitting his head, horror on his face.

He had forgotten about his brand new son.[59]

Phil was not a disciplinarian; Janey mostly handled that role. "He was always very tender with us," said James, "sometimes to a fault." The idea of getting a spanking from their father was never something the children dreaded. Once, when the boys were exceptionally loud, Phil came to their room carrying a shoe to deliver punishment. He tried to spank them through several layers of covers. It was loud but not painful. "All of us [were] simultaneously laughing and pretending to be crying," James recalled. On the few occasions that Phil did get angry, "It was always upsetting to us," said Walter, "because we hated to upset him. We all loved him so dearly."

Although exceptionally busy, Hart made a great effort to be with his family or at least to contact them. He was not off on the weekend playing golf or attending football games without them. His campaign staff tried not to schedule him for appearances on weekends because he wanted to be home. While Hart was lieutenant governor and on the road, reporter Jerald terHorst covered him and was impressed by his intense dedication to his family, an "unusual characteristic" for a politician. "Every evening," said terHorst, "he would find the time to stop and call one of the kids."[60]

Although Hart seemed perplexed around his babies, as the children grew he interacted effectively with most of them. He seldom lectured his children, but when they had a problem or a question he patiently listened, advised, and subtly taught. Ann Bronfman, Janey's close friend, was impressed with Hart's dialogue with the children: "Phil *listened* to his children. He enjoyed talking to them. Ideas were always flying around."

Hart drove the children to school, took them on tours of Civil War battlefields and to football and baseball games. At least part of the family went on vacations together. He and the children enjoyed moments of silent sharing, like traveling the back roads of Mexico and pausing to reflect on the natural beauty. He took pride in his children's accomplishments. After attending Ann's singing concert, he gushed, "She is great! She is really great!"

The children remembered his smiling face, wry humor, and open affection. When he greeted them, he hugged and kissed them even when they were grown. "Dad's capacity for love was breathtaking," said Walter. "There was never a moment in my life when I doubted his love for me. Along with that was a great capacity for forgiveness."[61]

In the late 1960s, the boys wore their hair long, and most of the older children were radical in their political philosophy. "They have very dim views, many days, of the system," Phil acknowledged. "I readily agree there are some absurdities, and I'm glad they question them. That's the kind of children I hope I have."

Before Christmas the senator's staff traditionally sent out thousands of cards, with a Hart family photograph, to close supporters in Michigan. In the late 1960s, when the boys had long hair and beards, a staff member worried that supporters would associate Hart's family with the hippie "flower children" and damage his reelection chances. Over lunch the staff member started to urge the senator not to send the photograph, but he cut him off. "I know exactly what you are thinking," he said. "You think that because the boys have beards that we would be better off not to send Christmas cards this year. Well, I've never been ashamed of my four boys, and I'm not ashamed of them now. And the cards will go out."[62]

However, the oldest child, Ann, had mostly dark, chilling memories of her father. She conceded he was a great senator who had genuine affection for his children, but she thought he practiced an "invisible version of fathering." Excessively distant, reserved, and preoccupied, "He was [mentally] somewhere else most of the time," she lamented, even when he was home. Year after year Phil would introduce himself to Ann's friends—the same friends. Sitting on the sofa, reading his newspaper, he failed to notice that "all hell" had broken loose with his children. Instead, he kept reading his newspaper. "The man could have been somewhere else for all he knew about what was going on with his children," said Ann. "He was certainly always gentle," she added. "It is easy, when you're disengaged, to be gentle."

Beginning in August 1954, when Ann, seven, fell ill with crippling polio, she spent almost a year in the hospital in Farmington, Michigan. "My father came to see me maybe twice," she recalled bitterly. Her father was more interested in furthering his own political career, she thought.

Janey Hart sharply disagreed with Ann's view and questioned some of her facts. Ann's overall assessment of her father was "distorted," said Janey. As for Phil's reaction to Ann's polio, Janey insisted that he did make weekly visits to Ann's hospital. "[Ann] just didn't remember," said Janey.[63]

James Hart agreed with Ann that Phil was often distant. His father had an "ethereal" approach to life, he believed. Otherwise, James took a different view of his father, one more representative of the attitude of his brothers and sisters. "He was the kind of guy I could sit in a room with . . . and feel very happy being there with [him] and not have to talk about everything." Phil wrote scores of letters to James whose travels included high school in Spain and schools and jobs throughout the United States. "He had a beautiful style of writing to me." While James was working on Mackinac Island in July 1968, Phil wrote from Washington, "All of us miss you and I just want you to know it." In a letter a month later he said, "Nicest part of my last trip to Michigan was seeing and being with you. I'm proud of you—which says it all."

His father's presence in the Senate helped bolster James's faith in the establishment at a time when he was increasingly disillusioned about the Vietnam War and flaws in U.S. society. "Knowing that dad was there helped me sustain a certain faith in the system," he remarked.[64]

In early July 1971, James, twenty, was charged with possession of a marijuana cigarette—less than a half-inch long—while in a park near the downtown area of Mackinac Island. He pleaded guilty to the charge and the judge gave him a stiff sentence: a $200 fine and twenty days in jail. The incident received extensive publicity in Michigan, and after the sentencing the Harts issued a statement from Washington: "Our reactions are no different from any parents. We are regretful. We desperately wish that it hadn't happened. But our affection for Jim is undiminished. The important thing now is that it not happen again."

"[Phil] was perfectly wonderful about it," James reflected about the incident, "and totally correct." Shortly after the arrest, Phil phoned James: "You know, Jim, we have always said that stuff is illegal." James said he understood, and resolved to pay the consequences. Phil's belief in equal justice made it impossible for him to seek special privileges for his son, but he visited James in jail and told him, "You know we love you." Later, James Brown, the prosecuting attorney in the case, wrote Hart that his son had not asked for favorable treatment and added, "I also appreciated the fact that neither you nor Jane asked for any special treatment and I admire you for it." Through thick or thin, James concluded, "I always had the fallback to rely on. He was a rare and loving man."[65]

Hart considered himself a staunch Catholic—"ais3270in capital letters," said an aide. He also struck most people as a deeply spiritual person. "One could easily have seen him going into the priesthood," said Burt Wides. "I often have wondered why Phil Hart did not pursue the ministry," said Senator John Pastore. "To me, he is a pious man." The politician should be a "lay priest," Hart said, one who had a mission to serve the public's interest. Ann Hart thought that her father aspired to sainthood. "We are talking [about] delayed gratification in a big way with the life of Phil Hart," she said. "We are talking [about] the after-life."

In the 1964 campaign, when Carolyn Burns scheduled him to visit a plant gate on Sunday morning, Hart said, "Carol, I've got to get to Mass!" In March 1966 in a letter to his son James, Phil made a request: "I would appreciate your saying a word for me now and again in prayer. I certainly have you in mine." Consistently, into the 1970s, when the senator traveled with Jerry Kabel, he kneeled next to his bed and prayed before going to sleep.

When the children were young, the entire Hart family went to Sunday Mass. As the children grew, Phil encouraged them to attend church, but he left the decision up to them and, for the most part, the children stopped going. So did Janey. For awhile Phil continued to attend church alone but in about 1968 he stopped attending Mass regularly on Sunday. "I'm afraid I influenced him on that," said Janey. She speculated that Phil came to the point at which he no longer believed that if he missed Sunday Mass he was going to hell. Yet he still prayed and made visits to churches. "I know he never lost his faith in God," said Janey.[66]

Although a spiritual man, Hart did not believe that legislative decisions should be based on religious principles. He was a senator who happened to be Catholic, not a Catholic senator. In 1965 he was the first Catholic to sign as Senate co-sponsor of a bill to provide research into population control problems and to disseminate birth control information in the United States and abroad. "I do not think that I as a Catholic, should impose my moral judgments in this area on others," he said. However, he insisted that government programs be free of even the hint of coercion or pressure. "I am thinking particularly of welfare cases," he said, "where recipients might be subtly, or not so subtly, pressured into action that might violate their own sense of moral responsibility."[67]

Hart remained proud of his service in the 4th Infantry Division, and he delighted in reunions with his former comrades. "Any event that occurred that involved the 4th Infantry Division," said Ferris, "he was going to be there." Occasionally, a veteran of the 4th would visit his Senate office and Hart would grab and hug him. "The joy he had at seeing these people was more than with any other human being," Ferris observed. "There was a strength of feeling that was impressive."

On 6 June 1969, Hart stood on Utah Beach in Normandy, France, where exactly twenty-five years earlier he and hundreds of thousands of Allied troops had poured ashore on D-Day. The beach looked beautiful. The sea was calm. The tide was out and three or four happy French kids were swimming. The scene had looked much different twenty-five years earlier. As he looked out on the channel water and recalled the formidable German defenses, he said to a former army colleague, "To this day I do not understand how we accomplished what we did."

Hart was at Utah Beach to celebrate the twenty-fifth anniversary of the invasion of Europe. He had been asked to deliver the main address at the dedication ceremonies of the new memorial monument to the 4th Infantry Division. "Coming here gives all of us an awareness of the decades of hope, vision and hardship that go into building a country," Hart told the gathering. "This day—the visit to yesterday—helps man endure by lifting his heart, by reminding him of the courage, honor, compassion, hope, pride, pity and sacrifice which has been the glory of his past. One who takes pride in and counsel from his past is more likely to make sound decisions about his future. . . . The story of honest patriotism is the story of men who served. Even under the worst of circumstances, man can and will prevail."[68]

Wealth allowed Hart the opportunity for expensive, wide-ranging leisure activities but his taste in leisure was mostly simple. His main hobby was reading for pleasure (mostly nonfiction); he devoured newspapers. He did not smoke and seldom drank, except for an occasional rum and ginger beer.

He loved railroads. When he became discouraged with the slow pace of legislation or harried by the frenzied atmosphere of the Senate, he quietly slipped out of his office and walked two blocks to Union Station. There, unrecognized by travelers, he would sip a cup of coffee, read a newspaper, and watch the trains pull in. "I was an old train hound," Phil wrote his son James, explaining the various trains he had taken in his youth. "Nothing like a locomotive steaming at the platform on a dark, snowy night. It was before ecology hung us up."[69]

Hart had his share of father-son games of catch and touch football, and with the children watched football and baseball on television. He enjoyed long conversations with his family and close friends. The dearest memories for the children were summers on Mackinac Island where the Harts maintained a summer residence. It was difficult for Phil to get there, but during his infrequent visits he would stroll downtown, shop at local stores, watch the bicycles speed by, and gossip with the islanders. Janey sailed on a friend's boat in the Caribbean. "I'd get lonesome for him," she recalled. She would phone Phil's secretary, arrange his schedule and buy an airplane ticket so he could join her on the sailboat.[70]

In the early 1960s, Janey bought a thirty-five-acre farm near Warrenton, Virginia. She renovated the two-story frame home, but in March 1967, it was totally destroyed by fire. The following August, Janey purchased a one-third interest in the ultra-plush Glade Valley Farm, near Frederick, Maryland. With four hundred acres, a lovely eighteenth-century farmhouse, five barns, and an indoor training track, Glade Valley was one of Maryland's outstanding horse-breeding farms. In the breeding season the farm had 250 mares and five stallions. Phil knew little about horses but enjoyed watching the mares and foals running around and playing. There he relaxed. On a cool, bright autumn day in 1969, he showed a reporter the farm. Looking out on the rolling hills, the horses grazing, and the sunlit pond in front of the house, he said, "Sometimes when I'm out here I really think I wouldn't mind losing an election, just so I could retire to this."[71]

But Hart had decided to run for reelection one more time.

NOTES

1. *Washington Post*, 19 March 1971; Saul Friedman, telephone interview, 17 May 1988; Janey Hart, interview, Washington, D.C., 1 and 2 April 1989; Michael Pertschuk, telephone interview, 13 April 1988; Robert Pisor, telephone interview, 21 March 1989; William Welsh, telephone interview, 23 April 1988; Burton Wides, interview, Washington, D.C., 29 March 1988.
2. Janey Hart, interview, Washington, D.C., 1 and 2 April 1989; Barbara Kincaid, telephone interview, 23 May 1988; Edmund Muskie, telephone interview, 13 July 1988; Florence Roth, interview, Washington, D.C., 29 March 1988; Jerald terHorst, telephone interview, 28 March 1989; Harrison Wellford, telephone interview, 3 May 1988; Burton Wides, interview, Washington, D.C., 29 March 1988.
3. Muriel Ferris, interview, McLean, Virginia, 26 March 1988; Barbara Kincaid, telephone interview, 23 May 1988; Donald Tucker, telephone interview, 11 April 1989; Burton Wides, interview, Washington, D.C., 29 March 1988.
4. Barbara Kincaid, telephone interview, 23 May 1988.
5. Richard Ryan, telephone interview, 19 May 1988; Jerald terHorst, telephone interview, 28 March 1989.

6. William Welsh, telephone interview, 23 April 1988.

7. Paul Douglas, *In the Fullness of Time* (New York: Harcourt Brace Jovanovich, Inc., 1971), 236; Patricia Bario, interview, Washington, D.C., 28 March 1988; Janey Hart, interview, Washington, D.C., 1 and 2 April 1989; Joseph Rauh, interview, Washington, D.C., 29 March 1988; Burton Wides, interview, Washington, D.C., 29 March 1988.

8. Memorandum, John Cornman, 4 June 1975, Box 441, Hart Papers, Bentley Library; clipping, Box 551, Hart Papers, Bentley Library; *Flint Journal*, 8 June 1975; Klein, "Saint," 35, 37; Vreeland, *Philip A. Hart*, 16; John Cornman, interview, Washington, D.C., 26 March 1988; Jerry Kabel, telephone interview, 24 February 1988; Lynn Sutcliffe, telephone interview, 22 April 1988; Harrison Wellford, telephone interview, 3 May 1988; Sidney Woolner, telephone interview, 12 and 14 January and 5 July 1988.

9. Clipping, Box 551, Hart Papers, Bentley Library; Patricia Bario, interview, Washington, D.C., 28 March 1988; Muriel Ferris, interview, McLean, Virginia, 26 March 1988; Alfred Fitt, telephone interview, 28 April 1989; Leila McKnight, interview, Washington, D.C., 25 March 1988; Florence Roth, interview, Washington, D.C., 29 March 1988; Sidney Woolner, telephone interview, 12 and 14 January and 5 July 1988.

10. *Washington Post*, 2 August 1964; Ann Bronfman, interview, Washington, D.C., 2 April 1989; John Cornman, interview, Washington, D.C., 26 March 1988; Walter Hart, telephone interview, 30 April 1988; Burton Wides, interview, Washington, D.C., 29 March 1988.

11. *New York Times*, 6 June 1975; William Welsh, telephone interview, 23 April 1988; Burton Wides, interview, Washington, D.C., 29 March 1988.

12. John Cornman, interview, Washington, D.C., 26 March 1988; William Welsh, telephone interview, 23 April 1988.

13. Burton Wides to Edward Kennedy, n.d., unprocessed Burt Wides Papers, Washington, D.C.; *Boston Globe*, 22 May 1987; Conkin, *Lyndon Baines Johnson*, 234; Jerry Kabel, telephone interview, 24 February 1988; Florence Roth, interview, Washington, D.C., 29 March 1988.

14. *Detroit Free Press*, 9 March 1969; *Detroit News*, 27 December 1976; *Washington Post*, 3 May 1970; Jerry Kabel, telephone interview, 24 February 1988; Sidney Woolner, telephone interview, 12, 14 January and 5 July 1988.

15. Vreeland, *Philip A. Hart*, 9; John Cornman, interview, Washington, D.C., 26 March 1988.

16. *Washington Post*, 5 November 1982; Carolyn Burns, telephone interview, 9 May 1989; Eugene McCarthy, telephone interview, 7 June 1988; William Simpson, telephone interview, 15 March 1989; Harrison Wellford, telephone interview, 3 May 1988.

17. *Bay City Times*, 30 October 1964.

18. Burt Wides to Edward Kennedy, n.d, Wides Papers; Jerry Cohen, interview,

Washington, D.C., 30 March 1988; John Cornman, interview, Washington,

D.C., 26 March 1988; Muriel Ferris, interview, McLean, Virginia, 26 March 1988; Alfred Fitt, telephone interview, 28 April 1989; Martin Hayden, telephone interview, 13 May 1988; Wallace Long, telephone interview, 9 May 1989; Michael Pertschuk, telephone interview, 13 April 1988.

19. *Washington Star*, 27 April 1970; Vreeland, *Philip A. Hart*, 7; Janey Hart, interview, Washington, D.C., 1 and 2 April 1989.

20. *New York Times*, 23 August 1964; John Cornman, interview, Washington, D.C., 26 March 1988; Barbara Kincaid, telephone interview, 23 May 1988.

21. William Welsh, telephone interview, 23 April 1988.

22. *New York Times*, 27 July 1962; *Memorial Addresses*, 85; William Beckham, telephone interview, 9 May 1988; Jerry Cohen, interview, Washington, D.C., 30 March 1988; John Cornman, interview, Washington, D.C., 26 March 1988; John Feild, telephone interview, 20 March 1989; Barbara Kincaid, telephone interview, 23 May 1988; Burton Wides, interview, Washington, D.C., 29 March 1988; Sidney Woolner, telephone interview, 12 and 14 January and 5 July 1988.

23. *New York Times*, 27 July 1962; John Cornman, interview, Washington, D.C., 26 March 1988.

24. *Flint Journal*, 8 June 1975; *New York Times*, 6 June 1975; Jerry Kabel, telephone interview, 24 February 1988; Barbara Kincaid, telephone interview, 23 May 1988; Florence Roth, interview, Washington, D.C., 29 March 1988.

25. *The Blade* [Toledo, Ohio], 27 June 1971; Burton Wides, interview, Washington, D.C., 29 March 1988.

26. "Dedication of the Philip A. Hart Senate Office Building," *Congressional Record*, 100th Cong., 2d sess., vol. 134, pt. 21:4; *Memorial Addresses*, 103; Klein, "Saint," 37; Saul Friedman, telephone interview, 17 May 1988; Sidney Woolner, telephone interview, 12 and 14 January and 5 July 1988.

27. Wallace Long, telephone interview, 9 May 1989; Eugene McCarthy, telephone interview, 7 June 1988; Donald Tucker, telephone interview, 11 April 1989.

28. *Washington Star*, 5 December 1976; Jerald terHorst, telephone interview, 28 March 1989; Eugene McCarthy, telephone interview, 7 June 1988; Edmund Muskie, telephone interview, 13 July 1988; Burton Wides, interview, Washington, D.C., 29 March 1988.

29. *Observer and Eccentric* [Farmington, Michigan], 12 June 1975.

30. Janey Hart, interview, Washington, D.C., 1 and 2 April 1989; Jerry Kabel, telephone interview, 24 February 1988; Neil Staebler, telephone interview, 27 August 1987; William Welsh, telephone interview, 23 April 1988.

31. Burt Wides to Edward Kennedy, n.d., Wides Papers; *New York Times*, 6 June 1975; *Oakland Press*, 12 March 1976; Klein, "Saint," 37; Harrison Wellford, telephone interview, 3 May 1988; Burton Wides, interview, Washington, D.C., 29 March 1988.

32. *Oakland Press*, 12 March 1976; *Washington Post*, 3 May 1970; *New Republic*, 15 January 1977, 6, 10, 11.

33. *Flint Journal*, 8 June 1975; Janey Hart, interview, Washington, D.C., 1 and 2 April 1989; Jerald terHorst, telephone interview, 28 March 1989.

34. Jerry Cohen, interview, Washington, D.C., 30 March 1988.

35. Donald Randall, interview, Washington, D.C., 28 March 1988.

36. Joseph Rauh, interview, Washington, D.C., 29 March 1988.

37. John Cornman, interview, Washington, D.C., 26 March 1988; Jerry Kabel, telephone interview, 24 February 1988

38. John Cornman, interview, Washington, D.C., 26 March 1988.

39. Javits, *Javits*, 262; Klein, "Saint," 37; Edmund Muskie, telephone interview, 13 July 1988.

40. *Observer and Eccentric*, 2 March 1975; Ray Courage, telephone interview, 13 May 1988; John Feild, telephone interview, 20 March 1989; Saul Friedman, telephone interview, 17 May 1988; Jerry Kabel, telephone interview, 24 February 1988; Richard Ryan, telephone interview, 19 May 1988.

41. Burt Wides to Edward Kennedy, n.d., Wides Papers; *Detroit Free Press*, 12 August 1968, 9 March 1969; Foley, *The New Senate*, 165; John Feild, telephone interview, 20 March 1989.

42. *The Blade*, 27 June 1971; *New York Times*, 20 May 1968; *Washington Post*, 15 February 1970; John Cornman, interview, Washington, D.C., 26 March 1988; Jerry Kabel, telephone interview, 24 February 1988.

43. Michael Mansfield to Philip Hart, 10 May 1971, Box 551, Hart Papers, Bentley Library.

44. Edmund Muskie, telephone interview, 13 July 1988; William Welsh, telephone interview, 23 April 1988.

45. *Detroit Free Press*, 9 March 1969; *Washington Post*, 14 July 1968; "Edward Kennedy," *Current Biography Yearbook, 1978*, ed. Charles Moritz (New York: The H. W. Wilson Company, 1978), 225-29; Saul Friedman, telephone interview, 17 May 1988; Janey Hart, interview, Washington, D.C., 1 and 2 April 1989; Florence Roth, interview, Washington, D.C., 29 March 1988; confidential interview.

46. *New York Times*, 20 February 1986; *Washington Star*, 29 July 1972; Klein, "Saint," 35, 37; John Cornman, interview, Washington, D.C., 26 March 1988; Eugene McCarthy, telephone interview, 7 June 1988; Howard O'Leary, interview, Washington, D.C., 28 March 1988; William Simpson, telephone interview, 15 March 1989; Thomas Williams, interview, Washington, D.C., 28 March 1988.

47. *Detroit Free Press*, 9 March 1969; *Washington Star*, 29 July 1972; Klein, "Saint," 35; *Memorial Addresses*, 91; Jerry Cohen, interview, Washington, D.C., 30 March 1988; William Simpson, telephone interview, 15 March 1989.

48. *Washington Post*, 3 March 1970; Janey Hart, interview, Washington, D.C., 1

and 2 April 1989; Sidney Woolner, telephone interview, 12 and 14 January and 5 July 1988.

49. *Detroit News*, 19 June 1970; *Washington Post*, 3 May 1970; *Washington Star*, 5 December 1976; Janey Hart, interview, Washington, D.C., 1 and 2 April 1989.

50. *Detroit News*, 19 June 1970; *New York Times*, 18 January 1970; *Washington Post*, 8 June 1969, 3 May 1970; *Washington Star*, 23 May 1967, 5 December 1976.

51. Clippings, Phil Hart File, Georgetown University Archives, Washington, D.C.; *Washington Post*, 17 October 1968, 3 May 1970.

52. *New York Times*, 17 January 1970; *Washington News*, 15 January 1970; *Washington Star*, 7 April 1970.

53. Helen Berthelot, telephone interview, 23 May 1988; Carolyn Burns, telephone interview, 9 May 1989; Mildred Jeffrey, telephone interview, 31 May 1988; Sidney Woolner, telephone interview, 12 and 14 January and 5 July 1988.

54. *Birmingham Eccentric*, 22 January 1970; *Detroit News*, 27 December 1976; *Parade*, 20 September 1970; Carolyn Burns, telephone interview, 9 May 1989.

55. *Washington Post*, 3 May 1970; *Washington Star*, 22 February 1968; Ann Anderson, interview, Washington, D.C., 26 March 1988.

56. *Washington Star*, 22 February 1968.

57. *Parade*, 20 September 1970; *Washington Post*, 3 May 1970; Cammie Conserva, telephone interview, 23 May 1988; Muriel Ferris, interview, McLean, Virginia, 26 March 1988; James Hart, telephone interview, 31 May 1989; Janey Hart, interview, Washington, D.C., 1 and 2 April 1989; Walter Hart, telephone interview, 30 April 1988.

58. William Beckham, telephone interview, 9 May 1988; Cammie Conserva, telephone interview, 23 May 1988; Janey Hart, interview, Washington, D.C., 1 and 2 April 1989; Walter Hart, telephone interview, 30 April 1988.

59. Janey Hart, interview, Washington, D.C., 1 and 2 April 1989.

60. Carolyn Burns, telephone interview, 9 May 1989; James Hart, telephone interview, 31 May 1989; Janey Hart, interview, Washington, D.C., 1 and 2 April 1989; Walter Hart, telephone interview, 30 April 1988; Jerald terHorst, telephone interview, 28 March 1989.

61. Ann Bronfman, interview, Washington, D.C., 2 April 1989; Muriel Ferris, interview, McLean, Virginia, 26 March 1988; James Hart, telephone interview, 31 May 1989; Janey Hart, interview, Washington, D.C., 1 and 2 April 1989; Walter Hart, telephone interview, 30 April 1988.

62. *Parade*, 20 September 1970; Muriel Ferris, interview, McLean, Virginia, 26 March 1988.

63. Ann Anderson, interview, Washington, D.C., 26 March 1988; Janey Hart, interview, Washington, D.C., 1 and 2 April 1989.

64. Philip Hart to James Hart, 15 July 1968; unprocessed James Hart Papers, Pasadena, California; Philip Hart to James Hart, 16 August 1968, unprocessed James Hart Papers; James Hart, telephone interview, 31 May 1989.
65. James Hart to author, 20 December 1989, James Brown to Philip Hart, 23 October 1973, James Hart Papers; *Detroit News*, 2 July 1971; *The State Journal*, 1 July 1971; James Hart, telephone interview, 31 May 1989; Walter Hart, telephone interview, 30 April 1988.
66. Philip Hart to James Hart, 18 March 1966, James Hart Papers; *Memorial Addresses*, 63; *Detroit Free Press*, 29 December 1976; Ann Anderson, interview, Washington, D.C., 26 March 1988; Carolyn Burns, telephone interview, 9 May 1989; James Hart, telephone interview, 31 May 1989; Janey Hart, interview, Washington, D.C., 1 and 2 April 1989; Walter Hart, telephone interview, 30 April 1988; Jerry Kabel, telephone interview, 24 February 1988; Eugene McCarthy, telephone interview, 7 June 1988; Burton Wides, interview, Washington, D.C., 29 March 1988.
67. *New York Times*, 21 August 1965; Cammie Conserva, telephone interview, 23 May 1988.
68. Clipping, unprocessed Werner Kleeman Papers, Flushing, New York; "Dedication of the 4th Infantry Division Monument" [brochure], 5 and 6 June 1969, Kleeman Papers; *Harper's Magazine*, October 1969, 112; Muriel Ferris, interview, McLean, Virginia, 26 March 1988; Werner Kleeman, telephone interview, 23 May 1989.
69. Philip Hart to James Hart, 25 March 1975, James Hart Papers; *Washington Post*, 6 June 1975; John Feild, telephone interview, 20 March 1989; Janey Hart, interview, Washington, D.C., 1 and 2 April 1989.
70. *Detroit News*, 28 December 1976; *Washington Post*, 3 May 1970; Janey Hart, interview, Washington, D.C., 1 and 2 April 1989.
71. Clipping, Philip Hart File, Georgetown University Archives; *Detroit News*, 14 June 1970; *Washington Star*, 9 August 1967; Janey Hart, interview, Washington, D.C., 1 and 2 April 1989.

CHAPTER 6

Conscience of the Senate

Early in 1970, Republican strategists, while conceding Phil Hart's popularity and the favorite's role for reelection, thought there was a chance to upset him. Independent voters would be more conservative in 1970, they reasoned, and as an "extreme" liberal, Hart was vulnerable. They planned to attack him as an advocate of big government and more spending as answers to everything, as an old-fashioned New Dealer, wedded to outmoded solutions, and as a coddler of criminals. Crime in the streets would be a major issue in the campaign, and in 1968 Hart had voted against the Safe Streets and Crime Control Act. (Only three other senators had joined him in opposition.) "Both 1958 and 1964 were really big Democratic years nationally," said one GOP member of Congress, "but Hart won't have that advantage this time. He must win on his own in a year when a Republican president is mighty popular and is doing mighty well."[1]

Hart may have been vulnerable, but Michigan Republicans badly botched their attempt to field a strong opponent against him. Polls taken by Democrats and Republicans long before the race began showed that the senator had broad support, but deeper surveys indicated that much of the support was tacit, and in the face of a vigorous, youthful opponent he might be vulnerable. Political observers particularly watched two promising young opponents, Northern Michigan's Congressman Phil Ruppe and 7th District congressman, Donald Riegle. Ruppe was handsome, wealthy, and a moderate with support within the GOP, but he showed no aggressive inclination to run. Riegle was eager to take on Hart and had put together elaborate plans for a campaign. He hoped his liberal antiwar positions would wean voters away from the senator. But Riegle's brash ambition, maverick style, and liberal views and voting record antagonized many powerful Michigan Republicans.

In late February and early March 1970, three hundred Republican leaders from throughout the state met in Lansing to select a consensus candidate for the U.S. Senate nomination. On 7 March, after several ballots, they chose Lenore Romney. Actually, the designation of Mrs. Romney had been more of a compromise than a consensus, and many Republicans and voters were upset with her selection and with the selection process. Some assumed that her prominent husband had pushed her on the party.[2]

Lenore Romney was the wife of George Romney, Michigan's governor from 1962 to 1968, who was currently President Nixon's secretary of Housing and Urban Development. Mrs. Romney, sixty-one, a frail-appearing mother of four and a grandmother of fifteen, was a fervent speaker, intelligent and sincere, kind and gracious, and had enjoyed wide popularity while her husband was governor. She was an alternative to the unacceptable Riegle. With her unlimited charm, extensive financial resources, support from the party organization, and name recognition throughout Michigan, she appeared to be an attractive candidate. There was a presumption that women would support her. Friends touted her as a warm-hearted and generous woman of high ideals and good intent who was anxious to lift the moral tone of politics.

When critics pointed out that she was short on political experience, Mrs. Romney cited experience as a Cabinet wife, her campaigning for her husband, and her leadership in volunteer civic organizations such as the YMCA and the National Conference of Christians and Jews. "Never before has the voice and understanding of women been so needed," proclaimed her campaign slogan. She proudly told audiences that she was the only woman running for the Senate in 1970, and that she hoped to join the only other woman in the Senate, Margaret Chase Smith, Maine's Republican.[3]

Whatever advantages Mrs. Romney seemed to possess were dashed, however, when State Senator Robert Huber (R.-Troy), an aggressive, conservative, maverick Republican, ignored the party's consensus designation and challenged her in the 4 August Republican primary. When Huber won 48.5 percent of the vote to Mrs. Romney's 51.5 percent, her surprisingly dismal showing crippled her candidacy.

Hart was relieved that he did not have to run against either Ruppe or Riegle. "I'm glad the Republicans didn't nominate one of [those] smart young Republican congressmen to run against me," he admitted late in the campaign. He knew, and said privately, that in running for the U.S. Senate Mrs. Romney was "out of her league." By the end of the campaign almost all political observers agreed with Hart's assessment. For, despite all of her attributes, Mrs. Romney had serious limitations as a candidate, most notably her inexperience in a high-profile political campaign.[4]

She tried to correct her embarrassing misstatements, but her explanations never caught up with her original remarks. She took a strong stand against civil disobedience, and then under sharp questioning found herself in the untenable position of opposing civil disobedience at all times—even when conducted by the recent martyr for the civil rights cause, Dr. Martin Luther King. Her position outraged many blacks.[5]

A particularly egregious blunder occurred in mid-October. At her speech at the Henry Ford Community College in Dearborn, a student asked if she thought criminal charges recently filed against the promoter of a Goose Lake rock music festival were fair. (Some believed that the promoter was prosecuted unfairly because others, over whom he had no control, had sold drugs at his music festival.) "Yes, he broke the law," responded Mrs. Romney. The student then countered with a rhetorical question: "What if deans were selling or allowing drugs to be sold on campus?" (The student was trying awkwardly to draw a parallel by asking if she believed deans should be prosecuted if drugs were sold on a campus.) Mrs. Romney totally misunderstood the student's question.

That evening she spoke before the Business and Professional Women's Club of Birmingham and recklessly referred to the three deans who were trafficking in narcotics at a nearby college. "We're going to follow through on this," she said, "but we couldn't at the time. It was a large assembly." She said the problem was haunting her. Subsequently, when reporters identified the college, its president, James McCann, angrily countered that "She'd better be sure of her facts. This is a very, very serious charge. I'm not about to buy any of her charges." Because Mrs. Romney had been completely wrong about her facts, she had to apologize the following day.[6]

Mrs. Romney was also ill-served by her amateurish campaign staff who confused motion with progress. She visited conservative Berrien County, which had only a small number of voters, three times in a week near the end of the campaign. "What she hoped to win there was difficult to assess," said a reporter.

In four face-to-face debates, and on other occasions during the campaign, Hart easily parried Mrs. Romney's charges. When she accused him of being a "Johnny-come-lately" in opposing the Vietnam War, he replied, "All I can say is that George Romney and Phil Hart changed their minds on the war at about the same time." In a debate she insisted Hart was wrong to change positions on defense spending, the Vietnam War, the extension of the draft and anticrime legislation. But the senator won the loudest applause of the night from the audience when he responded, "You are suggesting we find men and women who are infallible. I wish that my shift on Vietnam had been earlier." In another debate she charged that the Democratic party perpetuated the worst of the seniority system in Congress and cited important committee chairmen who supported the Vietnam War and retarded integration. In his soft sell response Hart indicated that as a result of the seniority system he was chairman of the Senate Antitrust and Monopoly Subcommittee, and he promised to fight for better antitrust legislation to help small business compete. When she accused him of being soft on crime because he voted against the Safe Streets and Crime Control Act of 1968, he countered that he had, indeed, voted against the measure because amendments loosened restrictions against wiretapping, bugging, and the use of tainted confessions, all of which he considered dangerous and unconstitutional.[7]

Hart refused to attack Mrs. Romney. "My hunch is whatever I say on Mrs. Romney will be interpreted as harsh political criticism, so I shan't say anything." He was genteel and gallant whenever they debated. After Mrs. Romney and Senator Hart debated on Lou Gordon's television program, and Gordon had handled her roughly, Hart told Gordon. "Lou, I think you were a little unfair to Lenore."

During their debate on foreign policy Hart refused to go on the offensive even when Mrs. Romney slipped badly. When she was asked what the U.S. policy should be toward South Africa, she treated the repressive, white-dominated nation as if it were just another emerging African state. Like other "preferential nations," she replied, South Africa should be favored in U.S. trade agreements. "It is important they realize we are interested in their integrity as a nation." There were audible gasps and laughter from the audience. Flustered by her comments, Hart tried to rescue her. "I think Mrs. Romney simply didn't understand the question," he said when it was his turn to address the issue. Commenting on the evening's debate, a political writer for the *Detroit Free Press* thought "Hart proved he will not take on Mrs. Romney even when her guard is down and she is open to attack."[8]

"Phil Hart never has, never will, run against anybody," George Googasian, the senator's campaign chairman, said stoutly during the campaign. "He runs on issues." Hart ran a confident, low-profile campaign, addressing many issues but steering away from controversy. Asked privately after the election if he thought he had a chance of losing, he replied, "No." Why, then, did he work so hard in the campaign? Because, he said, it was his only chance, every six years, to get the undivided attention of the citizens of Michigan. "I can tell them what I've done and what I want to do. I really don't campaign against anybody, or for myself. I really campaign on the programs that I'm in favor of," he said. "It is a great chance to get in touch with [the voters]."[9]

His standard campaign presentation emphasized the need to reorder the nation's priorities. One reason he hoped to stay in the Senate was that "I believe the 1970s have an excellent chance of going into the history books as the decade when this country really reshuffled its priorities":

> Most of our federal money is spent to protect our liberty from foreign threat, but more and more we are coming to realize that the forces that are really eroding our freedom are right here at home.
>
> Nearly half of all Americans are afraid to walk the streets at night—certainly their liberties are diminished.
>
> Every time another lake or stream gets polluted, we have lost some freedom of choice.
>
> And if a child's mind is dulled forever because he was undernourished in the first years of his life, then his options become very limited.

He hoped to see the United States "get out of Indochina very quickly," and added, "I want to see the $20 billion a year spent to cure our domestic ills. I would be a fraud if I pretended I could do that alone, so it is not a campaign promise, but it is what I think our goals should be."

Hart had fundamentally changed his position on the Vietnam War. He favored a specific public schedule for troop withdrawal. The Paris peace talks would be advanced if the South Vietnamese were told they would be on their own as of a specific date.[10]

Mrs. Romney kept trying to portray Hart as a dangerous advocate of civil disobedience who encouraged a disrespect for law. After considerable rethinking he had, indeed, modified his views on the issue. During the civil rights movement and the Vietnam war, civil disobedience became a standard form of protest. Fight unjust laws by breaking them; others, like Mrs. Romney, said the method would lead to anarchy. Hart said:

> I think, in this regard, that we are all the better for Dr. Martin Luther King's civil disobedience. We're talking about something that has haunted man ever since he assumed that he had an obligation to his conscience.
>
> This question has divided theologians as well as politicians and there is no tougher question. But I think . . . that there would be occasions when, unless you want to turn the formation of your conscience over to the State, you've got to take this position.
>
> There are some who [break the law] very casually with no purpose of social reform at all. They are either nihilists who want to destroy us or they are people who really don't think.
>
> But . . . isn't it going quite a ways to suggest that an individual surrender his conscience totally?. . . . What do you do if you, in good conscience, feel a law is wrong? At Nuremberg we said people should disobey laws that they feel are immoral. I think any country can enact a law that is immoral.[11]

Hart continued to win over audiences who might be expected to be hostile to his message. In early August he spoke in Iron Mountain at a "Faith in Our Country" rally. Before a large, shirt-sleeve crowd gathered to celebrate patriotism and listen to martial music, he praised the younger generation, "even these children of ours who have different hair styles than ours." The applause was warm and sustained from an audience who only moments earlier had clapped for a local politician whose speech denounced student troublemakers. "Hart's style is sincere and reassuring, as comfortable as the old-school blue blazer he wears," observed a reporter who covered the event. "It is a rational, quiet-spoken style that lets him get away with defending long-hairs to a crowd of crewcuts."[12]

However, one highly controversial issue placed Hart in an awkward position. On 28 February 1970, following a campaign fund-raising dinner in Royal Oak, the senator told reporters: "I would be in favor of, and fully support, amnesty for our Americans who are presently in Canada because of Vietnam." Initially, his comment in Royal Oak received little publicity. But six months later, in August 1970, Hart joined with Democrats Sander Levin, the party's nominee for governor, and Attorney General Frank Kelley in disavowing a controversial platform plank adopted at the Democrats' state convention in Grand Rapids that urged "a general amnesty for all opponents" of the Vietnam War.

Less than half of the 3,000 delegates were present on the convention floor when the motion was adopted. Many, including most party leaders, were attending caucuses and were shocked to learn that the controversial amnesty resolution had passed on the floor. "The panic in the Democratic headquarters," observed a political reporter, "was the realization that the party might have given the Republicans a hammer to defeat them with in November."

The joint statement signed by Hart, Levin, and Kelley declared: "We disagree with the amnesty resolution. Those who employ civil disobedience to protest a law or war must stand ready to accept whatever punishment is provided by the legal code. Moreover, condoning an illegal act on the part of some may encourage others to follow suit in a mistaken belief that eventual exoneration is a certainty."

Despite Hart's signature on the joint statement, the document did not accurately reflect his views. He was more sympathetic to amnesty than the statement indicated and was rethinking his views on civil disobedience. Like other Democratic candidates, however, he was worried that Republicans would use the issue of blanket amnesty to hammer Democrats in the campaign.

When asked about the apparent contradiction between his February and August statements on amnesty, through a spokesman in his Washington office the senator denied there was any contradiction. There might be an appearance of inconsistency, Hart said, "although I am satisfied there is not." In February in Royal Oak, he said, he was responding to a question about amnesty "after the conflict was ended." He thought the party resolution at Grand Rapids was premature; it would be "irresponsible for a public official to condone unlawful acts in advance." Moreover, he added, the party resolution endorsed general amnesty. "This, presumably, would include bomb throwers and those guilty of other violent acts. Such a sweeping amnesty I find unacceptable."

Hart found himself in the uncomfortable position of being on both sides of the controversial issue. One newspaper charged him with "making a subtle distinction which will escape most people." Hart's statement in February, said the newspaper, "did have the effect of condoning draft evasion in advance by supporting amnesty. What difference does it make whether the amnesty was to be granted in the present or following the war?"[13]

Despite his explanations Hart was caught in a crossfire between Democratic party leftists and Michigan Republicans. At a news conference, Al Fishman, co-chairman of the dissident New Democratic Coalition (NDC) that supported the amnesty resolution criticized the party's three leading Democrats for "chickening out on the issues." From the other perspective, Mrs. Romney accused Hart of not repudiating draft dodging or lawbreaking. "This nation can ill afford a leader who . . . encourages young men to sit out the draft until some president grants amnesty."

Later, in a debate with Mrs. Romney, Hart tried to clarify his position. He did not favor amnesty for draft dodgers while the Vietnam War was still going on. But, he said, he thought presidential amnesty should be granted selectively after the war ended. When Mrs. Romney criticized this position, he simply asked, "Are you opposed to amnesty forever?"[14]

In mid-September, controversial vice president Spiro Agnew barnstormed through Michigan for ten hours. As he had done to other Democrats, Agnew accused Hart of being a "radical liberal," part of "a little band of unwilling men who are holding back the will of the people." Agnew tried to breathe new life into the issue of amnesty, the one issue that seemed to be effective for Mrs. Romney. "Rest assured, my friends," said Agnew, "that there will be no amnesty for draft dodgers." Asked to comment on Agnew's charges, the senator said with classic understatement, "Campaigns are periods when shrillness sometimes substitutes for thoughtfulness." But Hart and other Democrats felt compelled to denounce left-wing demonstrators who tried to shout down Agnew and Mrs. Romney during their appearance in Saginaw. The young demonstrators chanted "Sieg Heil" at Agnew and heaped obscenities on Mrs. Romney. "The attempt to deprive Mrs. Romney and Vice President Agnew of the right to speak is an insult to every citizen who believes in democracy," Hart declared. "Political campaigns, by their nature, are times of controversy and debate. Any attempt to stifle that debate is not only an unforgivable affront to good manners but also a serious threat to a system that depends so heavily on a free exchange of ideas."[15]

Besides winning reelection, Hart had an important secondary goal during the campaign. He wanted to conduct a model election campaign that would serve as an example for securing federal election reforms, particularly public financing for the election of the president and members of Congress. Like many politicians, the senator detested the need to attend fund-raising functions to solicit campaign contributions from wealthy benefactors. "He just thought that was a form of prostitution," said Janey Hart. "He enjoyed meeting the people, [and] he didn't compromise his positions when he spoke with them, but he just thought it was a terrible thing a candidate had to do."

For the first time Hart used specialized campaign services, and Charles Guggenheim of Washington produced television commercials for him. During the campaign the senator promoted legislation that he had co-sponsored that would impose a ceiling on political campaign spending for television and radio advertising. His legislation would have limited candidates to a maximum of seven cents for each vote cast in the previous state election; it applied to congressmen, senators and governors. "Spending is getting out of hand," he said; the candidate felt like a "semijerk, running around putting contributors against the wall." After President Nixon vetoed the bill, Hart unsuccessfully sought to override the veto. "The present system favors those with great wealth and those who are willing to pass the hat everywhere and anywhere," he said in response to Nixon's veto. Nonetheless, Hart and Mrs. Romney agreed to limit their own campaign expenses, both setting the limit for advertising costs at $170,755, the same amount that would have been in effect had the campaign financing bill not been vetoed.[16]

Hart and his campaign staff invited a reporter from the *New York Times* to trace all of the money raised and expended in the Hart campaign from its source to its destination, "a trail," said the reporter, that "politicians traditionally tend to cloak in the deepest obscurity." For nearly two weeks the reporter examined bank accounts, ledgers, files, expense vouchers, receipt records and correspondence; he interviewed money managers and questioned outsiders.

Hart wanted Carolyn Burns, his finance secretary, to be exceptionally scrupulous when she accepted money. "He was greatly concerned that he not accept funds from people who [had] shoddy reputations or could be an embarrassment," said Sidney Woolner. When a $1,000 check came in from a Detroiter known to be involved with the Mafia, there was concern within the Hart campaign about how to handle the check. The man's name would be immediately recognized if it appeared on any list of contributors. Because of lax campaign finance rules, an unscrupulous politician could have laundered the money, like the conspirators in the Watergate scandal later would do. The *New York Times* story considered the options: "There were several well-tested solutions to the problem. The funds could have been 'scrubbed' by having the check rewritten to the Democratic Senatorial Campaign Committee and sent to Mr. Hart in a second, seemingly unrelated transaction. Or, the gift could have been sent to the Washington-based fund-raising committee. Such groups are not required to make even token public disclosures, and most senators appear to have one. But Mr. Hart does not. The most direct way would have been to take the check and simply fail to report it. The chances of discovery are very remote." But after some thought, another solution was found. The check simply was returned to the donor. (In addition, about five other checks totaling about $4,000 were returned to persons whose character Hart's managers thought was questionable.)

The Hart campaign sought only the minimum amount of special interest money. "We were not allowed to accept any cash donations," observed Carolyn Burns. "Every donation had to have a donor's identification." The campaign exhaustively documented the source and amount of every political contribution—amounting to over one hundred pages of entries—and his entire list was filed in Michigan and opened to the public.

By election day Hart's campaign had raised funds from 4,343 extraordinarily diverse sources. Prominent and wealthy persons did not dominate the list; most contributors gave $5 or $10, and checks came in from almost every state. Hart's primary and general election campaign cost $510,250, compared to $878,820 spent by Mrs. Romney.[17]

At the end of the campaign the *Detroit News* announced that it would not endorse Mrs. Romney because her campaign had been "vague, insubstantial and contradictory," but it also refused to endorse Hart. The newspaper's editorials condemned him for his "demagogic attack on business" and for his "astonishing attitude . . . of unremitting hostility toward the automobile industry." Phil had started off well enough in the Senate, said the *News*, showing clear-headedness and independent judgment. "But as time passed, he became an echo chamber of the views of labor union chiefs and his party's liberal wing." Hart also held a "charter membership in the Society of New Isolationists.

With dismaying recklessness and lack of perception he has opposed the Safeguard antiballistic missile system, so vital to national security, and urged a course of retreat and defeat in Vietnam."

In the final debate, Lou Gordon asked Hart to comment on the *Detroit News* editorials, specifically the charge that he had displayed "unremitting hostility toward the automobile industry." The senator pleaded innocence. He recognized that Michigan's economic future depended on a vibrant auto industry, but added that he had a duty to encourage cars designed and manufactured so they could be inexpensively repaired. He also supported federal efforts toward development of antipollution devices on internal combustion engines. "Your obligation [as a senator] really is to the public," Hart explained. "It's not to the industry, not to labor."[18]

"Campaigning takes me to Michigan too many times," Phil wrote his son James on 15 September. "Glad to get off the road November 4." Although tired, Hart sought to keep his campaign staff "charged up" and was upset with supporters who assumed he had the election wrapped up. "All I've got to worry about in November," he said, "is too much of an attitude that I don't have anything to worry about in November." Nonetheless, said an observer, "Hart is so far ahead that he's like a race driver who has lapped the field. He can slow down and save his engine."

Mrs. Romney's crippled campaign allowed Hart to campaign for other Michigan Democrats, particularly Levin who was running a close race against Republican governor William Milliken. Hart also cut his campaign budget, allowing Levin to raise funds more easily. On election day, although Republicans captured twelve of nineteen House seats in Michigan and retained the governorship by a slim margin, Hart earned 67 percent of the vote, winning by 886,246 votes. Except for five small counties, he carried every county in the state, including Republican strongholds.[19]

A few weeks after the 1970 election, Hart privately informed his two key staff members, Jerry Kabel and Sidney Woolner, that he did not intend to run for reelection in 1976. "That was my last campaign," he told Woolner. "I'm not going to run again. . . . I think eighteen years is enough. It's time for someone else to have a chance." But he wanted Woolner to run the office just as though he might run again because "I know all the problems of an office where [you are a lame duck]." He told Woolner, "The one thing I would like to do would be to emphasize our constituent services. The problem for most of us in the Senate is that the little people of this world can't get access to their senators. Our time is filled up; we're busy people and we just don't hear from the people who we should be hearing from." Hart encouraged Woolner to seek another job if he so desired, but Woolner said he would stay for the duration. Hart also wanted to free himself from the inhibitions and responsibilities inherent in political life. "I'm free of politics now," he told Kabel. "I can follow my own natural inclinations instead of accommodating to all the political whims." He emphasized, though, that he wanted to become a "voice for the voiceless," a spokesman for those without money, access, or influence.[20]

After meeting with Kabel and Woolner, Hart made a rare, emotional appearance at a meeting of his entire staff. While not directly indicating to them his intention to retire in six years, he spoke as if he were about to begin his last term in the Senate. He said he wanted to make his third term more important than the previous two. Referring to a disturbing visit he had recently made during the campaign to a public housing project in Detroit, Hart said he had come to realize that too little of his efforts had been aimed at improving the life of slum dwellers. "In my twelve years in the Senate, I really haven't been able to help these people," he said. While recognizing the heavy work load already burdening staff members, he asked them to redirect their priorities and to concentrate more on the needs of the urban poor, the disadvantaged, and the voiceless.[21]

Hart candidly discussed his frustrations and third-term goals with the Michigan press corps. He was trying to chart a new course for himself, he said:

> I'm as good as the average performer, in effort and the progress I have made. But I have the feeling we respond to the problems of people who have relatively few. We are engaged in pulling Trans World Airlines out of a financial hole, when there are families that don't have enough money to eat, let alone fly.
>
> You can be busy around here doing things which in and of themselves are appropriate—holding hearings, asking the right questions, voting on legislation. But over the long haul such things are much less important for our national survival than that which we do not do.
>
> We can't even get something done around here when no one is against it. Who opposes feeding the hungry? No one. So why don't we

stop hunger? Who is opposed to stopping the deterioration of our waters and our air? No one. So why isn't something done?

Yet Hart seemed uncertain of the effect he could have. He would hold hearings on a variety of topics but did not know if they would do any good. "Hearings themselves tend to convince people that the system doesn't work. We spend weeks holding hearings, and they are filed and forgotten." When a reporter suggested that he shed his thoughtful, gentle style of speaking and take on his adversaries with a "give-'em-hell" approach, Hart rejected the idea. "That would be theatrical and phony," he said.[22]

Hart managed his affairs differently after 1970, budgeting less time for politics and for Democratic county meetings in Michigan. Staff members of the Antitrust and Monopoly Subcommittee outlined new investigations of economic concentration. Out of the Commerce Committee's environmental subcommittee, Hart proposed bringing together environmentalists and the urban poor to try to improve the quality of life in urban areas. His office staff tried to implement his wishes. "We all tried our best," said Muriel Ferris of the staff's efforts to prioritize and reorganize their work. Periodically a staff member would ask, "What's happened to our priorities?" But the normal work load was too burdensome for the staff to fully implement the senator's goals. "You'd start off the morning with the phone ringing, and it never stopped all day long," observed Ferris. Scores of lobbyists and constituents showed up at Hart's office every week, frustrating the staff's efforts to do more for the voiceless.[23]

When Hart walked onto the Senate floor on 16 November 1970, he became the first incumbent senator in thirty-one years to sport a beard. "Is that for real?" asked a fellow senator. Another colleague walked right past Hart without recognizing him. The beard was the result of a promise made during suppertime banter before the 1970 election. His son James boasted a beard and urged one on his father. "OK," said Phil. "If I win the election in November, I'll grow a beard." After defeating Lenore Romney, Hart started growing his beard at Mackinac Island. On 16 November he admitted being sensitive about his stubble and knew he would absorb good-natured kidding. Indeed, colleagues teased him that he had "gone Lincoln" on them. It was "a good experience for every man to grow a beard other than while on a hunting trip," Phil said. Shortly after Hart started growing his beard, Senator Harold

Hughes (D-Iowa), began growing one as well, but Hughes' experiment lasted only two months. "I like Senator Hughes," Hart later kidded: "which is why I refrained from calling him a copycat." Hughes had grown most of his beard while on vacation in Nova Scotia, Hart told the press. "In a sense Hughes had to leave the country and go into hiding to grow a beard, which made his a foreign beard. Mine is strictly domestic."

The beard irritated some people. "I think you look like a cross between a billy goat and the emblem of your party, a jackass," someone wrote him. "The prevailing Senate sentiment is antibeard," reported the *Washington Post* in April 1971. In the same month, still the only senator with whiskers, Hart made it official, instructing his staff to send his latest portrait—bristly beard and all—when constituents requested his picture. His wire-trimmed glasses, high forehead, graying hair, together with his beard, gave him a professorial look.[24]

Shortly into his third term Hart initiated scores of proposals aimed at improving conditions for the poor. As chair of the Senate Select Subcommittee on Nutrition, he held hearings in Michigan in 1971 on why Michigan, one of the wealthiest states in the nation, was feeding less than half of the poor children who could qualify for school lunches. In the same year he and Senator Jacob Javits pressed for $310 million to provide 641,000 ten-week summer jobs for poor youths. With a reporter in 1971 he talked about spending a morning in the Commerce Committee listening to the financial complaints from airline presidents. He understood that airlines had problems, but what about the "guy who doesn't even have enough money to get to the airport?" Or the malnourished child? Or the child who was born with brain damage because his mother lacked an adequate diet? He was pessimistic that the Senate would ever focus on the "men and women who have the great problems." Instead, those "who have the means to get here, the status to get in, will be listened to, and it probably always will be that way. Only rarely is pressure heard from those who are faceless and voiceless."[25]

Hart still refused to temporize on racial issues, whether they involved equal opportunity, voting, civil rights, or busing. He was shaken by the Kerner Commission report of increasing racial polarization and was disturbed that the commission's findings had not galvanized government to implement corrective action. His controversial stand on busing, however, was mostly a lonely vigil in Michigan.

In 1971, after a federal judge ruled that it might be necessary to bus school children across district lines to end many years of segregation in Detroit's schools, the decision sparked almost hysterical reaction in Detroit's suburbs where many whites had fled to remove themselves and their children from deteriorating schools and increasing racial tensions in Detroit.

Worried about reelection, almost all the liberal politicians in Michigan scurried for cover. "Everybody ran for the hills," was the laconic comment of a Detroit politician. Sobered by the intense public reaction to busing, they quickly became converts to the antibusing cause. (In 1970, four school board members in Detroit who wrote a busing plan for integration had been recalled from office in an exceptionally successful recall campaign.)[26]

Of all the liberal politicians in Michigan, only Hart stood firm in his hope for brotherhood and integration. Judges should be free to use all necessary remedies to ensure the constitutional promise of equality, he said. Consequently, Michigan lawmakers who were once friends not only stayed away from busing but temporarily stayed away from the senator because he supported busing. Abusive and obscene phone threats condemning Hart's position poured into Democratic party offices in Detroit. Lou Gordon had dinner with Hart one evening and told him that his support of cross-district busing was wrong in principle and would cost him his Senate seat. "Lou," Phil replied, "something must be done for these black youngsters—they must get a decent education or they will have no chance in life."

On 6 October 1971, in the suburb of Roseville, two miles north of the Detroit city line, citizens formed the Roseville Action Group (RAG) to protest busing. At the meeting someone suggested that an example be made of Senator Hart, and a motion for a recall passed unanimously. A year earlier, Roseville had voted overwhelmingly for Hart's reelection, but on 19 October 1971, the Roseville-inspired state recall movement commenced. Under Michigan law, in a ninety-day period, the recall movement had to collect 664,041 valid signatures (one-quarter of all the votes cast for all candidates for governor in the previous election). A month later, two of RAG's leaders, Michael T. Broadbridge and Mrs. Linda Schmidt, claimed to have 25,000 signatures. "I believe Phil Hart was a very good man," said Mrs. Schmidt. "I don't know what made him decide to stop representing what most of the people believe in."[27]

"Of course I'm concerned," said Hart of the recall. "If you like the Senate—and I do—then you don't like to see those you work for so terribly upset." But, he added, he would not change his position: "Whenever there was a finding of deliberate school segregation in the South, I supported busing it that was the only way to correct it. If I were to change my position now that the issue has come home, Michigan would have a fraud for a senior senator."

Complaints from constituents, though, caused Hart to agonize privately over the issue. "He was not a happy man about busing," said Janey Hart. He felt guilty that his own children were in private schools. On a plane trip he sat near some constituents who angrily confronted him about their objections to busing. "Your kids haven't had to go into a john in a school where they might be physically threatened!" one constituent charged. Such confrontations did not worry Phil politically, but led him to question the morality of his own position. Was he morally right?

Because he still judged his position to be morally right, he persevered. In a Senate speech on 8 November 1971, he told his Senate colleagues that one was not a bigot to want his children educated at a nearby school or to be reluctant to have his child bused to a school where the education was the same or worse as the one within walking distance. Nor was it inappropriate to voice concern about possible tensions at the new school.

Having said that, he continued, the overriding issue was that the courts had outlawed racial segregation in the schools, and immediate relief from an unconstitutional situation could be achieved by busing. "Busing was found in that case to be the only reasonable remedy available."

"And if we outlaw the bus as a tool, what then?" Hart added. "Do we not signal that we are content with enforced segregation and that we are not about to fix it? Do we not signal that we are content with that most dangerous of conditions—a continued splitting of black and white?

"Whatever tensions and inconveniences we may feel in the desegregation process now, they will be nothing to the tensions we will endure twenty years from now if we do little or nothing in the meantime. One does not really have to be a prophet to see what will happen to us if black children grow up exposed only to one set of values and white children grow up exposed only to a totally different set."[28]

In the fall of 1971, Hart spoke in Clarksdale, Mississippi, at a get-out-the-vote rally to build black voting power in the state. He told his Mississippi audience:

> The North is going to have to take a new look at itself as a result of what men of good will—black and white—have done in the South. . . . For years—why blink it?—the North has been looking down its nose and asking, "You southerners down there, why don't you improve yourself and be good like us?" And now we are approaching the uncomfortable position where white and black southerners can look northward with the words, "We're doing fairly well. Why don't you try improving at the same rate?"

He edged close to the busing issue in Michigan when he said, "Segregation in the North has been tougher to get at because it was never written into the laws of our states." But ghettos were not accidents. They were perpetuated because of zoning laws and mortgage policies and a host of decisions by political and financial leaders. "All-black schools in the North are no accident," he said. "They happen because housing patterns are dictated and, sometimes, because school boundaries are deliberately drawn to create them. And now is past the time that the North takes its hands away from its eyes and realizes what is going on."[29]

Hart received some support from the Michigan media for his firm stand. The *Flint Journal* said the recall was being used as a "bludgeon" against the senator who had "never arrived at a position casually and who cannot be frightened by political threats into shifting gears. We are convinced that Hart would much prefer recall to knowingly taking a course he believes detrimental to the nation and his constituents." The *Journal* continued, "Over the years he has proved himself one of the most thoughtful, consistent members of the Senate—one who does not play political games with important issues, one not afraid of the unpopular stand, one who does not permit the uncertain winds of public opinion to sway him from what he determines to be the right course."

Lloyd Schwartz, reporter for the *Pontiac Press,* agreed, arguing that the recall campaign would have no effect on Hart's position: "The senator is not planning to yield on something as fundamental as integration, equal opportunity, and human dignity, no matter how shrill the din back home in Michigan, or how mindless and mean the personal attacks on him by those who suggest he be run out of Washington for early retirement."

The recall movement eventually fizzled out, and subsequently Hart led a Senate filibuster that killed antibusing legislation. The busing controversy had exhausted Hart. When Senator Edward Kennedy sought Hart's advice about a speech on busing Kennedy was scheduled to deliver in Boston, Hart advised, "Don't go."[30]

Hart continued to fight for consumer legislation. A leading congressional advocate of auto insurance reform, in February 1971 he introduced a package of five bills aimed at changing the insurance system and lowering the costs. The most important measure sought to establish a no-fault insurance system covering personal injury and property damage. His goal was to eliminate the tort liability system under which the person who caused an accident, or his insurance company, paid for the damages inflicted on others. Hart argued that insurance claims should be paid without considering who caused the accident; finding fault should be a separate concern, handled by the police and the courts, not insurance companies. The problem under the tort system was that it often took years of expensive legal wrangling in the courts to determine the guilty party. His no-fault insurance plan passed the Senate, but not the House; however, a number of states did adopt some form of no-fault insurance.[31]

Hart maintained his idealistic position on gun control, going further than most gun opponents. Senator Birch Bayh (D-Ind.) proposed to eliminate Saturday Night Specials, and others called for the licensing and registration of all firearms. Hart supported those measures, but pushed for more. "I have concluded," he said in 1972, "that privately owned handguns—of any type—simply have no place in today's society." His legislation would prohibit the possession of handguns by anyone except the military, the police, and approved security guards. Limited exceptions would be made for licensed target-pistol clubs and for inoperable collectors' items. For all practical purposes, under Hart's legislation, private citizens would have to be content with owning shotguns and rifles. "It is true that people kill people but I would have to add that handguns make the job a great deal easier—and possibly more tempting," said Hart. "And does not government have some responsibility to make it as difficult as possible for people to kill people?" However, his legislation won only a few votes in the Senate.[32]

On 28 July 1972, Democratic senators caucused to choose the president pro tem of the Senate, a post made vacant by the recent death of

Senator Allen Ellender of Louisiana. Traditionally, the post went to the senator with the most seniority in the majority party, in this case the Democrats. James Eastland had the most seniority and was clearly in line for the job. The post was largely ceremonial, except that its holder was third in line of succession to the presidency, ranking behind the vice-president and the Speaker of the House.

Every Democratic senator voted for Eastland—except Hart. Breaking with the tradition of the sacrosanct Senate, Hart opposed the elevation of a senior senator and friend to a largely ceremonial position. Although it was a remote possibility, Hart worried that Eastland might someday become president. In a gentle voice that sounded like thunderclaps in the hushed Senate caucus room, Hart explained his lone dissenting vote. Eastland had treated him kindly and affectionately, Hart told his colleagues. If it were only the ceremonial role for which Eastland was being considered, he would concur. "But there is . . . a second element involved in our decision this morning, and that is succession to the presidency of the United States. I would ask that you consider your own requirements with respect to the qualifications for this aspect of the office. For this I believe Jim Eastland is not qualified—the governance of our country." Therefore Hart asked to be recorded as voting no on the nomination. "I believe Jim Eastland would be an excellent president pro tem but an outrageous president."

Before the speech Hart had informed Eastland of his intentions. "Eastland's reaction was that he understood completely Hart's position and accepted it," said William Simpson. After the caucus broke up, a fellow senator told a reporter that Hart's solitary speech had been the "most courageous I ever heard." When Hart returned to his office, other senators phoned him to say he had been "absolutely right" and had been "most impressive." Later Hart expressed some disillusionment with the way his Senate colleagues had responded to his speech. "They all came over and congratulated me on my statement," he said. But when Phil asked them why they did not publicly concur, they told him it was too risky.[33]

Hart remained frustrated with the slow progress of antitrust. "What are we really doing?" he asked his staff director, Howard O'Leary. "What are we accomplishing? Will this do something for minority people and the poor?" O'Leary would counter that antitrust enforcement translated into lower prices, which enhanced the buying power of the poor proportionately more than others. "It does have an effect," O'Leary argued.

"It's indirect, but it's there." Hart would laugh and say, "OK. You tell me!"

In 1972 Hart devised a dramatic strategy to draw more attention to the issue of antitrust. In July he collected the long-awaited dividend from eight years of hearings on economic concentration when he introduced the Industrial Reorganization Act (IRA), a bill designed to give the economic system a good shaking.

Under Hart's legislation, "monopoly power" would legally exist if any of three things occurred: (1) a corporation's average rate of return on net worth after taxes topped 15 percent over a period of five consecutive years out of the previous seven; (2) there had been no substantial price competition among two or more corporations for three years out of the most recent five years; or (3) 50 percent of the business involved was controlled by four companies or fewer.[34]

An industrial reorganization commission would be established for fifteen years to prosecute companies that fit the definition of monopoly, to study other industries, and to propose reorganization programs. Hart's legislation singled out seven industrial families for automatic study: chemicals and drugs, electrical machinery and equipment, electronic computing and communication equipment, energy, iron and steel, autos, and nonferrous metals. Finally, an industrial reorganization court of fifteen judges would be created to try cases.

Because two-thirds of all manufacturing occurred in concentrated industries (or shared monopolies), Hart argued that the new legislation was needed to protect consumers from an economic *structure* as costly as the more familiar, and illegal, price-fixing *behavior*. The current antitrust approach was ineffective. Instead, his new approach would virtually strip the Justice Department of its antitrust powers and place them in the hands of the commission and court. If Hart's legislation passed, observed an article in the *Nation's Business*, "it will mean that for the first time a corporation will have to defend itself before the government whenever it reaches a size which the government will have decided in advance constitutes a threat to competition. And it must either restrain its growth or face mandatory dismantlement."[35]

Why had he introduced such a draconian proposal? Hart was asked. "Frustration," he replied. "I realized that if I and others like me around here did nothing but continue to make speeches on the dangers of concentration, nothing at all would happen. So my reaction was to say, 'For God's sake, let's have something specific that, if we can sell to the Congress, will maybe not cure the problem but at least reduce it.'

"Where a few firms dominate an industry, they can readily yet independently coordinate their pricing policies to maximize profits for the whole group," Hart declared. "Rarely are they forced to outright conspiracies, so dear to the hearts of antitrust lawyers, which can easily be prosecuted. In any event, it would take a couple of centuries of such cases to eradicate the economic concentration that haunts this country."

Although there were 400,000 manufacturing companies operating in the United States, a mere 200 controlled two-thirds of the assets. In the major sectors of the economy, markets were dominated by two, three, or four companies that "often behave as one when it comes to pricing policy." Hart believed that concentration of economic power had contributed to "waves of inflation that plague us so consistently."

He did not like to be considered a "giant-killer" for wanting to bust up huge companies; he claimed he was really out to save the free enterprise system. But he conceded that his decontrol bill might spell the end for General Motors, U.S. Steel, and General Electric. Not wedded to the details, the senator called his legislation a dialogue bill, and he circulated it widely among industries, antitrust experts, and economists.

Hart held stock in companies his legislation would break up (General Motors, 315 shares; Exxon, 104 shares). But he downplayed any significance in his stock holdings: "My holdings are so small that it is not to my credit that I seem to be attacking some of my interests because, hell, my interests are pipsqueak."[36]

When asked if his bill was too radical, Hart deadpanned, "No. It's just a reasonable little bill. In fact, when you think about it, it's really rather conservative." But spokesmen for industry disagreed and unleashed a chorus of criticism. "Drastic," "staggering," "revolutionary" were some of the polite descriptions of the legislation from spokesmen of industry. "What could be more powerful than a single government agency controlling the destiny of the nation's basic industries?" said Charles B. Overmiller, chief economist of the Exxon Corporation; "Senator Hart would do well to ponder the dangers of such a concentration of government power." Breaking up the oil industry could boomerang, Overmiller argued. "There are tremendous economies in vertical integration from oil well to gas station. To separate crude exploration or production from refining would only add needless cost burdens and push prices up."

If profits threatened to cross the 15 percent line, argued David Schwartzman, professor of economics at the New School for Social Research in New York, "then firms will become extravagant and inefficient. Such unanticipated effects will be difficult to avoid if the law is to depend on simple rules." Testifying on behalf of the National Association of Manufacturers, Lowell C. Smith argued that the bill would have a stifling effect on the economy. "The mere passage of the act would create a moral obligation on the parts of several large industries not to grow. Since bigness and success, by the definition of the act, are bad, is there any incentive to invest in the name of further efficiency or future growth?" Others charged that Hart's bill did not include concentration in labor unions. "Why, mightn't it be asked," said the *Nation's Business*, "should a union with a concentration of power in a particular industry, say, automobile manufacturing, be exempt from dismantlement?"

Republican senator Roman Hruska of Nebraska was certain that Hart's legislation would damage the U.S. economy: "If the Hart bill passes it would make the United States a third-rate trading nation. Big industries abroad have expanded 120 percent in the past five years. The rate of growth in this country has been only 60 percent. If that growth rate continues we will be outstripped in another four or five years. We can break up these industries here, but we can't break them up over there."

Another member of the subcommittee, who also opposed the bill, thought the legislation stood little chance of passage in the immediate future. "Phil Hart knows that and he just wants to keep the issue alive," the senator explained. "He's probing for the soft spots and will keep at it until something gives."[37]

In rebutting critics, Hart conceded that his proposal involved heavy governmental interference with the business system. But he distinguished his method from other kinds of regulation on the grounds that reforming individual companies and industries would be a one-time program, not a continuing activity. The commission would die in fifteen years, after which existing antitrust laws would sustain the competitive structure. In short, the bill provided the corrective surgery and then the patient was discharged.

The efficiency issue was critical, but he thought something more important than efficiency was at stake. "Suppose," he argued, "this never-never land did arrive and we had four or five giants who

CONSCIENCE OF THE SENATE   193

achieved monopoly power because of their superiority. No matter how much power is obtained, it is contrary to the political and social interests of the nation for it to be held in a few hands." He explained that what the bill said, without saying it explicitly, "is that we don't care if you met in the dark of night or if you were just a magnificent entrepreneur, there is a point after which you must be denied the fruits of your ingenuity."

Hart candidly conceded that the special court his legislation would create might find that industrial concentration was not so bad after all. "It may be that if you find an industry is overconcentrated you might be going from the frying pan into the fire to deconcentrate," he explained. "It's conceivable that this special court (and if I were on the court I might agree) could find there is concentration but that the costs of busting it up are greater than the costs of keeping it. Or that the benefits which might come from keeping an industry intact are greater than the benefits which would result from deconcentration."

Hart's legislation was too outrageous for Congress and had no immediate chance of passage, but he used it as a vehicle for holding hearings. The hearings continued until 1976. Occasionally, there were dramatic disclosures: that General Motors had retained its holdings in Nazi Germany and had made profits off both sides during World War II. "Most of the time, though, it was pretty boring," said one observer, "a parade of victims testifying that big corporations had shoved them out of business . . . and the corporation, in turn, covering their tracks under a mountain of obscure statistics and technical language." There seemed to be no political advantages to be gained but potentially many liabilities. Nonetheless, Hart kept plugging away at his hearings in the hope that someday, someone would have the fortitude to use the information he and his staff were amassing.[38]

Nation's Business asked Hart: "Is this awkward for you, being around these automobile executives at the same time you're trying to break up their companies?" The senator laughed, paused a moment and replied:

> I hadn't thought of it that way. But I'm sure their opinion of this proposal is that it's outrageous. I'm sure if I were in their positions I'd feel the same way.
>
> But, really, none of that group has discussed the bill with me seriously. Once in a while one of them will make a pleasant, light comment and make it clear what they think of the bill. I would add this, though.

If there were an imminent likelihood that this thing would become the law of the land, this light and casual treatment would damn sure become very serious and very direct.[39]

Although Hart sought to break up concentrated industries, he also defended them from unjust accusations. In 1971 a California-based antiwar group demanded a congressional investigation of the oil industry for coveting potentially rich oil leases off the coast of South Vietnam, which the group suggested was responsible for the "Nixon administration's failure to get our sons out of Vietnam." The charge provoked friction between the Senate Foreign Relations Committee and the State Department. Hart's Antitrust and Monopoly Subcommittee had studied the Vietnamese oil matter, and he judged the charges against U.S. oil companies inaccurate and misleading. Possibly there was oil off the coast of Vietnam, but the oil companies were not currently racing to develop the potential and were not responsible for continued presence of U.S. soldiers in Vietnam. "Truth has suffered enough as this war has dragged on," Hart said. "We who criticize the war and urge our involvement be ended have been acutely aware of the role of the half-truth in the Vietnam debate and have decried its use. This error must now be corrected," he said of the oil question, "to protect the effectiveness of the best antiwar tool—truth."[40]

The issue that most troubled Hart's conscience in his third term was abortion. In 1973 in *Roe v. Wade* the Supreme Court struck down state laws banning abortion during the first three months of pregnancy. Hart reluctantly supported the decision. The "right" liberal position was to be pro-choice, but his Catholic background had taught him to abhor abortion. At a meeting, a Catholic critic, noting that Phil opposed capital punishment, said that he assumed he also opposed abortion. There was a consistency in the critic's comment that bothered the senator. "Abortion made him uncomfortable," said Burt Wides. "There was a conflict within himself," added Florence Roth.

"We had the first vitriolic wave of the right-to-lifers knocking on our doors," recalled Donald Tucker of Hart's staff who was assigned to study the abortion issue. Hart met with a Michigan delegation opposed to abortion and carefully listened to their arguments. "He was extraordinarily sympathetic [and] understanding in a nonsolicitous way," said Tucker, "more of the becomforting clergyman in his approach to these people and their advocacy, than he was a condescending and politically adroit manipulator of constituents." Hart agreed with the delegation that life began at conception. "There is no question that it is a life or not a life," he told them. "It is a life." Nonetheless, he said, "I cannot honestly say that if my daughter would come to me and say that she had been raped . . . and wanted to abort the child, that I would say no. I cannot tell you I would say no." The Michigan delegation left the meeting with no apparent bitterness. They hoped he would eventually support their position, but they seemed to understand that he could not at the moment. "It was uncanny," thought Tucker of how amicable the meeting was.[41]

By 1970 Hart had changed his view on the Vietnam War and began voting with antiwar senators who urged reduced spending for the war, a negotiated settlement, and withdrawal of U.S. soldiers. Phil partly credited Janey and the children for convincing him to move toward an antiwar position. Moreover, after 1968 the Democratic party, freed from President Johnson's leadership, had moved toward the peace position.

In 1972 Hart spoke against resumption of bombing in Vietnam and the imposition of a sea blockade in North Vietnam. In a Senate speech in April Hart asked, "What end justifies the terrible costs which inevitably result from massive bombing?" and admonished, "Any nation contemplating the waging of war should not separate the costs of war from the end it seeks." Continuing, he said:

> What we have no answer to is the question which will not go away—what outcome of the war in Vietnam would be so harmful to our national interests that we are justified in resuming and in escalating to record proportions massive attacks which cannot help but destroy non-military and military personnel and buildings alike?

Hart introduced one of the first amnesty bills into Congress and tried to prick the conscience of his colleagues on the issue of amnesty. Every time Senator Harry F. Byrd introduced a resolution that would posthumously restore full citizenship rights to Civil War general Robert E. Lee, Hart threatened to amend the resolution to grant amnesty to the young men who refused to serve in Vietnam. While the Senate considered a bill to provide hundreds of millions of dollars for Vietnamese refugees, he stood up in an almost empty Senate and suggested that in welcoming the Vietnamese to America, it would also be appropriate to welcome home war resisters who had exiled themselves abroad. "It was very touching and compassionate and just so true," Senator Edward Kennedy later told a reporter. "Amnesty is not a terribly popular issue, but he's never looking for the easy way."[42]

Long before Watergate, Hart had suggested federal financing of elections in an effort to eliminate private money and private greed from the electoral process. Few took him seriously until the Watergate scandal exposed the need for election reforms. Twice in 1973 the Senate voted to tighten federal laws on the financing of political campaigns.

Whether or not campaign contributions actually bought votes, Hart thought, they gave the *impression* of it, and even the impression eroded confidence in the Congress. "The public believes large campaign contributions purchase votes in Congress, whether this is true or not," he argued in July 1973. "I suspect that view is less, rather than more, accurate; yet, it is true that a contributor gets access." That fact was well illustrated during the 1972 presidential campaign, he said, when the milk producers explained how a contribution opened White House doors for them. Once inside, they succeeded in turning the Nixon administration around on the "merits" of their case. "Cynics will say that the merit of the case was the size of the contribution," Hart said. "However it colored the merits, it did open the door. This is not to imply that a contributor may not have a real problem, but rather that the problem may not be one to which time is budgeted. As in any office, the most likely problems to be handled are those that come to one's desk. Under our present system, that petition, too often, is the one submitted by the contributor."[43]

Periodically, Hart looked back on his Senate career and asked, "Have I done any good? Have I *really* done any good being here?" When Saul Friedman once asked him, "Well, have you done any good, Phil?" he responded, "Yeah, I think I have," and he cited the Voting Rights Act and Sleeping Bear Dunes. For the most part, though, during Hart's third term he became deeply frustrated with himself and with the Senate.

"He expressed bitterness at the waste of time in the Senate, and a sense of the waste of his life," observed Mike Pertschuk. "He set such high standards for himself, and I think he never met them." He felt that many of his proposals merely adjusted an imbalance or redressed a grievance within the system. At best they were palliatives. Despite his massive hearings on the dangers of economic concentration, for example, the trend toward monopoly was continuing. Few seemed to care.

The Senate process was too slow and unresponsive, he thought, and the government's priorities were misplaced. He looked about the Senate and with a smile shook his head. "You know, the trouble is we believe all the things we say about each other in here. We think this is where it really happens. But it doesn't. It's happening out there—and in time, God willing, we finally react to it." There was nothing Congress liked to do better than "deliberate, deliberate, and deliberate," Hart said. "It is the conclusion we too seldom reach." He wryly remarked that "even a community of saints could not move legislation through [the Senate] more quickly."

The government's values and priorities helped create the myth that you increased national security by increasing armaments. "I don't know how many billions we've spent for weapons since I've been here but it's at least a trillion dollars. . . . And the whole world is doing it, and we're peddling arms to the poor nations. Every dollar spent that way is a dollar deprived the poor, health systems, educational systems. Last year, the world spent—I think it was $240 billion—for its 'security.' If we had taken 10 percent of that—$24 billion—and put it into technology to increase agricultural productivity so the world could better feed itself, a person would argue we would have contributed more toward security than we got from that $24 billion spent on weapons."[44]

"He had pretty much despaired of politics as a way to do very much," Eugene McCarthy thought. "I assume he didn't think he was being effective. Of course, some of us felt the same way, but we weren't as sensitive to it, or as distressed over it, as Phil was." Hart was particularly upset with the Senate's inability or lack of desire to address fundamental problems, like the plight of the urban poor. "The urban poor especially touched him," said Pertschuk. He displayed his melancholy and frustration in late May 1975 at the congressional black caucus's day-long hearing on the economic problems minorities faced. When Senator Hubert Humphrey presented a rousing, optimistic speech about the chances of full-employment legislation in 1975, Hart applauded enthusiastically. But when he was asked to speak, his outlook was different. "I'm not nearly as optimistic as my friend and colleague, Mr. Humphrey," Hart told the group. "In fifteen years we have not made even a dent in the task of redistributing wealth in this nation," he said. "Some 200 corporations still control most of the wealth. Until we do something about that appalling concentration of power—power that even overwhelms the Congress at times—we will be able to do little to improve matters for the poor. . . . It is right that we meet this morning and these days to talk about increasing employment opportunities. But in my book, until we make structural changes of such a basic nature that I don't see the will to even try, we are going to be constantly assembled talking about which Band-Aid now."[45]

Hart struck many as simply exhausted. He often just shrugged his shoulders. "You knew he was plain worn out," said Lynn Sutcliffe. "You could see it in his face and the way he carried his body." In 1973 Muriel Ferris approached the senator with a controversial proposal that she thought needed to be addressed. Looking bone-tired, Hart pulled out a three by-five card listing on both sides all the items people thought needed to be addressed. "This is what people have come to me [with]," Hart said, waving the card. "Will I do this? Will I take on that?" He suggested that Ferris take her problem to the senator on the committee that ordinarily handled the issue. Ferris responded that the senator had already refused to handle the problem because he was up for reelection. "It all got dumped to Phil Hart," reflected Ferris of the thorny problems and issues, "because he cared. . . . He was tired out for carrying all these burdens."[46]

Ironically, as Hart grew increasingly frustrated with his work, colleagues and political observers were increasingly lauding his character and his high moral principles. By the end of his third term, he was often being described as the conscience of the Senate. His reputation, especially in Washington, had grown partly because for years his staff had been telling everyone how wonderful their boss was. "So honest and good and humane," "so gentle and thoughtful," "among the brightest in the Congress," "so damn decent" were common phrases his staff used to characterize him.

In the fall of 1973, a widely publicized poll of legislative assistants in all senatorial offices highlighted Hart's uniqueness. The assistants were asked to rate all senators on their effectiveness, intelligence, work habits, and integrity. Of 100 senators Hart received the most votes for having the highest integrity and tied for honorable mention, behind Senator Jacob Javits, for being the most intelligent. Hart's name "always evoked sighs of admiration from secretaries and never failed to generate a strong note of approval from liberal and conservative members alike," Michael Foley discovered during his interviews with senators and their assistants.[47]

Stories circulated, some perhaps apocryphal, about Hart's exceptional qualities. When a Washington journalist wrote a book describing the senator as a man who was "widely regarded" as the gentlest and kindest in the Senate, former senator Paul Douglas, who had been asked by the author to read the galley proofs, sent the author back a penciled note: "Don't say that Phil Hart is 'widely regarded' as the gentlest and kindest in the Senate. Just say he *is*."

In his 1971 book *In the Fullness of Time*, Douglas singled Hart out as the saint of the Senate. Besides modestly concealing his many virtues, Hart had sought idealistic goals. Too often, Douglas argued, society sought compromises on vital issues to win either an election or a petty advance. There was a degree of truth in the position, Douglas thought. "Compromises must be made to attain the possible," but the "pragmatic approach sometimes becomes essentially negative and devalues all issues." Idealists like Phil Hart were "still needed to raise the standards higher," said Douglas. "Politics needs the much maligned idealists and saints."[48]

After the astronaut John Glenn was elected to the Senate in 1974, Senator Mike Mansfield gave him a tour of the Senate. Mansfield tugged at Glenn's sleeve and pointed out a frail figure across the room. "Phil Hart," Mansfield said, "There's one senator who never looked at a tally sheet before he voted."

"Every morning," wrote columnist Jack Anderson in the wake of the Watergate scandal, "my mail brings more expressions of disillusionment from people suddenly turned cynical. Reduced to simplest terms, their theme is 'all politicians are crooked.'" In contrast to the sordid corruption of the Watergate era, Hart stood out, said a *New York Times* reporter, "like a choir boy at a crap game."[49]

From 1974 to 1976, many columnists singled him out for special praise. "Hart is one of those rare men in public life," wrote Jerald terHorst, "whose ego is smaller than his talent; whose directness and sense of conscience have led others to regard him as the moral compass of the Senate." Columnist Colman McCarthy said Hart "has practiced as pure a style of politics as [the Senate] has ever seen, elevating not only the level of thought but also the vocation itself." Although the senator had said repeatedly that he had no presidential aspirations, his reputation for exceptional integrity caused his name to be bantered about as a possible Democratic nominee for president in 1976. An article in *The Washington Monthly* said that "a man who commands so much respect has too strong an appeal to be completely discounted."[50]

Hart was often credited with extraordinary moral authority over his peers. "He is the only man who can, with quiet argument and comments, actually change votes," said Edward Kennedy. "That's not usually done in debate, where minds are made up and there is only the formality of the vote. But Phil can do it, with intelligence, reason and compassion."

Part of the reason Hart was often called the conscience of the Senate was that he never sought the title. In the past some senators had seemed to actively campaign for the honor, but they were either self-righteous, caustic and abrasive, or purposely attracted attention to themselves. "Hart didn't operate that way," said Jerry Kabel. Senator Edmund Muskie agreed that Hart did not appoint himself to the role. "He never lectured the Senate, never chided the Senate," said Muskie. "He simply stated what he was for," but he said it so credibly, so clearly as a matter of conscience that his fellow senators regarded him and his views—even if they disagreed with him—"as the clearest demonstration . . . of what a senator of conscience ought to be." Mike Pertschuk thought Hart had an enormous effect in upholding a moral standard to the Senate—particularly on the issues of race, poverty and opportunity. "He was just so utterly decent and committed to a larger vision than many [senators] really were," said Pertschuk, "that he raised their vision, raised their sense of what statesmanship was all about."[51]

Hart was aware that people admired his "quiet courage" and were describing him as the conscience of the Senate, and he was flattered. He joked with intimates about the praise but publicly remained modest and self-deprecating. While reading over a brochure written by his staff, he deadpanned to a staff member, "There's nothing in here about my 'quiet courage.'" In the mail, Joe Rauh received a photo of Hart on which was written, "To Joe Rauh, the *real* conscience of the Senate with thanks and best wishes, Phil Hart." "That's incredible," reflected Rauh, because "he was so clearly [the conscience of the Senate.]"[52]

Since 1970 political observers had been speculating that Hart might not seek reelection in 1976. He declined to talk publicly about his plans, saying only that he would announce his decision by the end of the summer of 1975. Actually, there was no doubt in his mind what that decision would be. He remained firm in the plan he set shortly after the 1970 election: he would retire at the end of his term. "Going to Michigan this weekend," Phil wrote James Hart on 21 January 1975, "but such trips will be so few that the 'political observer' soon will report 'he is not going to run again.'"

In October 1974, he had suggested that the republic would be better served if senators and congressmen were required to retire at age sixty-five. There were exceptions—people of advanced age who still made great contributions—but the tasks heaped on a senator's shoulders were exceptionally difficult. It required energy and stamina to handle over-lapping committee meetings, hurry-up trips to the Senate floor, and endless requests from constituents. "I think it would be better if we had a mandatory retirement age in the House and Senate," he said. "This would guarantee that Congress was made up of people young enough to handle the work load." He also argued that it was better to have a person in the Senate who, however mistaken or misguided, sincerely believed he could change the world overnight once he got into office. "You and I know that he's not going to be able to do it, but he makes a better senator if he thinks he's going to be able."[53]

In 1975, while chatting with Edmund Muskie in the back row of the Senate chamber, Hart explained part of his rationale for not wanting to run again: "I just cannot go back through a campaign and make promises again, so many of which you can never keep."

He also wanted to enjoy his children and looked forward, in good health, to spending much of his time reading. (He often told Janey that a person really needed more than one lifetime—one of which should be devoted entirely to reading.) Moving into a large law firm and making a lot of money was a prospect he rejected. He would have liked to teach at Georgetown, and had discussed with university officials the possibility of teaching law and politics. When Jack Cornman suggested he write his memoirs after his retirement, Hart rejected the idea. "The books that sell for memoirs," he said, "are usually because they have some tales and stories about other people and usually not always kindly tales. That is not my style. I'm not going to be a kiss-and-tell politician."[54]

In announcing his retirement Hart decided not to hold a press con-ference or make a speech on the Senate floor. Instead, on 6 June 1975, he slipped a brief, modest statement into the *Congressional Record*. (Shortly before the announcement his staff sneaked out to reporters an unapproved memo listing his accomplishments.) He gave age as his rea-son for stepping down. No one should run for office "unless he believes that he will have the energy and stamina to be fully vigilant for the entire term sought." No person was irreplaceable, he said, no one insti-tution is all-important, and the guard should be changed with regular-ity. "When I complete this term I will be sixty-four and will have been a

U.S. senator for eighteen years. By the end of still another term, I would be seventy years old and would have served twenty-four years."

Looking forward to the remaining eighteen months of his term, he said he wanted to assure completion of Sleeping Bear Dunes National Lakeshore, help Michigan and Detroit cope with the recession, extend the Voting Rights Act, and continue "my poorly attended lectures on the evils of economic concentration." Finally, he hoped to convince more people that "all of us will be safer when we ban handguns," and that "amnesty for Vietnam War resisters is in keeping with our nation's noble traditions of tolerance and forgiveness."[55]

Many in the Washington press corps, often cynical about all politicians, quietly murmured about how they hated to see him go. "The man has class," said the *Oakland Press* of Michigan. "There will no doubt be a lot of promising persons eager to capture his Senate seat," the newspaper said. "For the one who finally wins it, there will inevitably be days when he or she will feel like a little boy trying on his father's shoes. And he may hope someday he'll grow into them. In the meantime, we hope he at least keeps them shined."

A top aide of a Senate leader wrote his boss in a despairing effort to convince Hart to remain in the Senate: "How do you convey to a man whose humility leads him to doubt his own uniqueness that his qualities of mind and conscience (not least, that very humility) are the qualities that define his uniqueness?"[56]

Six weeks after his retirement announcement Hart discovered a lump under his arm and went for tests at Bethesda Naval Hospital. Hoping it was a virus, doctors gave him ten days of medication. When the medication failed, a biopsy revealed that he had malignant melanoma, a particularly deadly form of cancer that spread rapidly throughout the body. "I knew exactly what that meant," Janey thought when a doctor informed her. "There is nothing you can do about it." (Phil probably had cancer long before it was discovered, and the undiagnosed illness may have caused his mysterious loss of energy.)

After the doctors told him the seriousness of his illness, Phil was naturally upset. Recalling that his mother had died of cancer, he told his daughter Cammie, "All my life I've been worried that I'll get this, and now I guess I won't have to worry about it anymore." After the initial shock, though, he adjusted and did not slip into depression.[57]

In early September, Hart was admitted to Bethesda Naval Hospital for tests to find the primary source of the cancerous growth. One operation removed a cancerous tumor from under his arm. A second removed a small nodule from his right lung, which doctors feared was malignant, but was later discovered to be benign. "Men as well as women can have breast surgery," Hart said on 8 October 1975, as he announced he would have a third operation to clean out the lymph nodes in his right breast. The operation removed fifty-four lymph nodes, thirty-two of which later proved to be cancerous. However, doctors never were able to determine the primary source of his cancer. In early November, Hart began outpatient treatment of monthly immunotherapy and bimonthly chemotherapy to halt the spread of his melanoma.

The chemotherapy made him sick. He vomited so much during one period of treatment that he became dehydrated. "There wasn't any progress," Janey observed. After several rounds of unsuccessful treatment, doctors discontinued their efforts to cure him, and Phil let the cancer take its course. He tried to ease the embarrassment and awkwardness of those who came to console him. "He made it easy for me," said Florence Roth, "That's what he would do, make it very easy for others."

For more than a year after the cancer was discovered, Hart continued to maintain a regular schedule. However, the debilitating effects of the operations, the chemotherapy, and the progressing cancer increasingly stole his strength. As he lost buoyancy and energy, he skipped committee meetings and only appeared on the Senate floor for vital matters.[58]

Because of his hospitalization for cancer treatment, Hart missed the early sessions of the Senate Select Committee on Intelligence, which was investigating the abuses of the FBI. Under J. Edgar Hoover's direction, the bureau had repeatedly engaged in illegal or questionable activities—burglaries against "domestic subversive targets," harassment of dissident and political protest groups within the United States, and an intensive campaign to discredit Dr. Martin Luther King, Jr. In November 1975, Hart made his first appearance and heard the disturbing testimony about the FBI's actions against King and other dissidents. He moved many of his colleagues and the audience with a brief monologue. His children had been correct, he said, when they warned him in the 1960s about FBI abuses. He had "been told for years by, among others, members of my own family that this is what the Bureau has been doing all this time. As a result of my superior wisdom and high office, I assured them that they were on pot—it just wasn't true. [The FBI] just wouldn't do it. . . . I am glad I got back in time to be persuaded of what my own family had not been able to persuade me of for so long."[59]

In October 1975, in an unexpectedly close vote, the Senate narrowly defeated legislation Hart originated to prevent oil producers from also owning refineries, pipelines and retail outlets. Years of testimony before the senator's subcommittee had led him to conclude that a few major oil companies had received favorable tax treatment and had amassed monopoly control of oil reserves, pipelines, and retail outlets. Regulation and antitrust efforts had failed mainly because of the power of the oil companies. Case after case had been filed against the industry, only to have them settled by watered-down consent decrees or dropped entirely. The oil industry, he believed, had achieved "power inconsistent with the basic values of a democracy." Hart's legislation lost by only nine votes, 45-54. He had been recuperating from surgery at the time the legislation reached the Senate and received a standing ovation when he stepped out on the Senate floor to cast his vote for the measure.

The drive to break up the large oil companies resumed in 1976 and this time it looked like legislation would pass. The legislation moved out of the Judiciary Committee in May, but the Senate leadership never brought it to the senate floor. "It was an election year," said one observer, "and many senators weren't ready to choose between voters and the oil companies."[60]

At the end of his third term Hart began calling for a radical program to assist the poor. "What we really need in this country is income redistribution," he told *Forbes*. "I probably would not confess it if I were going to stay in office, but I have come to see that as long as we have the profit motive, there'll be damn little redistribution. Everybody says, 'I've fought like hell to get where I am. . . .'"

In short, Hart would just as soon abolish the profit system:

> If I could see a way to eliminate the bad distribution of an economy fueled by profit, I might soften my statement. But what we've got is a machine purring along and no one to insure equitable distribution of the machine's output. As long as relatively few influential people benefit, Congress won't change things.
>
> Unless a revolution comes, we'll always find that income disparity. With profit as the engine, you can't expect people who have wealth to give it up. I don't.

Why not? asked *Forbes*. Why not redistribute the wealth he and Janey possessed? Phil was taken aback. "Well," he hesitated, "I admire monastic orders and I do give a pretty fair share to charity, but, but . . . that's a tough question. I never asked myself that."[61]

Hart remained frustrated with politics. At times his pessimism seemed to border on gloom. On 29 December 1975, columnist John McKelway of the *Washington Star* reported that at a recent joint appearance on "Meet the Press," Phil and Janey Hart "just barely hinted there was some reason to struggle into 1976." Liberalism had peaked, Phil said. "I think that it's correct to say that the optimism which we brought in 1958—that whatever the problem was we could get a handle on it—we don't have that kind of optimism any more." Janey was hardly more encouraging. "There are times," she said, "when I'm so discouraged that I wonder whether it makes the slightest difference at all who is president or who is governor or who is mayor." McKelway concluded by taking a swipe at both Harts: "It is hard to picture either Hart in a funny hat New Year's Eve."[62]

Hart was stung by McKelway's comments. In an open letter, he referred specifically to the "Meet the Press" program. "My concern," he wrote, "is with stories which reported that Janey and I were discouraged by recent events, and that our dismay was representative of the decline of liberalism." He was not a doomsayer, he contended, for while he was, indeed, disappointed with the lack of sustained progress in domestic reforms, he remained confident in the goals and the possibility of future progress:

> Certainly those of us who hoped the programs of the 1960s would be effective in reducing poverty and hunger and improving schools and housing and health have reasons to be discouraged with the results of some of those programs, but not with the goals we sought.
>
> Those of us who hoped to close the gap between the many at the lower end of the economic scale and the affluent few during the years of economic expansion have reason to be disappointed by the failure to achieve any real change, but not with the goal.
>
> Those of us who believed that the time had come when we could at last deliver on the promise of our founding fathers that all persons were created equal have reason to be discouraged by the discrimination still with us, but not with the goal.

Mistakes were made, he pointed out in his letter, beginning with support for the Vietnam War, and then voting war funds without raising taxes, "a failure which had more to do with inflation than spending on domestic programs." Other domestic programs were poorly conceived or poorly administered, and Congress had not paid close enough attention to how the programs were being carried out.

Also, he said, Congress too often tinkered with, rather than changed, the structure. For example, "We sought to help the poor by rewarding the rich with tax incentives to invest in low-cost housing, and paid consultants to help fill out poverty grant applications. Where we dealt with the structure— as we did in passing the Voting Rights Act—we were effective:

> But let us also remember that many of the programs were inadequately funded and conducted for very short periods of time. The lesson of the 1960s is not that liberals sought unwise or unobtainable goals, but that we should have known all along: it is easier to solve physical problems—putting men (but not women) on the moon—than social problems.[63]

At the Democratic National Convention in July 1976, Hart talked openly and thoughtfully about his progressing cancer with Remer Tyson of the *Detroit Free Press*. The cancer was spreading throughout his lymph glands, he said, and his chemotherapy treatments were ineffective. Sooner or later the cancer would put him "out of business." He was frank about his feelings: "The damn illness affects you when you get it, emotionally or psychologically. . . . [You] would be a fool to tell yourself that emotionally you are the same the day after you learn about it as you were the day before." He admitted to worrying about future pain. "It isn't that you ask for a cure, but that either you will be spared long periods of pain or that you will handle it with some measure of decency and dignity."[64]

Hart's family rallied around him. Family friends Robert and Margaret Boylan spent many weekends with the Harts at their Maryland farm in the summer of 1976. "Watching him with his entire family was a lovely thing to see," said Margaret Boylan. "All those husky sons, so affectionate with each other and with him, those robust young men sitting on the sofa with their arms around him." Robert Boylan observed Phil's sons "embracing him almost in the continental manner, with no self-consciousness. There is open love on the part of all of them."

By August 1976 Hart looked terminally ill. Alone with his father at the farm in Maryland, young James Hart felt compelled to express his feelings. "I understood he was dying," recalled James, who worried that he was not articulate enough to express himself. "I was in tears. And I told him how sorry I was that this was happening and how unfair it was . . . he should die without enjoying the benefits of not having the job be a daily grind for him and not having the time to go off and enjoy the grandchild that he had at the time." Phil told him not to worry, that his father loved him, and that James should enjoy his own life.[65]

Although drained of energy, Hart was vigilant to the end of his term, making one last effort on behalf of antitrust. In the summer and fall before adjournment, he fought for the passage of the Hart-Scott-Rodino Antitrust Bill, the first major legislation to stiffen antitrust laws in twenty-five years. In a two-year legislative battle business forces had lobbied to defeat it or at least dilute key provisions.

The bill had followed an unusually complex legislative path through Congress, having survived two Senate filibusters and a last-minute attempt by the House to defeat it. The final version was drafted informally, without a conference, to avoid another filibuster. The Senate's leadership was adamant that the bill receive a vote. "If it was Phil Hart's bill, it was going to get a vote!" observed Howard O'Leary of Senator Mansfield's attitude. "A major force behind the bill's progress," the *Wall Street Journal* reported, "was the desire of many senators to pass it as a farewell monument to Senator Philip Hart."

Although Hart was in pain, he showed up on the floor and sat in his seat the substantial part of every day the bill was being considered. "He was in on every key consultation," said Senator Muskie. In the last days of Congress, as his disease progressed, he left his seat occasionally to rest privately in a reclining chair outside the Senate chamber.

The compromise bill that finally passed had three sections. The most extensively debated portion authorized state attorneys general to bring triple damage antitrust suits in federal court on behalf of citizens. (The suits were called *parens patriae*, a legal term indicating that the attorney general was serving as "parent of the state.") Another controversial section directed companies of a certain size to give thirty days' notification to the Justice Department and the Federal Trade Commission before consummating a merger. (Supporters argued that the government needed time to block illegal mergers in advance because it was nearly impossible to unscramble companies once they had merged.) The final section significantly expanded the Justice Department's authority to gather information for potential antitrust suits.

Hart would have preferred a more fundamental assault on monopoly power but seemed satisfied with at least a small victory. "We have an expression in our family that progress consists in climbing molehills—and as long as we have a modest definition like that, why, most things are progress," he commented on the bill. "This is a little better than a molehill."

On 30 September 1976, President Ford signed the law, renamed the Antitrust Improvements Act. It was hailed as the most important antitrust law in decades and a significant safeguard for consumers. Earlier, after the bill had passed Congress, Senator Mansfield said Phil Hart's "wisdom, his intelligence, his quiet effective manner and his courage and tenacity primarily have been responsible for the passage of what is considered to be a monumental piece of legislation which will long benefit the people of this nation. I salute a good man and a cherished colleague . . . the noblest of us all."[66]

In September, the Michigan press corps hosted a reception in his honor and gave him two birch trees to be planted outside the Visitors Center at Sleeping Bear Dunes. Because he had lost so much weight, his brown suit no longer fit. "I'm sorry I have this ill-fitting suit on," Hart said, "but I didn't know if it was worthwhile investing in another." He said it in a light-hearted tone and everyone laughed. Later, though, most of the reporters were wet-eyed. "This was a man probably everybody loved," reflected Richard Ryan of the *Detroit News.*[67]

On 29 September, Hart made his last public appearance. The Michigan congressional delegation hosted a reception for him and for the Honorable James G. O'Hara, who was leaving Congress, in the Cannon House Office Building. Hart walked in very slowly, seemed extremely tired, and sat through most of the reception. It was the usual "boozy, noisy retirement party, the rhetoric competing with chatter, and losing," said a reporter. Until it was time for Hart to say a few words. Then the room became silent—no talking, no clinking of glasses or ice cubes. His brief, moving speech summarized part of his political philosophy and reflected his unfinished agenda.

Members of Congress were lucky, he said, his voice weak and pace slow. He was grateful for his own opportunity. "As I look around, I see the press who know you're not as smart as your claims would suggest and know that they can make anybody look to be an idiot if they undertake it, but who nonetheless restrain themselves."

He praised his fellow politicians and the profession of politics:

> There are people who fill books describing or vaguely suggesting the evils that occur in these halls. If they could listen to the conversations I've listened to since '58, if it was evil they were curious about, they would have long since left.
>
> In my book, politicians maintain a higher level of integrity than most other categories. The temptations are great but hopefully the discipline of the press and others is equally great. Most people say "thank you, but no."
>
> I hope that younger people understand that politics is a very dangerous business but what effective weapon isn't? And it's a weapon that will mean somebody is interested and if they will just understand that it does not demean them and that it does not expose them to more than they would be exposed to if they were a teller in a bank or an associate in a law office, then we might be assured of a more constant, steady stream of the best of them—and we need them.

Looking over the people gathered in the room, he said somewhat resignedly that "we've seen some little growth, some improvements but it's still an awfully white audience out there and it's a pretty affluent audience." He could only hope that "fifty years from now . . . the complexion and the Dun and Bradstreet rating and the ages of a group like this would be dramatically changed to reflect more in keeping with what we are as a country."

"This is the last time for me and I close as I began, by thanking all of you for trusting me."

When he finished, said Sidney Woolner, "I don't think there was a dry eye in the house."[68]

"If he had been there, Phil Hart would have blushed," observed the *Detroit News* of the laudatory tributes Hart's Senate colleagues gave him at the end of the fall of 1976 Senate session. Hart did not sit in the senate chamber to listen to the tributes. In a statement inserted into the *Congressional Record*, he thanked the senators and said, "I leave as I arrived, understanding clearly the complexity of the world into which we were born and optimistic that if we give it our best shot, we will come close to the goals set for us years ago."[69]

When Phil was certain he was dying, he said to Cammie, "I think we better discuss the program," meaning the plan for his death. He assumed he would enter the hospital, but the family thought otherwise. Rather than the sterile hospital environment, the Harts decided to take care of him themselves at their home on Calvert Street. That way Phil could talk to family members at any time.

The children came home from their various pursuits around the country to help care for their father. For six weeks, from mid-November to late December, Janey and the eight children surrounded Phil with "twenty-four-hour-a-day love and care" at home. Janey rented a hospital bed and placed it in his room. Cammie, a nurse, taught family members how to give shots. The boys bathed him in the bathtub until he became too weak; then they bathed him in his bed. They cut his hair and trimmed his beard. One member of the family stayed in the bed next to him every night. He kept worrying that caring for him was too much of a burden on the family. "We assure him it is not a burden but a privilege," Janey said. "It was really a very wonderful time for us as a family," reflected Cammie. "We changed so much for the better."

Hart rejected any extraordinary life support efforts, including intravenous feeding. There was no effort to cure him; the pills and shots he took were to relieve his pain. The pain-killing drugs kept him reasonably comfortable but also disoriented him at times. "He still has moments of brightness and lightness and we all enjoy that," Janey said in early December.[70]

Friends visited his bedside. Detroit columnist Lou Gordon found that Hart was still concerned about issues, especially poverty. "Lou, you have been concerned about Detroit for a long time, does it have a chance?" Gordon responded that he thought Detroit was a dying city, but while there was life there was hope. After his visit Gordon told his readers about Gordon Strachan, an aide to H. R. Haldeman, who had said pessimistically during the Watergate hearings that young men should never come to Washington. Lou Gordon disagreed: "I say, 'Dear God, this country needs more men like Phil Hart'—young men, do come to Washington and try and emulate Hart's life and style."

Eugene McCarthy and Edmund Muskie came to visit. In June, Muskie had hosted a last reunion of Hart's Senate friends. Several eulogized him. Senator Edward Kennedy delicately injected humor to the occasion. "Teddy managed to keep the equilibrium of the group at a time when they all might have broken down in tears," said a person who attended the gathering. "He kept up the spirits of the group when they all knew they were probably seeing Phil for the last time." Muskie described for Hart a funeral "Mass of Joy" given for an old friend of Muskie's. The idea was that death was not an end, but a joyous beginning, and that love survived. Phil responded positively and said to Janey, "I now understand what has happened and I am glad."

Hart usually wanted to see Edward Kennedy. When his medication made him delirious, in his confused state he worried about Senate legislative matters. "Who would you like to see?" Janey asked when he was agitated. "I would like to see Ted," Phil would say. Every time Janey called Kennedy, he graciously came over and reassured Phil about whatever was currently bothering him. After one visit, Kennedy hugged Janey and cried.[71]

As Hart lay in bed he occasionally thought about life after death; talking about it relieved some of his anxiety. How would his loved ones fare? "I want to come back," he told Ann Bronfman. "I don't want to come and spy on everyone, but I just want to see how things are going for the people I love!"

Christmas, 25 December 1976, was the last day Phil was conscious. The Hart family attempted to have a normal holiday at home. They exchanged gifts around the tree, ate a turkey dinner, and in the evening listened to a small professional group sing Christmas carols. At about 6:45 P.M., everyone assembled in Phil's room and the group sang carols to him for fifteen minutes. Janey held his hand during the singing, and he seemed to smile. A family friend observed, "He looked at his children. A tear came out of his eye and on his cheek. I remember Janey wiping it away. We all felt after that at peace. He knew everyone there loved him. He was not alone." Janey reflected, "We had such a lovely Christmas." The following day, 26 December 1976, the entire family was with him when he died at 1:05 P.M. Some were holding his hands; Cammie was rubbing his brow. "We were telling him we love him," said Janey.[72]

The eulogies following his death emphasized his exceptional integrity and held him up as an inspiring model for the politician. "The man was a legend," said the *Detroit Free Press*. "And now he is gone. And saying goodbye is not easy at all." "Phil Hart was a liberal," the conservative *Detroit News* said. "Unlike some other liberals, he held his viewpoint because he believed in it, not because he thought it would win votes for him. His was not an easy, sleight-of-hand liberalism." "He was not only pleasing to God," Eugene McCarthy wrote in his eulogy to Hart; "he also met the sometimes more difficult test of being pleasing to man."

It would be a long time, editorialized the *Washington Post*, "before anyone in the Senate matches his integrity, diligence and compassionate humanism. . . . Others will come along, of course. And they will have few models—for professional politics and personal character—more deserving of study than Philip Hart."

Columnist Coleman McCarthy labeled Hart as the most trusted man in American politics: "How many owed something to Hart when he died Sunday can't be known, but it can be said that because of the moral substance of his positions and the depth of his character, it was not an accident that he was the trusted man of American politics. He fronted for no one. His alliances were to timeless ideals, not upstart lobbies. As though he were the wildest of gamblers, he bet that the common vanities of hack politics—images, smiles, calls for brighter days—counted for little. Instead, he wagered that conscience and persistence could matter."[73]

While Hart was still lucid, one of the last things he had talked about was his disappointment in not securing blanket amnesty for draft evaders and deserters who were not allowed to return to their families. Therefore, when President Gerald Ford phoned a few hours after Phil's death to express his condolences and asked, "Is there anything I can do?" Janey said, "Yes. There is just one thing I wish you would do and that is to give amnesty to the Vietnam protesters, deserters and draft evaders." "Well," President Ford responded, "I'll give it another hard look." The news that Ford, who was leaving his office on 20 January, was considering a blanket amnesty attracted extensive publicity. "I thought a great deal of him," said Ford, explaining why he seemed to be changing his mind after having said many times during the 1976 presidential campaign that he would not grant blanket amnesty. Subsequently, under intense media questioning, Ford backed off, indicating that his basic thinking on amnesty had not changed despite his promise to review the issue. "I just said that at the request of her I would look at it," he said.[74]

"The Hart family wanted everything very simple," said the funeral director who handled arrangements. Indeed, Hart had insisted that his funeral be simple and inexpensive. His Antitrust and Monopoly Subcommittee had once investigated the funeral industry, and he was appalled at the high cost of funerals. "If I die in office and you spend more than $250 on my funeral," Phil had told Janey, "I am going to get up and walk out." Through a local Washington burial society, Janey found a carpenter who made a simple pine coffin for $150.

As Hart had requested, his body was cremated, a practice forbidden by the Catholic church until only a few years earlier. Those who wished to contribute to his memory were asked to donate to a scholarship fund at tiny Lake Superior State College in Sault Ste. Marie. Phil had selected the college because it was located in an economically deprived area, and many of the students who wanted to attend were in financial need.

On 27 December, Hart's body rested in the closed pine coffin in the glassed-in porch of the Hart home. Wrapped in the sheet from the bed in which he died, his body had been placed in the coffin by his four sons. The following day a solemn crowd of 1,200 attended a funeral mass at St. Matthew's Cathedral in downtown Washington. "The rich and powerful were there, dressed in tailored suits and fine furs," observed a reporter. "So, too, were the poor and powerless, dressed in jeans and parkas." Father Vincent Hart, who first met the senator forty-five years earlier at Georgetown, delivered the eulogy. The priest told the mixed crowd of conservatives and liberals that people disagreed at times with Phil's judgment, "but we shall never disagree with him in the openness of his mind. Would that all our minds are so open as Phil Hart's."

After the service in Washington, Phil's ashes and the Hart family were flown by U.S. Air Force transport to upper Michigan and then by helicopter to Mackinac Island. On Wednesday morning, 29 December, in near-zero temperature, horse-drawn sleighs transported friends and family to St. Anne's Catholic Cemetery in the middle of the island to bury Phil next to Philip, Jr. who had died thirty years earlier. There was no fancy canopy—only trees arched overhead. The box with his ashes was lowered in the grave by his son Clyde. It had all been unpretentious: a simple funeral and a simple burial for a simple man.[75]

NOTES

1. *Washington Post*, 15 February 1970.
2. *Detroit Free Press*, 5 November 1970; *Detroit News*, 4 November 1970.
3. Clippings, unprocessed Wallace Long Papers, Detroit, Michigan; *Detroit Free Press*, 1 October 1970, 5 November 1970; *Detroit News*, 4 November 1970; *Parade*, 20 September 1970, 4, 6.

4. *Detroit News*, 6 July 1970, 4 November 1970; Wallace Long, telephone interview, 9 May 1989.

5. Clipping, Wallace Long Papers; *Detroit News*, 4 November 1970; *Iron Mountain News*, 28 October 1970.

6. *Detroit News*, 20 October 1970, 21 October 1970.

7. *Birmingham Eccentric*, 29 October 1970; *Detroit Free Press*, 26 June 1970; *Detroit News*, 23 October 1970, 4 November 1970; *Parade*, 20 September 1970, 4.

8. Clipping, Wallace Long Papers; *Detroit Free Press*, 11 August 1970; *Detroit News*, 4 November 1970, 10 November 1976; Wallace Long, telephone interview, 9 May 1989.

9. Clipping, Wallace Long Papers; *Parade*, 20 September 1970, 4; Basil Briggs, telephone interview, 15 March 1990.

10. *Detroit News*, 12 June 1970, 19 September 1970; Wallace Long, telephone interview, 9 May 1989.

11. *Detroit News*, 11 October 1970; *Kalamazoo Gazette*, 9 December 1976.

12. *Detroit Free Press*, 11 August 1970.

13. Clippings, Wallace Long Papers; *Detroit News*, 25 August 1970.

14. *Detroit Free Press*, 1 October 1970, 29 October 1970; *Detroit News*, 25 August 1970.

15. Clippings, Wallace Long Papers; *Detroit News*, 27 December 1976; Jerry Kabel, telephone interview, 24 February 1988.

16. *Detroit News*, 13 October 1970, 2 November 1970; *New York Times*, 8 November 1970; Vreeland, *Philip A. Hart*, 6; Janey Hart, interview, Washington, D.C., 1 and 2 April 1989.

17. *The Sunday News* [Detroit], 6 September 1970; *New York Times*, 8 November 1970; Vreeland, *Philip A. Hart*, 6; Basil Briggs, telephone interview, 15 March 1990; Carolyn Burns, telephone interview, 9 May 1989; Sidney Woolner, telephone interview, 12 and 14 January and 5 July 1988.

18. *Detroit News*, 22 October 1970, 28 October 1970, 29 October 1970.

19. Philip Hart to James Hart, 15 September 1970, James Hart Papers; *Detroit Free Press*, 11 August 1970, 5 November 1970; *Detroit News*, 13 October 1970; Basil Briggs, telephone interview, 15 March 1990.

20. Jerry Kabel, telephone interview, 24 February 1988; Sidney Woolner, telephone interview, 12 and 14 January and 5 July 1988.

21. *Detroit Free Press*, 14 February 1971; Vreeland, *Philip A. Hart*, 2; Muriel Ferris, interview, McLean, Virginia, 26 March 1988; Michael Pertschuk, telephone interview, 13 April 1988.

22. *Detroit Free Press*, 14 February 1971.

23. Ibid.; Muriel Ferris, interview, McLean, Virginia, 26 March 1988; Jerry Kabel, telephone interview, 24 February 1988; Michael Pertschuk, telephone interview, 13 April 1988.

24. *Congressional Record*, 100th Cong., 2d sess., vol. 134, pt. 21:5; *Detroit News*, 17 November 1970; *Kalamazoo Gazette*, 9 December 1976; *National Observer*, 1 February 1975; *Parade*, 28 November 1971, 7; *Washington Post*, 16 February 1971, 13 April 1971.

25. Clipping, Philip Hart File, Georgetown University Archives; *The Blade* (Toledo, Ohio), 27 June 1971.

26. *Detroit News*, 7 November 1970; *Pontiac Press*, 17 November 1971.

27. *The Ann Arbor News*, 27 December 1976; *Detroit Free Press*, 27 December 1976; *Detroit News*, 7 November 1971, 10 November 1976; Adelaide Hart, telephone interview, 2 March 1988.

28. *Flint Journal*, 8 June 1975; *Pontiac Press*, 17 November 1971; Burton Wides, interview, Washington, D.C., 29 March 1988.

29. *Pontiac Press*, 17 November 1971.

30. *Detroit Free Press*, 27 December 1976; *Flint Journal*, 7 December 1971; *Pontiac Press*, 17 November 1971.

31. Clipping, Wallace Long Papers; *Congressional Quarterly: Almanac 1971*, 675.

32. *Muskegon Chronicle*, 3 March 1975; *Washington Post*, 27 July 1972; Burton Wides, interview, Washington, D.C., 29 March 1988.

33. Memo [unidentified], 28 July 1972, unprocessed Burt Wides Papers, Washington D.C.; *Detroit News*, 29 July 1972, 27 December 1976; *Washington Post*, 27 December 1976; John Cornman, interview, Washington, D.C., 26 March 1988; William Simpson, telephone interview, 15 March 1989; Burton Wides, interview, Washington, D.C., 29 March 1988.

34. *Christian Science Monitor*, 19 March 1973; *The Progressive*, July 1975, 26; Howard O'Leary, interview, Washington, D.C., 28 March 1988.

35. *Christian Science Monitor*, 19 March 1973; *National Observer*, 1 February 1975; *Nation's Business*, November 1973, 26.

36. *Christian Science Monitor*, 19 March 1973; *National Observer*, 1 February 1975; *Nation's Business*, November 1973, 26.

37. *Nation's Business*, November 1973, 27, 35; *National Observer*, 1 February 1975.

38. Klein, "Saint," 37; *Nation's Business*, November 1973, 34; *National Observer*, 1 February 1975.

39. *Nation's Business*, November 1973, 32.

40. *Washington Star*, 31 March 1971.

41. John Cornman, interview, Washington, D.C., 26 March 1988; Janey Hart, interview, Washington, D.C., 1 and 2 April 1989; Florence Roth, interview, Washington, D.C., 29 March 1988; Donald Tucker, telephone interview, 11 April 1989; Burton Wides, interview, Washington, D.C., 29 March 1988.

42. *New York Times*, 3 June 1974; *Washington Star*, 5 December 1976; Vreeland, *Philip A. Hart*, 12, 20; John Cornman, interview, Washington, D.C., 26 March 1988.

43. Clipping, Box 551, Hart Papers, Bentley Library; *Congressional Quarterly: Almanac 1973,* 741; Philip Hart, "The Future of the Government Process," *The Annals of the American Academy of Political and Social Science* 408 (July 1973), 99; John Cornman, interview, Washington, D.C., 26 March 1988.

44. Clipping, Box 551, Hart Papers, Bentley Library; *Detroit News,* 18 June 1975; *Washington Post,* 29 December 1976; *Washington Star,* 5 December 1976; Philip Hart, "Future of Government Process," 98; Saul Friedman, telephone interview, 17 May 1988; Michael Pertschuk, telephone interview, 13 April 1988.

45. *Detroit Free Press,* 27 December 1976; *New York Times,* 6 June 1975; Eugene McCarthy, telephone interview, 7 June 1988; Michael Pertschuk, telephone interview, 13 April 1988.

46. Muriel Ferris, interview, McLean, Virginia, 26 March 1988; Lynn Sutcliffe, telephone interview, 22 April 1988.

47. Clipping, unprocessed Florence Roth Papers, Washington, D.C.; Lauralyn Ballamy, "Senate Aides Rate Senators," *Capitol Hill News Service,* 26 October 1973, Washington, D.C.; Foley, *The New Senate,* 196.

48. *Memorial Addresses,* 13; Douglas, *Fullness of Time,* 236.

49. Clipping, Box 551, Hart Papers, Bentley Library; *Kalamazoo Gazette,* 9 December 1976; *New York Times,* 6 June 1975.

50. *Detroit Free Press,* 12 February 1976; *Detroit News,* 18 June 1975; *The Washington Monthly,* March 1975, 27-28.

51. *Detroit Free Press,* 27 December 1976; Jerry Kabel, telephone interview, 24 February 1988; Edmund Muskie, telephone interview, 13 July 1988; Michael Pertschuk, telephone interview, 13 April 1988.

52. John Cornman, interview, Washington, D.C., 26 March 1988; Barbara Kincaid, telephone interview, 23 May 1988; Joseph Rauh, interview, Washington, D.C., 29 March 1988.

53. Philip Hart to James Hart, 21 January 1975, James Hart Papers; *Detroit News,* 9 March 1975; *The Iron Mountain News,* 22 October 1974; *Washington Post,* 27 December 1976.

54. John Cornman, interview, Washington, D.C., 26 March 1988; Janey Hart, interview, Washington, D.C., 1 and 2 April 1989; Edmund Muskie, telephone interview, 13 July 1988.

55. *Memorial Addresses,* 33; *Courier-Post* [Camden, New Jersey], 9 June 1975.

56. *Courier-Post,* 9 June 1975; *Detroit News,* 26 June 1975; *Oakland Press,* 12 March 1976.

57. *Detroit News,* 27 December 1976; Cammie Conserva, telephone interview, 23 May 1988; Janey Hart, interview, Washington, D.C., 1 and 2 April 1989.

58. *Detroit News,* 27 December 1976; *New York Times,* 6 September 1975, 12 September 1975, 18 September 1975, 9 October 1975; Ann Anderson, interview, Washington, D.C., 26 March 1988; Janey Hart, interview, Washington, D.C., 1 and 2 April 1989; Florence Roth, interview, Washington, D.C., 29

March 1988; Burton Wides, interview, Washington, D.C., 29 March 1988; Sidney Woolner, telephone interview, 12 and 14 January and 5 July 1988.

59. *Atlantic Monthly*, 13 February 1976, 14, 16; *Congressional Quarterly: Almanac 1975*, 408-9; *Washington Post*, 29 December 1976.

60. *Congressional Quarterly, Weekly Report*, 10 April 1976, 827; *Detroit Free Press*, 12 February 1976; Klein, "Saint," 37; Philip Hart, "An Advocate's Perspective on Divestiture," *Michigan Challenge*, July/August 1976, 10-11.

61. *Forbes*, 15 July 1975, 60.

62. *Washington Star*, 29 December 1975.

63. Clipping, Box 551, Hart Papers, Bentley Library.

64. *Detroit Free Press*, 18 July 1976.

65. *Washington Star*, 5 December 1976; James Hart, telephone interview, 31 May 1989.

66. *Congressional Quarterly: Almanac 1976*, 431-35; *Washington Star*, 5 December 1976; Klein, "Saint," 37; Howard O'Leary, interview, Washington, D.C., 28 March 1988.

67. Richard Ryan, telephone interview, 19 May 1988.

68. *Detroit News*, 27 December 1976; *Washington Star*, 5 December 1976; Barbara Kincaid, telephone interview, 23 May 1988; Burton Wides, interview, Washington, D.C., 29 March 1988; Sidney Woolner, telephone interview, 12 and 14 January and 5 July 1988.

69. Clipping, Burt Wides Papers; *Detroit News*, 3 October 1976; *New York Times*, 27 December 1976.

70. *Detroit News*, 27 December 1976; *Washington Star*, 5 December 1976; Ross, *Friend and Foe in Senate*, 168; Cammie Conserva, telephone interview, 23 May 1988; Janey Hart, interview, Washington, D.C., 1 and 2 April 1989.

71. *Detroit News*, 10 November 1976; *Washington Star*, 5 December 1976; Ross, *Friend and Foe in Senate*, 168; Ann Bronfman, interview, Washington, D.C., 2 April 1989; Janey Hart, interview, Washington, D.C., 1 and 2 April 1989.

72. *Memorial Addresses*, 1-3; Ann Bronfman, interview, Washington, D.C., 2 April 1989; Janey Hart, interview, Washington, D.C., 1 and 2 April 1989.

73. *Detroit Free Press*, 28 December 1976; *Detroit News*, 27 December 1976; *Washington Post*, 28 December 1976, 29 December 1976; Ross, *Friend and Foe in the Senate*, 28.

74. *Memorial Addresses*, 2; *Detroit Free Press*, 29 December 1976; *Detroit News*, 28 December 1976; Janey Hart, interview, Washington, D.C., 1 and 2 April 1989.

75. *Detroit Free Press*, 29 December 1976; *Detroit News*, 28 December 1976, 29 December 1976; Janey Hart, interview, Washington, D.C., 1 and 2 April 1989.

Epilogue

On 20 May 1987, Phil Hart's friends, family, and Senate colleagues dedicated the Philip A. Hart Senate Office Building. Earlier, much had been written about the disparity between the grandiose, pretentious structure and the simple, unpretentious senator. Those in attendance at the dedication, however, were there to listen to the dignitaries honor Phil's memory. Senator Carl Levin (D-Mich.) said he idealized Phil's sense of public trust.

"The last thing Phil Hart ever wanted was a building in his name," said Senator Edward Kennedy, the principal speaker. "But we went ahead and named it for him anyway because we loved him."

"He was not a Speaker of the House of Representatives, but now he ranks with Cannon, Longworth, and Rayburn. He never served in the Senate leadership, but he ranks with Russell and Dirksen now. And all of us who knew him would put him in the pantheon of the greatest senators of all, Webster, Calhoun, and Clay." Kennedy was overcome with emotion when he said, "He was like a brother to me."

Janey Hart was particularly pleased with the words inscribed above the main entrance to the Hart Building. "You should read the dedication," she later instructed an interviewer. She hoped that every young person who was thinking of entering politics would read the inscription and say, "That is the way I can be."

The inscription says:

This building is dedicated by his colleagues to the memory of Philip A. Hart with affection, respect and esteem. A man of incorruptible integrity and personal courage strengthened by inner grace and outer gentleness, he elevated politics to a level of purity that will forever be an example to every elected official. He advanced the cause for human justice, promoted the welfare of the common man and improved the quality of life. His humanity and ethics earned him his place as the conscience of the Senate.[1]

NOTES

1. *Congressional Record*, 100th Cong., 2d sess., vol. 134, pt. 21:1-4; *Boston Globe*, 22 May 1987; Janey Hart, interview, Washington, D.C., 1 and 2 April 1989.

Sources

This essay does not include a complete list of all the sources used for this study. Readers should consult endnote citations for specific sources.

MANUSCRIPTS

There are several important manuscript collections relating to the life of Philip Hart. More than 600 boxes of the Philip A. Hart Papers are located with the Michigan Historical Collections at the Bentley Historical Library, University of Michigan. The Janey Hart Papers (private collection, Washington, D.C.) contain over 200 valuable and compelling handwritten letters by Phil to Janey during World War II. In the James Hart Papers (private collection, Pasadena, California) are handwritten letters by Phil to his son James during the 1960s and early 1970s. Phil's military service records during World War II are in two locations: the Veterans' Administration Papers (Milwaukee, Wisconsin) and the Department of the Army Papers (St. Louis, Missouri). Georgetown University kept a noteworthy collection of newspaper clippings in its Philip Hart File (Georgetown University Archives, Washington, D.C.). The Wallace Long Papers (private collection, Detroit, Michigan) include an important newspaper clipping file on Hart during the 1970 election. The Sidney Woolner Papers (in my possession) also contain valuable clippings.

Phil's academic records are contained in the Waldron Academy Papers (Merion, Pennsylvania), West Philadelphia Catholic High School for Boys Papers (Philadelphia, Pennsylvania), Georgetown University

Papers (Washington, D.C.), and the University of Michigan Law School Papers (Ann Arbor, Michigan).

Some useful information was found in the Werner Kleeman Papers (private collection, Flushing, New York), Florence Roth Papers (private collection, Washington, D.C.), Sleeping Bear Dunes Papers (Empire, Michigan), Neil Staebler Papers (Michigan Historical Collections, Bentley Historical Library, University of Michigan), and the Burton Wides Papers (private collection, Washington, D.C.). Several individuals and institutions sent me their collections for photocopying.

BOOKS AND ARTICLES

No biography of Phil Hart exists. Two items proved helpful for understanding portions of his life. After Phil's death his Senate colleagues memorialized him in *Memorial Addresses and Other Tributes in the Congress of the United States on the Life and Contributions of Philip A. Hart* (95th Cong., 1st sess., Senate Document No. 95-37, Washington, D.C., 1977). Nena Vreeland, *Philip Hart,* Ralph Nader Congress Project: Citizens Look at Congress (Grossman Publishers, 1972), analyzed Phil's voting record in the Senate.

Several books about political colleagues shed light on Phil. Among the most helpful were the following: Paul Douglas, *In the Fullness of Time* (New York: Harcourt Brace Jovanovich, Inc., 1971), Joseph Bruce Gorman, *Kefauver: A Political Biography* (New York: Oxford University Press, 1971), Hubert Humphrey, *The Education of a Public Man* (Garden City, New York: Doubleday and Company, Inc., 1976), Jacob Javits, *Javits: The Autobiography of a Public Man* (Boston: Houghton Mifflin Company, 1981), and Frank McNaughton, *Mennen Williams of Michigan: Fighter for Progress* (New York: Oceana Publications, Inc., 1960).

Two other noteworthy books with material on Phil are Ross Baker's *Friend and Foe in the Senate* (New York: The Free Press, 1980) and Michael Foley's *The New Senate: Liberal Influence on a Conservative Institution, 1959-1972* (New Haven: Yale University Press, 1980).

Important articles about Phil include Ralph Bennett, "Behind the High Cost of Auto Repairs," *Readers Digest* (September 1969); "The Case for/against No-Fault Auto Insurance," *Popular Science* (January 1971); Paul Clancy, "All the Presidential Men," *The Washington Monthly* (March 1975); Mark Green, "The Senate's Reluctant

Trustbuster," *The Progressive* (July 1975); Joe Klein, "The Saint in the Senate," *Rolling Stone* (30 December 1976); Vernon Louviere, "Sen. Philip Hart: Is He Big Business' Biggest Bogeyman?" *Nation's Business* (November 1973); Eugene McCarthy, "Philip Hart," *New Republic* (15 January 1977); "Senator Philip A. Hart," *Motor Trend* (April 1970); Herbert Shuldiner, "Your Outrageous Car-Repair Bills," *Popular Science* (June 1969); and Sanford Unger, "Two Who Won't Be Back," *Atlantic Monthly* (14 February 1976).

Phil presented his own ideas in several articles, including "New Dimension," *The Progressive* (May 1961); "Swindling and Knavery, Inc.," *Playboy* (August 1972); "The Total Landscape of Sleeping Bear Dunes," *American Forests* (January 1969); "Change Antitrust Laws to Increase Private Suits," *Trial* (February/March 1968); "Self-interest the Key," *The Progressive* (February 1973); "The Future of the Government Process," *The Annals of the American Academy of Political and Social Science* (July 1973); "Truth in Housing," *American Home* (July 1973); "The Discount on 'Gorgeous,'" *The Nation* (23 October 1967); and "Truth in Packaging," *The Nation* (29 June 1963).

Newspapers and Periodicals

Research into forty-five different newspapers proved exceptionally time-consuming, but the results were indispensable. Those studied most comprehensively were the *Ann Arbor News*, (1961-1964, 1976), *Detroit Free Press* (1954-1976), *Detroit News* (1954-1976), *Lansing State Journal* (1954-1971), *New York Times* (1961-1976), *Washington Post* (1961-1976), and the *Washington Star* (1972-1976).

I also discovered useful information in *Blue and White* [West Philadelphia Catholic High School for Boys, yearbook] (1928-1930), *Congressional Quarterly Almanac* (1965-1976), *The Hoya* [Georgetown University, newspaper] (1933-1934), *Michigan Law Review* (1936-1937), *Michiganensian* [University of Michigan, yearbook] (1937), and *Ye Domesday Booke* [Georgetown University, yearbook] (1934).

Interviews

Valuable, intimate material was gathered in interviews with seventy-two persons. All the interviews were conducted by the author. One-fifth were personal interviews; four-fifths were telephone interviews. A few interviews were brief; some persons were interviewed at length or more than once. Almost all the interviews were tape-recorded. All the taped interviews are in my possession and, at some future date, I intend to donate them to a historical depository. Finally, I also gathered some important information from personal correspondence with sixteen persons.

Anderson, Ann. Interview. Washington, D.C., 26 March 1988.
Bangert, Charles. Interview. Washington, D.C., 28 March 1988.
Bario, Patricia. Interview. Washington, D.C., 28 March 1988.
Barreto, Antonio. Telephone interview. 22 October 1990.
Barrett, Richard. Telephone interview. 25 January 1989.
Beckham, William. Telephone interview. 9 May 1988.
Bernhard, Berl. Telephone interview. 21 February 1990.
Berthelot, Helen. Telephone interview. 23 May 1988.
Bickwit, Len. Telephone interview. 2 May 1990.
Bouie, Alonzo. Telephone interview. 9 August 1989.
Briggs, Basil. Telephone interview. 15 March 1990.
Bronfman, Ann. Interview. Washington, D.C., 2 April 1989.
Burns, Carolyn. Telephone interview. 9 May 1989.
Clark, John. Telephone interview. 4 October 1989.
Cohen, Jerry. Interview. Washington, D.C., 30 March 1988.
Conserva, Cammie. Telephone interview. 23 May 1988.
Cornman, John. Interview. Washington, D.C., 26 March 1988.
Cotterall, William. Telephone interview. 5 July 1988.
Courage, Ray. Telephone interview. 13 May 1988.
Feild, John. Telephone interview. 20 March 1989.
Fenlon, Edward. Telephone interview. 16 October 1989.
Ferris, Muriel. Interview. McLean, Virginia, 26 March 1988.
Fiset, Lew. Telephone interview. 11 May 1989.
Fitt, Alfred. Telephone interview. 28 April 1989.
Friedman, Saul. Telephone interview. 17 May 1988.
Hart, Adelaide. Telephone interview. 2 March 1988.
Hart, Clyde. Telephone interview. 8 August 1988.
Hart, Janey. Interview. Washington, D.C., 1 and 2 April 1989.
Hart, Vincent. Telephone interview. 16 May 1989.
Hart, Walter. Telephone interview. 30 April 1988.
Hart, James. Telephone interview. 31 May 1989.
Hayden, Martin. Telephone interview. 13 May 1988.
Heide, Herman. Telephone interview. 29 April 1988.

Hickey, Frances. Telephone interview. 4 April 1988.

Horn, Stephen. Telephone interview. 5 February 1990.

Howard, Milton. Telephone interview. 15 February 1989.

Jeffrey, Mildred. Telephone interview. 31 May 1988.

Kabel, Jerry. Telephone interview. 24 February 1988.

Keefe, Albert. Telephone interview. 17 May 1988.

Kincaid, Barbara. Telephone interview. 23 May 1988.

Kleeman, Werner. Telephone interview. 23 May 1989.

Long, Wallace. Telephone interview. 9 May 1989.

MacMullan, Russell. Telephone interview. 5 July 1988.

McCarthy, Eugene. Telephone interview. 7 June 1988.

McGarvey, William. Telephone interview. 7 May 1988.

McKnight, Leila. Interview. Washington, D.C., 25 March 1988.

Moon, Charles. Telephone interview. 23 February 1989.

Murray, John. Telephone interview. 18 July 1988.

Muskie, Edmund. Telephone interview. 13 July 1988.

O'Leary, Howard. Interview. Washington, D.C., 28 March 1988.

Pertschuk, Michael. Telephone interview. 13 April 1988.

Pisor, Robert. Telephone interview. 21 March 1989.

Randall, Donald. Interview. Washington, D.C., 28 March 1988.

Rauh, Joseph. Interview. Washington, D.C., 29 March 1988.

Richards, Eleanor. Telephone interview. 20 March 1989.

Roth, Florence. Interview. Washington, D.C., 29 March 1988.

Ryan, Richard. Telephone interview. 19 May 1988.

Simpson, William. Telephone interview. 15 March 1989.

Slattery, Paul. Telephone interview. 16 May 1988.

Staebler, Neil. Telephone interview. 27 August 1987.

Sullivan, Cajetan. Telephone interview. 15 June 1989.

Sutcliffe, Lynn. Telephone interview. 22 April 1988.

Taylor, William. Telephone interview. 26 January 1990.

terHorst, Jerald. Telephone interview. 28 March 1989.

Tucker, Donald. Telephone interview. 11 April 1989.

Valentine, Joe. Telephone interview. 8 September 1989.

Wellford, Harrison. Telephone interview. 3 May 1988.

Welsh, William. Telephone interview. 23 April 1988.

Wides, Burton. Interview. Washington, D.C., 29 March 1988.

Williams, Nancy. Telephone interview. 20 March 1989.

Williams, Thomas. Interview. Washington, D.C., 28 March 1988.

Woolner, Sidney. Telephone interview, 12 and 14 January and 5 July 1988.

CORRESPONDENCE

Allen, Charles, to author, 24 January 1989.
Balter, George, to author, 4 February 1989.
Barrett, Richard, to author, 14 January 1989.
Bradley, Wilmer, to author, 17 June 1988.
Doherty, Walter, to author, 8 July 1988.
Gill, Daniel, to author, 21 June 1988.
Hall, Robert, to author, 18 July 1988.
Hannigan, Thomas, to author, 25 June 1988.
Hart, Clyde, to author, 9 April 1988.
Hart, Janey, to author, 1 July 1991.
Hayes, E. Kirby, to author, 6 June 1988.
Heyns, William, to author, 20 January 1989.
Kayser, Victor, to author, 25 January 1989.
Keidan, Jacob, to author, 11 January 1989.
Murray, John, to author, 12 July 1988.
Smoyer, Stanley, to author, 7 February 1989.

Index

A

Adams, Sherman, 69
Agnew, Spiro, 178
Alger, Fred, 59
Americans for Constitutional Action, the, 82
Americans for Democratic Action, the, 82
Anderson, Jack, 199
Antitrust Improvements Act, the, 207-8
Arnett, Judd, 85

B

Balter, George, 21, 22
Bangert, Charles, 111, 113
Bario, Patricia, 111, 112, 113, 134
Barton, Raymond O., 28, 33, 35, 42, 43, 44, 45
Battle of the Bulge, the, 44
Bayh, Birch, 188
Beckham, William, 91
Berthelot, Helen, 59, 156
Blakeley, Harold W., 45
Bosco House, the, 58
Boylan, Margaret, 206
Boylan, Robert, 206

Bradley, Omar, 44
Bradley, Wilmer, 14, 15
Briggs, Janey. *See* Hart, Janey
Briggs, Walter O. "Spike," Jr., 13, 18, 19, 20, 29, 30
Briggs, Walter O., Sr., 29, 30, 58, 61
Broadbridge, Michael T., 185
Bronfman, Ann, 159
Brown, James, 161
Bryn Mawr, PA, 5-6, 10
Bryn Mawr Trust Company, the, 5, 6, 19
"Bumper bill," the. *See* Motor Vehicle and Cost Savings Act
Burke, Fred, 95
Burns, Carolyn, 59, 63, 156, 162, 179, 180
Byrd, Harry F., 195

C

Carswell, G. Harrold, 123
Case, Clifford, 109
Center for Christian Renewal, the, 155
Christian Brothers, the, 8
Civil Rights Bill, the, 92-94
Clyde, Anna. *See* Hart, Anna

Cobo, Albert E., 67
Cohen, Jerry, 87, 91, 111, 139, 145-46
Consumer Federation of America, the, 82
Coolidge, Calvin, 11
Cornman, John, 81, 135, 138, 149, 201
Cotterall, William, 9
Courage, Ray, 149
Cox, James M., 36

D

Daley, Richard, 124
Davis, John W., 11
Dawson, John P., 22
Detroit race riots, the, 102
Dewey, Thomas, 40-41
Dichter, Ernest, 106
Dirksen, Everett, 94, 112, 145
Dodd, Thomas, 112
Dole, Robert, 51, 142
Douglas, Paul, 133, 150, 199

E

Eastland, James: and civil rights, 93, 153; and Estes Kefauver, 89; and Phil Hart, 123, 150, 151-54, 189
Eisenhower, Dwight, 44, 69, 89
Ellender, Allen, 189
Equal Employment Opportunities Commission, the (EEOC), 94
Erwin, Sam, 112, 123, 137, 153

F

Faubus, Orval, 69
Feild, John, 94
Ferency, Zolton, 100
Ferguson, Homer, 67
Ferris, Muriel, 81, 85, 138, 162, 183, 198
Filibuster, the, 92

Firestone, Betty, 20
Fiset, Lew, 28, 31, 32, 39, 44, 45, 46, 50
Fishman, Al, 178
Fitt, Alfred, 63, 64
Fitzgerald, George B., 61
Ford, Gerald, 212
Fortas, Abe, 121-22, 123
Fourth Infantry Division, the (U.S.), 28-29, 35, 38, 42, 44
Fraser, Douglas, 143
Friedman, Saul, 121, 131, 149
Fulbright, J. William, 109

G

Georgetown University, 11-12
Gerdes, Wylie, 149
Glade Valley Farm, the, 164
Glenn, John, 199
Goldfine, Bernard, 69
Goldwater, Barry, 98
Googasian, George, 175
Gordon, Lou, 174, 181, 185, 210
Green, Mark, 112
Griffiths, Hicks, 57
Griffiths, Martha, 57
Guggenheim, Charles, 179
Gulf of Tonkin Resolution, the, 107

H

Hall, Robert, 17
Hart, Adelaide, 59
Hart, Ann: birth of, 55; and Eugene McCarthy, 123, 124; and her parents' relationship, 156-57; illness of, 62, 160; and Phil Hart, 97, 107, 124, 158, 160, 162
Hart, Anna, 5, 6-7, 19
Hart, Cammie, 55, 158, 210, 211
Hart, Clyde (brother), 5, 6, 7
Hart, Clyde (son), 55, 213
Hart, Father Vincent, 13, 14, 16, 17, 213

Hart, James, 55, 123, 158, 159, 160-61, 183, 207

Hart, Janey: activity in politics of, 58, 154-57; arrest of, 155-56; and the Catholic Church, 155, 162; childhood of, 29; and death of Flip, 55; disillusionment of with politics, 205; illness of, 94; and Jews, 38, 39; and the New Deal, 40; and Phil Hart, 29-31, 36, 48, 131, 156-58, 160, 162, 164, 210, 211; and Phil Hart's depression, 96-97; and Phil Hart's political career, 56, 60, 61, 66, 70, 156; and the Philip A. Hart Senate Office Building, 219; travels of, 158; and the Vietnam War, 123, 157; wealth of, 61; and the women's liberation movement, 155

Hart, Laura, 55

Hart, Mary, 55

Hart, Michael, 55, 96

Hart, Philip A., Jr.: and Abe Fortas, 122, 123; and abortion, 194-95; and Albert E. Cobo, 67; and antitrust legislation, 114-18, 189-94, 204, 207; appointment as Corporation and Securities Commissioner, 58; and the arms race, 71, 197; attendance record of, 137; attitude toward blacks, 39-40, 58, 90; and auto repair cost hearings, 118-19, 181; and Barry Goldwater, 98; and the Battle of the Bulge, 44-45; beard of, 183-84; and the Bill of Rights, 82-83; birth of, 5; and the Bosco House, 58; and busing issue, 184-88; and campaign reforms, 179, 196; campaigning style of, 59-60, 63-64, 70, 72, 73, 98-99, 174-75; cancer of, 202-3, 206; as Chairman of Senate Antitrust and Monopoly Subcommittee, 86, 88, 89-90, 111-20, 146-47; character of, 131-50; and Charles Potter, 69-70, 71, 73, 74; childhood of, 6-7; and civil disobedience, 176, 177; and

civil rights, 65, 71, 90-94, 99, 101, 102-5, 184-88; colleagues' opinion of, 1,2, 67, 89, 133, 148, 198-200, 208, 209, 219; committee assignments of, 79; consideration of for Supreme Court Justice, 121-22; and consumer rights legislation, 86-88, 101, 105, 118, 188; and D-Day, 34-36; death of, 211; decision to retire, 181, 200-202; depression of, 47, 49-51, 94-97; and the Detroit Tigers, 58; as Director of the Office of Price Stabilization, 60; and draft resistors, 110-11, 176-78, 195, 202, 212; and Dwight Eisenhower, 71; and D. W. Stone, 31; and Edmund Muskie, 150; education of, 7-9, 11-19, 20-22; and Edward Kennedy, 150-51, 211; election as democratic precinct delegate, 56; election as lieutenant governor, 61, 64, 67; and Elly Peterson, 99, 100-101; and Ernest Hemingway, 45; and Estes Kefauver, 88, 89; and Eugene McCarthy, 123-24, 150; and family, 158-61, 163, 206; financial disclosures of, 139-40; and Franklin Delano Roosevelt, 11; frustration with ineffectiveness of Senate, 182-83, 196-98, 205-6; fundraising of, 179-80; funeral of, 212-13; at Georgetown University, 11-19; and G. Mennen Williams, 58, 60-61, 62, 64-65, 67, 68, 75; and gun control, 121, 188, 202; and Hubert Humphrey, 123; and the Industrial Reorganization Act, 190-94; and the infantry, 31-32; and James Eastland, 150, 151-54, 189; and Janey Hart, 29-31, 32-35, 40-41, 43, 46, 47-48, 55, 154, 155, 156-58; and Jews, 38-39, 47; and Joe Rauh, 72, 200; judiciousness of, 141-43; lack of assertiveness of, 144-45; lack of presidential aspirations of, 124-25, 144; last weeks of, 210-11;

law practice of, 55; and legislation for Michigan, 83-84; leisure activities of, 163-64; and Lenore Romney, 173, 174-75; as lieutenant governor, 66-67; and Lyndon B. Johnson, 80, 92, 123, 157; and McCarthyism, 60, 62-63, 107; and the Michigan Bar Exam, 22; and the *Michigan Law Review*, 20; and Mike Mansfield, 2-3, 150; modesty of, 1, 8, 17, 59, 63, 133-35, 200; and the National Commission on the Causes and Prevention of Violence, 121; and the New Deal, 40-41, 62; and the Newspaper Preservation Act, 117; and 1924 Democratic convention, 11; and 1932 Democratic convention, 11; and 1958 campaign for election as senator, 69-75; 1964 reelection campaign of, 98-100; and 1968 Democratic convention, 124-25; 1970 reelection campaign of, 171, 173, 174-81; and no-fault insurance, 188; office staff of, 80-81, 111, 198; and oil industry antitrust legislation, 204; and open housing legislation, 103-5, 137; and organized labor, 82; and pharmacy ownership hearings, 119-20; and Phi Delta Phi, 21; philosophy on truth, 106-7; political background of, 9-11, 22; and politics as a career, 60, 70, 137, 209; and the Pontiac Urban League, 58; and pornography, 83; post-retirement plans of, 201; and prayer in schools, 141; press coverage of, 1, 2, 63, 73, 85, 90, 106, 137, 145, 149, 180-81, 187-88, 199, 202, 205, 211-12; privacy of, 131, 154; and programs for the poor, 99, 184, 204-5; and railroads, 163; and Raymond O. Barton, 28, 42, 45; reading of, 22, 40, 91, 163, 201; recall campaign against, 185-86, 188; relationship with the press, 65, 67,

74, 131, 132, 148-49, 208; religion of, 41-42, 46, 91, 161-62; and the Reserve Officers' Training Corps (ROTC), 14-15; revisit to Utah Beach, 163; role in World War II, 27-29, 31-51; and the Russians, 47; and the Safe Streets and Crime Control Act, 171, 174; Senate influence of, 149-50; sense of humor of, 135; shyness of, 131; skill as debater, 13-14, 17; and Sleeping Bear Dunes National Lakeshore, 84-86, 125, 196, 202; speaking style of, 143-44; and Spike Briggs, 13, 18, 19, 20; stock holdings of, 191; and television, 72, 144; third-term goals of, 181-83; toughness of, 145-48, 154; and the Truth in Packaging Act, 105; at the University of Michigan, 20-22; and the Vietnam War, 107-8, 109, 174, 175, 195; and the Voting Rights Act of 1965, 1, 101-2, 196, 202, 206; war injury of, 35-37; and women's liberation movement, 155

Hart, Philip A., Sr., 5, 6-7, 10, 19

Hart, Philip, Jr. (Flip), 33, 39, 51, 55

Hart-Scott-Rodino Antitrust Bill, the. *See* Antitrust Improvements Act

Hart, Walter, 55, 96, 110, 123, 157, 158, 159

Hartke, Vance, 79

Hayden, Martin, 97, 139

Hayes, E. Kirby, 18

Haynsworth, Clement, 123

Heide, Herman, 12, 18-19

Hemingway, Ernest, 45

Hershey, Lewis B., 110

Hoffa, James R., 57

Howard, Milton, 22

Hruska, Roman, 89, 112, 192

Huber, Robert, 172

Hughes, Harold, 183-84

Humphrey, Hubert, 92, 93, 94, 107, 110, 123, 197

I

Industrial Reorganization Act, the
  (IRA), 190
Inouye, Daniel K., 51
Irish Americans: and the Democratic
  Party, 10; discrimination against, 9-
  10

J

Jackson, Henry, 107
Javits, Jacob, 2, 148, 184, 198
Jeffrey, Mildred, 63, 68, 156
John Birch Society, the, 82
Johnson, Lyndon B.: and civil rights,
  92, 101; decision to retire, 110; and
  freshmen senators, 79, 80; and Phil
  Hart, 122, 123; and the Truth in
  Packaging Act, 105-6; and the
  Vietnam War, 98, 107; and the
  Voting Rights Act, 101

K

Kabel, Jerry: and Antitrust and
  Monopoly Subcommittee, 111; and
  influence peddling scheme, 95, 96;
  and Phil Hart, 81, 82, 96, 109, 121,
  134, 162, 181, 200; and Sleeping
  Bear Dunes National Lakeshore, 84,
  109, 125
Kefauver, Estes, 88-89, 150
Kelley, Frank, 177
Kelly, Harry F., 57
Kennedy, Edward: and Antitrust and
  Monopoly Subcommittee, 112; and
  Chappaquiddick, 151; and the Philip
  A. Hart Senate Office Building, 2,
  219; and Phil Hart, 1, 142-43, 150-
  51, 188, 196, 200, 210-11
Kennedy, Robert, 109
Kilmer Club, the, 8
King, Stanley, 156
Kincaid, Barbara, 140

Kleeman, Werner, 39, 43, 44, 45, 50
Know-Nothing Movement, the, 9
Kopechne, Mary Jo, 151
Kriegel, Glenn, 118
Ku Klux Klan, the, 11

L

Lawyers' Liberal Club, the, 22
Lee, Oner, 154
Lend-Lease Program, the, 27
Levin, Carl, 219
Levin, Sander, 177, 181
Lewis, John, 42

M

McAdoo, William G., 11
McCann, James, 173
McCarthy, Coleman, 199, 212
McCarthy, Eugene: and 1968 presiden-
  tial race, 108; and Phil Hart, 96, 137,
  143-44, 145, 150, 151, 197, 210,
  212; and the Vietnam War, 108-9
McClellan, John, 112
McGee, Gale, 107
McKelway, John, 205
MacMullan, Eleanor, 7, 9
MacMullan, Russell, 6, 7, 8, 9, 10
McNamara, Patrick, 67
Mannes, Marya, 86
Mansfield, Mike: as anticommunist,
  107; and Phil Hart, 2-3, 93, 104,
  134, 150, 199, 207, 208; and the
  Vietnam War, 109
Merrick Debate, the, 16-17
Michigan Democratic Club, the, 57
Michigan Law Review, the, 20
Milliken, William, 181
Mitchell, Clarence, 153
Mitchell, John, 154
Mitchell, Martha, 154
Monaghan, Joseph, 55
Monaghan, Peter, Jr., 55
Mondale, Walter, 104

Montgomery, Bernard, 44
Moon, Charles, 20, 21, 22
Motor Vehicle Information and Cost
  Savings Act, the, 119
Murray, John, 17
Muskie, Edmund, 2, 72, 109, 132,
  143, 148, 150, 200, 207, 210, 211

N

Nader, Ralph, 144-45
Nast, Thomas, 10
National Commission on the Causes
  and Prevention of Violence, the, 121
National Organization for Women, the
  (NOW), 155
National Rifle Association, the (NRA),
  121
Neuberger, Maurine, 86
New Democratic Coalition, the
  (NDC), 178
Newspaper Preservation Act, the, 117
Nixon, Richard, 179

O

O'Boyle, Cardinal Patrick, 155
O'Hara, James G., 208
O'Leary, Howard "Buck," 111, 189,
  207
Open Housing Act of 1968, the, 105
Overmiller, Charles B., 191

P

Pastore, John, 2, 161
Pertschuk, Mike, 81, 111, 196, 197,
  200
Peterson, Elly, 98, 99-101
Peterson, W. Merritt, 100
Phi Delta Phi, 21
Philodemic Society, the, 14
Pisor, Robert, 83, 131
Pontiac Urban League, the, 58
Potter, Charles, 68, 69, 72-73, 74

R

Randall, Donald, 111, 113, 119, 146-
  47
Rauh, Joe, 72, 133, 147, 200
Reid, Clarence A., 62
Reuther, Walter, 56
Riegle, Donald, 171-72
Robertson, A. Willis, 141
Romney, George, 98, 99, 172
Romney, Lenore, 172-75, 176, 178,
  179
Roosevelt, Franklin Delano, 11
Roseville Action Group, the (RAG),
  185
Roth, Florence, 81, 96, 132, 134, 136,
  151, 194, 203
Ruppe, Phil, 171
Russell, Richard, 137
Ruthven, Alexander, 20
Ryan, Richard, 132, 149, 208

S

Safe Streets and Crime Control Act,
  the, 171, 174
Schmidt, Linda, 185
Scholasticism, 12
Scholle, August, 56-57
Schwartz, Lloyd, 187
Schwartzman, David, 192
Senate Antitrust and Monopoly
  Subcommittee, the, 86, 88, 89
Senate Select Committee on
  Intelligence, the, 203
Shriver, Sargent, 99
Sigler, Kim, 57
Simpson, William, 138, 152
Slattery, Paul, 8
Smith Act, the, 60
Smith, Alfred E., 11
Smith, Lowell C., 192
Smith, Margaret Chase, 172
Smoyer, Stanley, 82

Sodality of the Blessed Virgin, the, 13
Sputnik, 69
Staebler, Neil, 57, 68, 90, 144
Stennis, John, 141
Stone, D. W., 31, 35, 45, 46
Strachan, Gordon, 210
Sullivan, Cajetan, 33, 46, 50
Sutcliffe, Lynn, 111, 118, 198

T

Talmadge, Herman, 141
terHorst, Jerald, 90, 159, 199
Tet offensive, the, 108
Toohey, Father John, 14
Truth in Packaging Act, the, 105
Tucker, Donald, 143, 194

U

United Auto Workers, the (UAW),
  56

V

Vietnam War, the: and Lyndon B.
  Johnson, 98, 107; Phil Hart's opinion
  on, 107-8, 109, 174, 175, 195;

Senate involvement in, 107-8, 109;
  Tet offensive, 108
Voting Rights Act, the, 101-2

W

Waldron Academy for Boys, the, 7-8
Waldron, Mother Patricia, 7
Wallace, George, 141
Warren, Earl, 121
Watts riots, the, 102
Wellford, Harrison, 132, 144
Welsh, William, 81, 95, 107, 125, 136
West Philadelphia Catholic High
  School for Boys, the, 8
Wides, Burt, 81, 131, 132, 161, 194
Williams, Gerhard Mennen "Soapy":
  campaign style of, 64; education of,
  21; as governor, 56, 57, 58, 65, 67-
  68, 75; and the 1960 presidential
  race, 68, 75; and Phil Hart, 21-22,
  58, 59, 60, 64-65, 68, 138
Williams, Nancy, 59
Wilson, Woodrow, 10
Wolfson, Louis E., 123
Women's Advisory Council, the, 98
Woolner, Sidney, 60, 81, 125, 156,
  179, 181-82